Digital Assets

The ecosystem of digital assets continues to change exponentially. In post-COVID times, digital assets may be seen as a cheaper, more liquid, and transparent safe haven compared to that offered by more traditional asset types. Inclusion of new digital assets, especially cryptocurrencies, in portfolios of standard financial assets has been the subject of some academic study, but the theoretical and practical implications of this new trend are not yet fully understood. *Digital Assets* is the first book to present a comprehensive review of studies on the valuation and pricing of cryptocurrencies and digital assets. Outlining a new research agenda aimed at understanding the fundamental drivers of the value of cryptocurrencies, it brings together an impressive line-up of academics and practitioners to provide a timely perspective on government responses and regulatory approaches towards digital assets, including the setting of new legal frameworks.

REENA AGGARWAL is Robert E. McDonough Professor of Finance and Director, Psaros Center for Financial Markets and Policy at Georgetown University's McDonough School of Business. She specialises in global financial markets, market regulation, exchange traded funds, initial public offerings, institutional investors, private equity, FinTech, and environmental, social, and corporate governance. She has received several research awards including the 2015 BlackRock-National Association of Corporate Directors Global Challenge for Innovation in Corporate Governance Award.

PAOLO TASCA is a renowned economist and professor, notable for his work in the web3 sector. He founded the Centre for Blockchain Technologies at UCL, DEC Institute, Quant Network, and DLT Science Foundation. He also holds visiting positions at the University of Zurich and LSE. An advisor in blockchain and CBDCs, he consults for Fortune 500 companies and Web3 firms like Hedera and Ripple. He contributes to the ISO's TC307 on blockchain and advises international bodies, including the UN and the EU Parliament. Previously, he was a lead economist at the Deutsche Bundesbank.

NIKHIL VADGAMA is an expert in web3 and emerging technologies, specialising in AI and blockchain. He co-founded the DLT Science Foundation and the UK Centre for Blockchain Technologies. He is an Associate Professor at UCL where he oversees and teaches in various programmes including fintech and digital technologies. He is a pioneer in digital technology education, having created and run many executive and online programmes and MOOCs. Additionally, he has substantial industry experience, having launched a challenger bank and worked in global investment banking. He also represents UCL on the Hedera Governing Council.

JIAHUA XU is an Associate Professor in Financial Computing at UCL and Programme Director of the MSc Programme in Emerging Digital Technologies. She also serves as the Head of Science at the DLT Science Foundation. Her interdisciplinary research, spanning DLT, blockchain economics, and financial risk management, is widely published and acclaimed.

Digital Assets

Pricing, Allocation and Regulation

Edited by

REENA AGGARWAL
Georgetown University, McDonough School of Business

PAOLO TASCA
University College London, The DLT Science Foundation

NIKHIL VADGAMA
University College London, The DLT Science Foundation

JIAHUA XU
University College London, The DLT Science Foundation

CAMBRIDGE
UNIVERSITY PRESS

CAMBRIDGE
UNIVERSITY PRESS

Shaftesbury Road, Cambridge CB2 8EA, United Kingdom

One Liberty Plaza, 20th Floor, New York, NY 10006, USA

477 Williamstown Road, Port Melbourne, VIC 3207, Australia

314–321, 3rd Floor, Plot 3, Splendor Forum, Jasola District Centre, New Delhi – 110025, India

103 Penang Road, #05–06/07, Visioncrest Commercial, Singapore 238467

Cambridge University Press is part of Cambridge University Press & Assessment, a department of the University of Cambridge.

We share the University's mission to contribute to society through the pursuit of education, learning and research at the highest international levels of excellence.

www.cambridge.org
Information on this title: www.cambridge.org/9781009362313

DOI: 10.1017/9781009362290

First published 2025

A catalogue record for this publication is available from the British Library

A Cataloging-in-Publication data record for this book is available from the Library of Congress

ISBN 978-1-009-36231-3 Hardback
ISBN 978-1-009-36230-6 Paperback

Contents

Editorial Board Members

Reena Aggarwal, Psaros Center for Financial Markets and Policy McDonough School of Business, Georgetown University.

Dr Reena Aggarwal is Robert E. McDonough Professor of Finance and Director, Psaros Center for Financial Markets and Policy, McDonough School of Business, Georgetown University. Dr Aggarwal has held various positions including Vice Provost for Faculty for Georgetown University, Interim Dean and Deputy Dean of the McDonough School of Business; Distinguished Scholar at the Reserve Bank of India's Centre for Advanced Financial Research and Learning (CAFRAL); Visiting Professor of Finance at MIT's Sloan School of Management; Financial Industry Regulatory Authority (FINRA) Academic Fellow; Academic Fellow at the US Securities and Exchange Commission; Visiting Research Scholar at the International Monetary Fund; Fulbright Scholar to Brazil; and Member of the World Economic Forum's Global Agenda Council on the Future of Financing and Capital.

Dr Aggarwal specialises in global financial markets, market regulation, ETFs, IPOs, institutional investors, private equity, FinTech, and ESG. She is a prolific scholar and has received several research awards, including the 2015 BlackRock-National Association of Corporate Directors Global Challenge for Innovation in Corporate Governance Award. She has been named among 'Outstanding Faculty' in the *Businessweek* guide to the best business schools and has been voted an outstanding professor by Executive MBAs. She was honoured with the Allan N. Nash Distinguished Doctoral Graduate Award by the University of Maryland and the Distinguished Alumni Award by Birla Institute of Technology and Science (BITS) Pilani.

Dr Aggarwal serves on the boards of Cohen and Steers, Dimensional Funds, and Nuveen Churchill Direct Lending. Her research and analysis has been cited in the *Financial Times*, the *Wall Street Journal*, the *New York Times*, the *Washington Post, Fortune*, and *CNBC*, among others. She received a PhD in finance from the University of Maryland and an MMS from BITS Pilani, India.

Paolo Tasca, UCL Centre for Blockchain Technologies, The DLT Science Foundation.

Dr Paolo Tasca is a distinguished professor and economist renowned for his contributions to the Web3 sector. He is the founder of several prominent organisations, including the Centre for Blockchain Technologies at University College London (UCL CBT), the DEC Institute, Quant Network, and the DLT Science Foundation (DSF). In addition to his foundational roles, Dr Tasca holds visiting academic positions at prestigious universities worldwide, including the University of Zurich and the London School of Economics (LSE). This involvement further cements his status as a leading figure in the academic study of digital currencies and blockchain technology. Widely recognised as an expert advisor in the fields of blockchain, Central Bank Digital Currencies (CBDCs), and Web3, Dr Tasca has provided consultancy services to numerous Fortune 500 companies and leading Web3 firms such as Hedera, NEXO, Algorand, and Ripple. He also plays a pivotal role as a member of the TC307 Technical Committee on blockchain at the International Organization for Standardization (ISO), among other significant positions.

Dr Tasca's expertise extends to advising policymakers and international organisations, including the United Nations, the European Parliament, the Federal Reserve, the European Central Bank, and various central banks in Italy, Chile, Brazil, Colombia, and Canada. His prior experience includes a key role as the lead economist for digital currencies and P2P financial systems at the German Central Bank (Deutsche Bundesbank).

Nikhil Vadgama UCL Centre for Blockchain Technologies, The DLT Science Foundation.

Nikhil Vadgama is a distinguished expert in web3 and emerging technologies specialising in artificial intelligence (AI) and blockchain. He is a co-founder and director of the DLT Science Foundation and deputy director of the UCL Centre for Blockchain Technologies. He is also an associate professor, programme director, and esteemed lecturer for several of University College London (UCL)'s world-class programmes, including financial technology, emerging digital technologies, and others. He also represents UCL on the Hedera Governing Council.

He has pioneered many new emerging digital technology education initiatives, including executive education, online education, accredited education, and education standards. He also has extensive industry experience in financial services, having launched a challenger bank in multiple countries, and previously working for large global investment banks.

Jiahua Xu, UCL Centre for Blockchain Technologies, The DLT Science Foundation.

Dr Jiahua Xu is Associate Professor in Financial Computing at UCL, where she teaches blockchain technologies and machine learning in finance. She is an award-winning researcher at the university's Centre for Blockchain Technologies and serves as Programme Director of the MSc Emerging Digital Technologies in the Computer Science Department. Dr Xu teaches FinTech courses at various institutions, including École Polytechnique Fédérale de Lausanne (EPFL), London Business School, EDHEC Business School, and the Center for Latin American Monetary Studies. She has visited and has ongoing research collaborations with Harvard Business School, Imperial College London, and Vienna University of Economics and Business. Her research interests lie primarily in blockchain economics, behavioural finance, and risk management. She has published academic papers in top-tier conferences in computer science and renowned journals in economics and finance.

James J. Angel, McDonough School of Business, Georgetown University.

Dr James J. Angel is an Associate Professor at Georgetown University's McDonough School of Business) specialises in the market structure and regulation of global financial markets, and he has visited over 75 financial exchanges around the world. He teaches undergraduate, MBA, and executive courses, including in Fintech and investments. Dr Angel has testified before Congress about issues related to the design of financial markets. In addition, he has been quoted in hundreds of newspaper articles and has appeared numerous times on radio and television. Dr Angel began his professional career as a rate engineer at Pacific Gas and Electric, where he worked on

Federal Energy Regulatory Commission (FERC)- and California Public Utilities Commission (CPUC)-related issues. Along the way, he has also worked at BARRA (later part of Morgan Stanley), where he developed equity risk models. He has also served as Visiting Academic Fellow in residence at the National Association of Securities Dealers (now FINRA) and also as a visiting economist at the Shanghai Stock Exchange. He has also been the chairman of the Nasdaq Economic Advisory Board, a member of the OTC Bulletin Board Advisory Committee, and has served on the board of directors of the Direct Edge Stock Exchanges (later part of BATS Global Markets). From 2012 to 2014, he was a visiting associate professor at the Wharton School of the University of Pennsylvania. Dr Angel is a co-inventor on 12 FinTech patents.

Silvia Bartolucci, Department of Computer Science, UCL.

Dr Silvia Bartolucci is a lecturer in the Department of Computer Science and an associate of the Centre for Blockchain Technologies at UCL. Her research interests include applications of distributed ledger technologies in finance and mathematical modelling and data analysis of current trends and issues emerging in digital economies and financial markets. She has previously worked as Research Associate of the Centre for Financial Technology at the Imperial College Business School, which she is currently affiliated to. She has gained industry exposure by working at a London-based start-up, where she produced more than 20 FinTech patents on the design of new blockchain protocols to improve anonymity, security, and network scalability.

Giovanna Massarotto, Center for Technology, Innovation and Competition (CTIC), University of Pennsylvania.

Dr Giovanna Massarotto is an international expert on antitrust, intellectual property (IP) law, and economic regulation in the field of information technology. She is Academic Fellow at the University of Pennsylvania Law School's Center for Technology, Innovation & Competition and an affiliate at UCL CBT. Dr Massarotto attained a PhD from Bocconi University in Milan, where she researched and taught competition law as Adjunct Professor. She was Academic Visitor at the University of Oxford (UK) and a visiting fellow at Fordham University in New York. Dr Massarotto has been invited to lecture on antitrust and legal issues related to blockchain and digital markets by several organisations in the US and the EU, including the Organisation for Economic Co-operation and Development Harvard, the Global Antitrust Institute in Washington, DC, the Competition and Markets Authority, and the University of Oxford.

Alberto Rossi, McDonough School of Business, Georgetown University.

Dr Alberto Rossi is Professor of Finance, McDonough School of Business, Georgetown University. He is also Director of the AI, Analytics, and Future of Work Initiative at Georgetown and Academic Fellow of the Luohan Academy. His research interests include FinTech, household finance, machine learning, and asset pricing. His recent work studies how robo-advisors can help individuals make better financial decisions and how to predict stock market returns using machine learning algorithms. He has worked extensively in analysing big data, and has collaborated with major brokerage houses, FinTech firms, and asset managers around the world.

Dr Rossi's work has been published in leading academic journals, such as the *Journal of Finance*, the *Review of Financial Studies*, the *Journal of Financial Economics*, and *Management Science*. Before McDonough, he was Associate Professor with tenure at the R. H. Smith School of Business, University of Maryland. He also worked as an economist at the Board of Governors of the Federal Reserve System in Washington, DC. He received his PhD in economics from the University of California, San Diego.

Acknowledgements

We acknowledge support from the University College London Centre for Blockchain Technologies and the Psaros Center for Financial Markets and Policy at Georgetown University's McDonough School of Business. We are also grateful to the University Blockchain Research Initiative and the DLT Science Foundation for their support. We thank Alice Ng for her excellent editorial assistance.

PART I

Institutionalisation of Digital Assets

1 *Institutionalisation of Digital Assets*

REENA AGGARWAL AND CHRIS MATTURRI

1.1 Introduction

Are digital assets a great bubble or will their underlying technology, blockchain, transform the world of finance? People have debated this question since Bitcoin and other digital assets took off in late 2017. Bitcoin was the first digital asset, developed in response to the financial crisis of 2007–2008, and a growing distrust towards banks and other financial institutions that contributed to the crisis. In the original 2008 Bitcoin Whitepaper, Bitcoin's anonymous, pseudonymously known as Satoshi Nakamoto, claimed, 'what is needed is an electronic payment system based on cryptographic proof instead of trust, allowing any two willing parties to transact directly with each other without the need for a trusted third party' (Nakamoto, 2020).

A decade later, this thesis laid the groundwork for the future of digital assets and blockchain technology that some argue has the potential to revolutionise the world.

Although Bitcoin is the most popular cryptocurrency today and represents 75% of the total market cap of digital assets, it is still just one small piece of this ecosystem. To clarify, Bitcoin is a cryptocurrency, which is a subsegment of the entire digital asset class. A cryptocurrency is essentially a digital instrument that uses encryption to conduct monetary transactions without the need for a bank or third party. Cryptocurrencies have use cases ranging from payments to stores of value to enabling of smart contracts. Another example of a digital asset can be a stablecoin, which uses the same blockchain technology as other cryptocurrencies but is backed by a traditional fiat currency or even a tangible asset.

Blockchain is the underlying technology that makes all these cryptocurrencies and digital assets usable. A blockchain is a distributed ledger that can be used to record anything. In other words, a blockchain is the digital bookkeeping of any transaction. The 'blocks' that are part of the blockchain are linked together and create what is known as a 'chain'. This seamlessly allows all cryptocurrency or digital asset transactions to be recorded on one massive ledger, for everyone to see. While cryptocurrencies made blockchain popular, there are countless use cases for blockchain technology outside the digital asset world.

1.2 Current State of Institutionalisation of Digital Assets

The digital asset space has matured some over the past few years, although there is still a long way to go. They have become more institutionalised than many may realise and are already being embraced by some of the largest banks, exchanges, and investment firms in the world. At the same time, cryptocurrencies have also been marred with problems with Bitcoin being associated with purchases of illegal drugs from the Silk Road or the Mt. Gox Bitcoin exchange hack in 2014. Cryptocurrencies have also been criticised because of their usage in ransomware attacks. Next, we discuss products and services that are helping in the institutionalisation of digital assets.

Bitcoin Futures Contracts on Chicago Mercantile Exchange

One of the earliest and most prominent financial institutions to introduce a regulated digital asset product was the Chicago Mercantile Exchange (CME), the world's largest exchange. CME announced in October 2017 their intention to launch a Bitcoin Futures contract by the end of the year shortly after the Chicago Board Options Exchange (CBOE) had also announced plans to create the first regulated Bitcoin Futures contract. The CME and CBOE products existed together for some time, but the CBOE delisted its contract a year later (Rooney, 2019). The successful introduction of a cryptocurrency futures product was seen as one barometer for the institutional growth of digital assets.

New futures products often follow a 'hockey-stick trajectory', of very slow growth at first, followed by a strong uptick in volume as the contract matures and more entrants to the market create a 'network' effect enabling more participants to trade among each other. However, CME's Bitcoin Futures launch saw immediate adoption, indicating demand in a regulated venue to trade digital assets. The Average Daily

Volume and Open Interest across CME's Bitcoin Futures market have consistently grown since inception.

In 2019, CME's Bitcoin Futures contract had average daily volume of 6,365 contracts, which is equivalent to 31,825 Bitcoin and represents a notional transactional value of nearly $250 million per day. As a result, Bitcoin Futures finished as CME's 55th largest futures contract by volume in 2019 (Daily Exchange Volume and Open Interest, 2020).

There was a steady growth in Open Interest of CME's Bitcoin Futures contract during the period 2018–2020. Unlike volume, which measures the number of contracts transacted, Open Interest indicates how many open positions exist, or in other words, how much risk traders are taking or hedging against. There are two ways to observe the growth in Open Interest at CME, through the total number of contracts or by looking at the number of large open interest holders (LOIH). To classify as an LOIH, a market participant must hold over 25 contracts in a specified futures market. For example, to appear as an LOIH, someone must own over 25 contracts of Bitcoin Futures at the time of disclosure. As seen, not only has CME set an Open Interest record of 13,600 contracts, but they have also grown to 93 LOIH, which is up from nearly 45 at the start of 2020 (Bitcoin Futures and Options on Futures, 2020). CME's Bitcoin Futures market has provided a quick way for investors to gain exposure to cryptocurrencies, sometimes as a hedge to their traditional portfolio.

CME has become one of the most important venues to transact Bitcoin. With an average daily turnover of 31,825 Bitcoin at CME in 2019, CME now ranks as the largest venue in the world to transact USD Bitcoin (Bitcoin Trading Volume, 2020). Unlike many of these 'spot' cryptocurrency exchanges that are more retail oriented and not regulated, it is much more difficult to open a futures account to trade on CME. All futures trading is regulated by the Commodity Futures Trading Commission (CFTC). Thus, looking at CME's volume is much more indicative of institutional adoption than just observing the volume of cryptocurrencies in totality at non-regulated crypto spot exchanges.

Based on interest from investors, CME started calculating an Ethereum Reference Rate in May 2018 (CME Group, 2018) and launched a Bitcoin Options contract in January 2020 (CME Group, 2018). Micro Bitcoin and Micro Ether futures and options contracts have also been introduced. These additions are a sign that there is interest in additional digital asset products.

Bitcoin Exchange Traded Funds and Trusts

Aside from directly purchasing or trading cryptocurrencies themselves, there are a growing number of ways to access the digital asset market. One investable digital asset product is the Grayscale Bitcoin Trust (GBTC). A division of Digital Currency Group, Grayscale, introduced GBTC in September 2013. In early 2020, Grayscale registered with the SEC as a reporting company.

Grayscale has seen assets under management (AUM) in GBTC product increase, reaching as high as $6 billion (Grayscale, 2020). GBTC traded at a premium compared to the price of its underlying Bitcoin for a while but has recently been trading at a significant discount (Grayscale Investments, 2020). Grayscale credits the interest in the product to its institutional customer base of hedge funds, family offices, and endowments.

There have been two main types of digital asset exchange traded fund (ETF) filings: physical-based filings and futures-based filings. Physical-based filings would hold 'physical' cryptocurrencies for their underlying exposure in the ETF. Whereas a futures-based filing would hold futures contracts traded on an exchange for their exposure. A physical-based filing would replicate what is traditionally seen in the equity space, where an ETF holds the underlying shares of stocks or other instruments that make up the basket in the ETF. On the other hand, a futures-based filing would be similar to most commodity-based ETFs that get their exposure through holding futures contracts based on the underlying asset.

A Bitcoin or digital asset-pegged ETF would give institutional and retail investors another way to access this market. However, regulators have expressed several concerns about spot ETFs.

Hedge Funds and Venture Capital

Some of the largest hedge funds have begun allocating funds to digital assets. In 2020, Renaissance Technologies, which manages $75 billion in total assets, disclosed they had begun trading digital assets (Chaparro, 2020). Similarly, the hedge fund manager Paul Tudor Jones announced that the firm has put 2% of its assets in Bitcoin, arguing that 'bitcoin reminds me of gold when I first got into the business in 1976 and the most compelling argument for owning Bitcoin is the coming digitisation of currency everywhere, accelerated by COVID-19' (Schatzker, 2020).

Another key indicator of institutionalisation in digital assets is the growing number of hedge funds focused exclusively on strategies related to cryptocurrencies. As reported by PWC & Elwood Asset Management in their annual Crypto Hedge Fund Report, the total AUM of cryptocurrency hedge funds increased from $1 billion in 2019 to $2 billion in 2020 (PWC, 2020). In addition, they found that the average AUM of a crypto hedge fund increased from $21.9 million in 2019 to $44 million in 2020. The growth in total assets in funds with digital asset strategies is another indicator that institutional investors are gaining exposure to digital assets through allocations to cryptocurrency hedge funds.

Many actively managed cryptocurrency funds today employ either a basic cross-exchange arbitrage or levered beta strategy (Koutoulas, 2020). The cross-exchange arbitrage strategy effectively exploits arbitrage opportunities across various cryptocurrency exchanges but is subject to operational risks. Many of these exchanges are at risk of hacks or poor infrastructure that could crash and lead to catastrophic losses for funds trading on them. The other common strategy actively managed crypto funds follow is a levered-beta product, which is essentially highly levered exposure to digital assets. However, many of these levered-beta funds charge extremely high fees (as high as 3% management and 30% performance), and it is not clear whether they deliver any true 'alpha' other than leveraged, long exposure to digital assets. In addition, they are not providing any downside protection and can have huge drawdowns.

There is also a growing number of venture capital (VC)-style investment firms that provide exposure to the digital asset space through investments in new blockchain start-ups. Unlike actively managed crypto hedge funds, crypto VC firms have a much longer-term holding period. According to research from Hutt Capital, a blockchain VC fund of funds, as of April 2020, there were over 65 venture funds managing over $4 billion in assets – an increase from 49 funds with an aggregate of $3.8 billion in assets a year prior. (Hutt Capital, 2020).

In addition, Hutt Capital estimates that of the $4 billion AUM in blockchain VC funds, nearly $1–1.5 billion is available as dry powder and ready to invest. This represents roughly 0.5% of dry powder for all VC funds, which is a slightly undersized amount since blockchain start-ups raised 1.1% of all VC capital and accounted for 2.8% of all deals in 2019 (Hutt Capital, 2020). This suggests that VC blockchain funds are putting their capital to work more quickly than traditional VC funds, as they are finding more attractive deals in the blockchain start-up space.

Some of the largest and most successful blockchain VC investment firms include Pantera Capital ($750 million AUM), Polychain Capital ($1 billion AUM), and A16z Crypto ($860 million AUM fund part of VC firm Andreessen Horowitz) as of the end of 2020.

Other Indicators of Institutionalisation

Goldman Sachs established a trading desk looking to offer non-deliverable forwards, an over-the-counter derivative-based swap, to their clients (Rooney, 2018).

Similarly, Fidelity Digital Assets, a division of Fidelity focused on building out custody and execution services surrounding cryptocurrencies. They published a report on the state of institutionalisation in cryptocurrencies (Baker, 2020). Fidelity surveyed 774 institutional investment firms from both the United States and Europe and found that 36% of respondents already had some sort of exposure to digital assets, with hedge funds and VC firms as their primary source of exposure. Somewhat surprisingly, European institutions had more exposure than US- based firms (45% vs 27%). Fidelity also found that 80% of investors they surveyed found 'something appealing about the asset class,' perhaps indicating this is just the beginning of a trend.

1.3 The Future of Institutionalisation of Digital Assets

There has been growth in the institutionalisation of digital assets in recent years. However, with a total market cap of only $360 billion, as of 2020, the size of digital assets markets is still small compared to the entire investable universe today. There are many inefficiencies related to volatility, regulatory clarity, and the introduction of custodians and prime brokers, among others, that need to be addressed before they can be truly institutionalised. We next examine the opportunities and challenges in institutionalisation to reach the next stage of development.

Valuation, Volatility, and Correlation

Cryptocurrencies such as Bitcoin have a trading price, but investors don't know how to value them in a traditional sense. There is no cash flow analysis approach that can be applied as is the case with equity. Even with gold and silver, some valuation approaches have been applied. Even though individual cryptocurrencies are scarce and have a finite supply, however, there is no limit on creating new cryptocurrencies, and thousands of them exist even today.

Another major problem is their high volatility that limits their wide adoption. According to research from Nasdaq, Bitcoin's one-year realised volatility is almost 10 times that of more traditional assets such as equities, bonds, gold, real estate, or foreign exchange.

Digital assets, such as Bitcoin, have a low correlation with most investable asset classes. According to research from Van Eck Associates, from February 2012 to June 2020, Bitcoin's highest correlation came from the S&P 500 at just 15bps. However, during periods of market stress, the correlations become much higher, and it is too early to tell whether there are benefits from diversification.

Regulatory Uncertainty

Digital assets are still very new and carry considerable risk. It is prudent of regulators to cautiously approach regulation. At the same time, the markets are looking for clarity from financial regulators.

One roadblock to Securities and Exchange Commission (SEC) approval of spot ETF approval has been the concern with the underlying, unregulated spot crypto exchanges. Since most cryptocurrency trading gets done on unregulated exchanges, price manipulation conducted on these offshore exchanges can influence the prices across the entire market. Thus, subjecting even regulated, US-based exchanges to potential price manipulation.

It has been reported that much of the 'reported' cryptocurrency volume across exchanges is fake. Bitwise Asset Management published a report in March 2019 illustrating this phenomenon and found that over 90% of the reported cryptocurrency volume is fake.

In May 2014, following the hack of the largest digital asset exchange at the time, Mt. Gox, the SEC published a warning on the risks associated with investing in 'Bitcoin and Other Virtual-Currency Related Investments' arguing that:

The rise of Bitcoin and other virtual and digital currencies creates new concerns for investors. *A new product, technology, or innovation – such as Bitcoin – has the potential to give rise both to frauds and high-risk investment opportunities.* Potential investors can be easily enticed with the promise of high returns in a new investment space and also may be less sceptical when assessing something novel, new and cutting-edge (Securities and Exchange Commission, 2014).

A few years later, in July 2017, the SEC made a ruling on Initial Coin Offerings (ICOs) in the decentralised autonomous organisation (DAO) Token report. In their investigation, the SEC concluded that:

tokens offered and sold by a 'virtual' organisation known as 'The DAO' were securities and therefore subject to the federal securities laws. The Report confirms that issuers of distributed ledger or blockchain technology-based securities must register offers and sales of such securities unless a valid exemption applies. Those participating in unregistered offerings also may be liable for violations of the securities laws. Additionally, securities exchanges providing for trading in these securities must register unless they are exempt (Securities and Exchange Commission, 2017).

This meant that many ICOs exhibit the same characteristics as basic securities and must be treated as such under regulation.

In September 2015, the CFTC officially declared Bitcoin as a commodity. A few years later in October 2019, CFTC Chairman Heath Tarbert followed with a similar ruling on Ethereum, the second-largest digital asset in the world:

We've been very clear on bitcoin: bitcoin is a commodity under the Commodity Exchange Act. We haven't said anything about ether – until now. It is my view as Chairman of the CFTC that ether is a commodity, and therefore it will be regulated under the CEA. And my guess is that you will see, in the near future, ether-related futures contracts and other derivatives potentially traded ... It's my conclusion as Chairman of the CFTC that ether is a commodity and therefore would fall under our jurisdiction (CFTC, 2019).

The New York State Department of Financial Services (NYSDFS) has set up a designation called a 'BitLicense'. A BitLicense is a permit that allows a firm to participate in any digital currency-related businesses in the state of New York. According to the NYSDFS, without a BitLicense, a firm is not allowed to take part in the following (Department of Financial Services, 2020):

- receiving Virtual Currency for transmission or transmitting Virtual Currency;
- storing, holding, or maintaining custody or control of Virtual Currency on behalf of others;
- buying and selling Virtual Currency as a customer business;
- performing exchange services as a customer business; or
- controlling, administering, or issuing a Virtual Currency.

There are nearly 200 cryptocurrency exchanges across the world that mostly go unregulated. Unlike a stock exchange that must receive approval before listing new securities, cryptocurrency exchanges often list thousands of highly illiquid cryptocurrencies. Dozens of different spot exchanges claim significant portions of market share, with the largest being Coinbase, Kraken, and Bitstamp (Bitcoin Trading Volume, 2020).

Originally, much of the appeal to cryptocurrencies was their decentralised nature and the fact that they were outside the control of the banks or regulators. This allowed digital assets, like Bitcoin, to act like a safe-haven asset and offered protection against inflation or changing monetary policies from central banks. However, this '*laissez-faire*' attitude must change if digital assets are to be truly adopted by institutions. Proper regulation must exist and there can no longer be unanswered questions as to what and who truly regulates digital assets else institutional investors will continue to wait on the sidelines.

Custody and Prime Brokerage of Digital Assets

Another important requirement for the institutionalisation of digital assets is the ability to custody them. In traditional markets, custodian banks act as third-party agent that holds assets and securities on behalf of their customers. Two of the largest custodian banks in the world, BNY Mellon and State Street, have nearly $70 trillion in assets under custody combined (Trefis Team, 2019). Custodian banks safeguard these assets and even offer services such as transaction settlements, interest payments, and tax support. One of the major barriers preventing true institutional adoption of digital assets is that large custodian firms have not begun offering custody services for institutional investors.

There are several potential reasons why traditional custodians have not yet begun offering custody solutions for digital assets. The first, and perhaps most obvious reason, is a lack of comfort with digital assets. Second up until recently, there was a lack of regulatory clarity on holding and storing digital assets.

While custodianship of any financial instrument is vastly complicated, storing digital assets presents an even greater challenge. Since cryptocurrencies have a history of being hacked and stolen, owners of digital assets tend to keep their holdings in a 'cold wallet', or in storage that is not connected to the internet – much like a thumb drive device. The preference of large holders of digital assets to self-custody, with their own cold storage devices, plays up to the decentralised intention of cryptocurrencies but also acts as a major hurdle, preventing institutions from entering the space since it is not what they are accustomed to for other markets.

In addition, the prime brokerage model that exists in traditional markets must be replicated for digital assets. Most institutional investors are used to the full-encompassing services in the traditional prime brokerage model offered by banks, such as trade settlement/clearing, connectivity to exchanges, securities lending, access to leverage, and institutional research reports. Prime brokers play a vital role in the institutional trading and investing space. For example, without a prime broker, many hedge funds would be unable to short stocks or trade derivative contracts. Hedge funds rely on their prime broker for connectivity to exchanges and settling their trades. Since many of the traditional prime brokers that hedge funds and investment firms use do not yet offer these services in the digital asset space, they feel uncomfortable participating in these markets.

Since very few custodians and prime brokers exist in the digital assets space, cryptocurrency exchanges are beginning to offer some of these services. Gemini and Coinbase, two of the leading cryptocurrency exchanges, recently dipped their toes into the custody and prime brokerage spaces. Investment banks such as Goldman Sachs and JP

Morgan have even begun to offer some basic prime brokerage services, like the settlement and clearing of digital asset futures contracts. However, it is clear that the custody and prime brokerage space is one of the biggest areas of growth needed for digital assets to become further institutionalised.

Tokenisation of Assets

Tokenisation is a way to digitise physical assets or other traditional financial instruments and is becoming a way for more institutions to use digital assets. tokenisation has become somewhat popular in the real-estate sector and is beginning to catch on with securities/ETFs and potentially even commodities. Tokenisation can allow individuals to access assets that they would not normally be able to. In a paper on digital assets, Deloitte states, 'we foresee that tokenisation could make the financial industry more accessible, cheaper, faster and easier' (Laurent, 2018)

Central Banks Digital Currencies

Another step in digital asset adoption will be central banks introducing a virtual currency of their own. Some of the most technologically advanced countries in the world have even begun testing digital assets pegged to their currency, effectively creating their own stablecoin. In August 2020, *The Wall Street Journal* reported that China has begun testing a digital currency pegged to the Yuan, in a pilot program led by the People's Bank of China (Xiao, 2020). The currency, referred to as 'DC/EP', short form of 'digital currency/ electronic payment', has been rolled out in some of China's most populous cities such as Beijing, Hong Kong, and Tianjin for trials. Over the past few years, many of the largest Central Banks, including in the US and EU, have announced their intentions to potentially launch a CBDC as well.

A digital currency can provide a mechanism for governments to quickly disburse payments to its citizens. After millions of Americans lost their jobs due to the pandemic, Congress passed the CARES Act in March to send a $1,200 stimulus check to nearly 100 million Americans. From the time Congress passed this Act, it took months for most Americans to receive checks or direct deposits. If a digital dollar existed, Americans could have been sent their payments almost instantly, giving them much-needed aid during the pandemic.

Ultimately, until there are legitimate use cases for digital assets, there will not be serious adoption by institutions. While some progress is being made, it appears we are still years away from having usable digital assets readily available for the public to use, and until this happens, institutions will continue to be sceptical about the benefits of investing in them.

1.4 Conclusion

There is still a long way to go before digital assets reach a point where they can be adopted by institutions in a meaningful way. Until there is more regulatory clarity, institutional investors are likely to stay on the sidelines. Further, while there have been some offerings in the custody and prime brokerage space, it will still take some time before institutions feel comfortable getting on board. Finally, until there are legitimate use cases for digital assets, we are unlikely to see meaningful institutional adoption.

There is some proof of institutionalisation of digital assets. Large institutions including Fidelity, BlackRock, and several large investment banks have started providing services to satisfy the needs of their clients. Hedge funds and VC funds are also investing in digital assets. It is yet to be seen whether there will be wide-scale adoption of these assets.

Bibliography

Baker, Paddy. 'Number of Institutions Buying Crypto Futures Doubled in 2020: Fidelity Report'. Coin Desk, 9 June 2020, www.coindesk.com/institutions-crypto-futures-doubled-fidelity-report. Accessed 5 September 2020.

'Bitcoin Futures and Options on Futures'. CME Group, 23 August 2020, www.cmegroup.com/market-data/volume-open-interest/exchange-volume.html. Accessed 23 August 2020.

'Bitcoin Trading Volume'. Bitcoinity, 25 September 2020, data.bitcoinity.org/markets/volume/2y?c=e&t=b. Accessed 18 October 2020.

CFTC. 'Chairman Tarbert Comments on Cryptocurrency Regulation at Yahoo! Finance All Markets Summit'. CFTC, 10 October 2019, www.cftc.gov/PressRoom/PressReleases/8051-19. Accessed 18 October 2020.

Chaparro, Frank. '75 Billion Hedge Fund Renaissance Technologies Is Eyeing the Bitcoin Futures Market'. The Block, 18 April 2020, www.theblockcrypto.com/post/62322/75-billion-hedge-fund-renaissance-technologies-is-eyeing-the-bitcoin-futures-market. Accessed 1 September 2020.

CME Group. 'CME Group and Crypto Facilities Launch Ether Reference Rate and Ether Real Time Index'. CME Group, 14 May 2018, www.cmegroup.com/media-room/pressreleases/2018/5/14/cme_group_and_cryptofacilitieslaunchetherreferencerateandetherre.html. Accessed 25 August 2020.

'Daily Exchange Volume and Open Interest'. CME Group, 23 August 2020, www.cmegroup.com/market-data/volume-open-interest/exchange-volume.html. Accessed 23 August 2020.

Department of Financial Services. 'BitLicense FAQs'. DFS, www.dfs.ny.gov/apps_and_licensing/virtual_currency_businesses/bitlicense_faqs. Accessed 20 October 2020.

Grayscale. Grayscale Bitcoin Trust, grayscale.co/bitcoin-trust. Accessed 2 September 2020.

Grayscale Investments. '1.4 Billion in First Half of 2020'. Medium, 15 July 2020, medium.com/grayscale-investments/1h2020-grayscale-record-3c95652bc219. Accessed 2 September 2020.

Hutt Capital. 'Hutt Capital's Blockchain VC Fund Landscape (2020 Edition)'. Medium, 13 April 2020, medium.com/@HuttCapital/hutt-capitals-blockchain-vc-fund-landscape-2020-edition-29abdbeddfd7. Accessed 18 September 2020.

Koutoulas, James. Personal Interview. 24 September 2020.

Laurent, Patrick. 'The Tokenisation of Assets Is Disrupting the Financial Industry. Are You Read?' Thibault Chollet, Michael Burke, Tobias Seerrs, Deloitte, October 2018, www2.deloitte.com/content/dam/Deloitte/lu/Documents/about-deloitte/Inside/lu-inside19-full.pdf. Accessed 5 November 2020.

Nakamoto, Satoshi. 'Bitcoin: A Peer-to-Peer Electronic Cash System'. Bitcoin, bitcoin.org/bitcoin.pdf. Accessed 23 August 2020.

PWC. 'Crypto Hedge Fund Report'. PWC, Elwood, May 2020, www.pwc.com/gx/en/financial-services/pdf/pwc-elwood-annual-crypto-hedge-fund-report-may-2020.pdf. Accessed 5 September 2020.

Rooney, Kate. 'CBOE to Stop Listing Bitcoin Futures as Interest in Crypto Trading Cools'. CNBC, 18 March 2019, www.cnbc.com/2019/03/18/cboe-to-stop-listing-bitcoin-futures-as-interest-in-crypto-trading-cools.html. Accessed 23 August 2020.

Rooney, Kate. 'Goldman Sachs CFO Says Bank Is Working on Bitcoin Derivatives for Clients'. *CNBC*, 6 September 2018, www.cnbc.com/2018/09/06/goldman-sachs-cfo-calls-reports-of-shutting-down-crypto-desk-fake-news.html. Accessed 25 August 2020.

Schatzker, Erik. 'Paul Tudor Jones Buys Bitcoin as a Hedge against Inflation'. Bloomberg, 7 May 2020, www.bloomberg.com/news/articles/2020-05-07/paul-tudor-jones-buys-bitcoin-says-he-s-reminded-of-gold-in-70s. Accessed 1 September 2020.

Securities and Exchange Commission. 'Investor Alert: Bitcoin and Other Virtual Currency-Related Investments'. SEC, 7 May 2014, www.sec.gov/oiea/investor-alerts-bulletins/investoralertsia_bitcoin.html. Accessed 17 October 2020.

Securities and Exchange Commission. 'SEC Issues Investigative Report Concluding DAO Tokens, a Digital Asset, Were Securities'. SEC, 25 July 2017, www.sec.gov/news/press-release/2017-131. Accessed 20 October 2020.

Trefis Team. 'State Street or BNY Mellon: Which Custody Banking Giant Uses Its Asset Base More Efficiently?' *Forbes*, 5 November 2019, www.forbes.com/sites/greatspeculations/2019/11/05/state-street-or-bny-mellon-which-custody-banking-giant-uses-its-asset-base-more-efficiently/#421265767953. Accessed 22 October 2020.

Xiao, Eva. 'China to Expand Testing of a Digital Currency'. *Wall Street Journal*, 14 August 2020, www.wsj.com/articles/china-to-expand-testing-of-a-digital-currency-11597385324?mod=hp_lista_pos2. Accessed 5 November 2020.

2 How and When Are Cryptocurrency Predictable? Backtesting Their Portfolio Economic Value

MASSIMO GUIDOLIN AND MANUELA PEDIO

2.1 Introduction

Cryptograms – among them, in particular, Bitcoin – represent one of the most popular and persistent 'hypes' of the new millennium.[1] As the interest in crypto-assets has kept growing steadily, with trading volume accounting towards a monetary equivalent of several billion USD, a new debate concerning the institutionalisation of these new opportunities has emerged in the literature (see, e.g., Bekemeier, 2021). This leads to the necessity to answer two crucial questions, that is, what is exactly the nature of this asset class (see, e.g., Liu et al., 2019) and whether they can represent an investment opportunity that is palatable to institutional and retail investors.

In this chapter, we attempt to answer both these questions by investigating the role played by a few of the most important digital currencies in the optimal portfolios of risk-averse investors when predictability (of crypto-assets as well as of traditional investment vehicles, such as stocks and bonds) is taken into account. In assuming the predictability of crypto-assets, we consider both crypto-specific and macroeconomic factors, in the attempt to disentangle whether the latter plays any role in driving their returns.

Our research questions and empirical findings fill distinctive gaps in our knowledge of the role and economic value played by cryptocurrencies. On the one hand, there seems to be a consensus in the literature on the fact that cryptocurrencies have been struggling to come to play the role that their very name attributes to them, that

[1] The creation of Bitcoin in 2008 spurred the creation of many new cryptocurrencies known as altcoins. These altcoins use similar cryptography technology but employ different algorithmic designs. Many of these altcoins were introduced with different purposes or to address the weaknesses of Bitcoin, such as the high-energy consumption caused by its proof-of-work (PoW) consensus algorithm or the supply limit of 21 million coins, among others (see, e.g., Ciaian and Rajcaniova, 2019).

is, that of currencies (see, e.g., Yermack, 2015). Although a variety of factors have been cited to support this prediction, the excessive volatility of crypto-asset returns has often been indicated as the Achilles heel of digital currencies (see, e.g., Baur et al., 2018). On the other hand, there is a persistently raging debate on the measurement of the diversification power and economic value of cryptocurrencies in optimised investors' portfolios.[2] Crypto-asset returns are expected to have low or negative correlation with the returns of traditional asset classes like bonds and stocks. In fact, there is some evidence that their inclusion in traditional portfolios may increase expected returns per unit of risk (see Bouri et al., 2017). Briere et al. (2015) and Chuen et al. (2018) use mean–variance spanning tests and find that investments in Bitcoin provide (in some exercises, significant) diversification benefits. Corbet et al. (2018) use a time and frequency domain analysis to support the idea that crypto-assets constitute a new investment asset class since they are interconnected to each other but disconnected from traditional financial assets. Dyhrberg (2016) and Symitsi and Chalvatzis (2019) have investigated the diversification properties of Bitcoin within the context of a diversified mean–variance portfolio and reported significant economic value.

However, Yermack (2015) argues that Bitcoin is uncorrelated with the majority of fiat currencies and is much more volatile, therefore being of limited usefulness for risk management purposes and diversification (see also Baur et al., 2018). Chuen et al. (2018) show that although cryptocurrencies are mildly correlated with traditional asset classes so that they expand the efficient frontier, they fail to lead to a large improvement in the utility of mean–variance investors when predictability is taken into account. A growing literature in empirical finance has documented that although often modest, predictability can hardly be dismissed in asset allocation problems across a variety of asset menus and applications (see, e.g., Kandel and Stambaugh, 1996). Recently, Bianchi et al. (2020) have shown that crypto-assets may be

[2] Another literature has examined a related question, that is, whether crypto-assets may represent a 'safe haven', that is, an asset class characterised by zero or negative correlations with other, major assets, such as stocks, bonds, and commodities (see, e.g., Bouri et al. (2017), Smales (2019), and Shahzad et al. (2019)). Even though such a research question is admittedly interesting, in this chapter, we shall devote no specific attention to the safe-haven hypothesis, also because in our perspective such a property would be subsumed by the potential of digital currencies to be characterised by large and positive hedging demands.

segmented from other asset classes because they are less predictable (from a common, homogeneous set of instruments derived from earlier literature). Such a lack of statistical predictability translates then into the lack of risk-adjusted realised performance generated by the major cryptocurrencies in a recursive, expected utility-maximising portfolio exercise.

In this chapter, we re-examine the question of the portfolio value of the three major digital currencies (Bitcoin, Litecoin, and Ripple) under predictability and using recent data. Consistently with a rather prolific literature, the predictors are represented by eight principal components extracted through factor analysis techniques in Ludvigson and Ng (2009) from an extensive set of 132 variables selected to represent broad categories of macroeconomic time series (real output and income, employment and hours, real retail, manufacturing and sales data, international trade, consumer spending, housing starts, inventories, orders, labour costs, capacity utilisation measures, price indexes, interest rates and interest rate spreads, and foreign exchange measures). Such factors are supplemented by a number of predictors that have emerged in earlier research on cryptocurrencies (see Bianchi et al. (2022) and Liu et al. (2019)). However, differently from past research, we apply a key finding from the field of forecasting: with few known exceptions, combining forecasts according to pooling schemes that may range from very simple (equal weighting) to sophisticated ones (e.g., the discounted mean squared prediction error (DMSPE), approach) yields less biased and less variable predictions than any of the individual forecasts.[3]

In practice, with reference to monthly data for a 2011–2020 sample concerning Bitcoin, Litecoin, and Ripple returns (or shorter series, as available in Coinmetrics), we uncover three key results. First, consistently with what has been argued by Rapach et al. (2010), forecast combinations perform better than most of the individual predictors for most cryptocurrencies and, generally, asset classes; however, the

[3] Xiao and Sun (2020) have experimented with model averaging applied to autoregressive distributed lag models of cryptocurrency returns. While forecast combinations (of which averaging is just special, albeit popular, case) apply transformations directly to the forecasts generated by a set of models, forecast model averaging outputs predictions from a single metamodel, the coefficients (more generally features) of which represent an average of the features obtained from a set of models.

out-of-sample (OOS) R-square characterising all digital currencies is generally modest and appreciable only in the case of Bitcoin and for the full 2011–2020 sample. In fact, most of the individual predictive regressions fail to outperform the historical mean benchmark, so the predictive accuracy entirely derives from the combination schemes. Second, among the crypto-specific factors, Bitcoin lagged returns and the 3-month time series momentum are the only predictors that outperform the benchmark mean model, originating OOS R-squares of 12.7% and 5.8%, respectively; however, when crypto-specific factors are added to the set of predictors in forecast combination schemes, the difference is negligible. Indeed, the best combination (DMSPE) scheme yields an OOS R-square of 5.8% when crypto-specific predictors are excluded, which increases to 5.9% when they are included (see, e.g., Panagiotidis et al., 2019).

Third, when we add either Bitcoin or all cryptocurrencies together to an asset menu that also includes stocks, public real estates (real estate investment trust (REITs)), a precious metals index, two corporate bond indices (AAA- and BBB-rated), 10-year Treasury bonds, and T-bills to recursively compute optimal mean–variance weights and the corresponding realised OOS risk-adjusted performance measures (Sharpe ratio (SR) and realised utility), we obtain that over the full 2011–2020 sample, the optimised portfolios based on the predictive models outperform those based on the historical mean, irrespective of the level of risk aversion and on whether cryptocurrencies are available to investors. Moreover, an investor will benefit from the inclusion of cryptocurrencies in their portfolio, regardless of the predictive model they select, even though these gains tend to be larger when predictability is exploited, with an increase in the realised certainty equivalent of up to 6% in annualised terms. In fact, a mildly risk averse investor characterised by $\gamma = 2$ ought to allocate on average 13–14% of their portfolio in Bitcoin. When, on a shorter 2015–2020 sample, also Litecoin and Ripple are included in the asset menu, while the evidence in favour of the power of forecast combinations remains intact (even if milder), the support for the inclusion of cryptocurrencies in the asset allocation fades away. This represents a warning against confusing Bitcoin with cryptocurrencies at large and also against comparing inferences drawn from heterogeneous samples.

The rest of this chapter is structured as follows. Section 2.2 describes the data and reports key summary statistics. Section 2.3 presents our methodology and research design. Section 2.4 discusses the key findings on realised OOS predictability, while Section 2.5 reports empirical results concerning risk-adjusted performance deriving from adding crypto-assets and/or from considering predictability. Section 2.6 concludes.

2.2 Data

We consider three major cryptocurrencies, namely Bitcoin, Litecoin, and Ripple. We collect their monthly data from Coinmetrics for a sample period spanning January 2011–December 2020 in the case of Bitcoin and January 2015–December 2020 Litecoin and Ripple.[4] As for traditional asset classes, equity is represented by the S&P 500 Index (dividend included) retrieved from CRSP (similar to Welch and Goyal, 2008); precious metals are proxied by the Dow Jones Precious Metals Index; real estate is represented by the FTSE NAREIT Index (All Equity REITs)[5]; investment grade and high-yield bonds are proxied by the ICE BofA AAA US Corporate Total Return Index and the ICE BofA BBB US Corporate Total Return Index, respectively; finally, we also include the 10-year US Treasury bond in the asset menu. The risk-free rate is proxied by the US 1-month T-bill rate.[6]

Table 2.1 reports the summary statistics and the correlations for the monthly asset returns over the sample period 2011–2020 (with the exclusion of Litecoin and Ripple, which are only available for the shorter period 2015–2020; the correlations are computed on the common sample). We notice that cryptocurrencies display large monthly average returns (ranging from 11.20% for Ripple to 20.65% for Litecoin) but also massive volatilities (as much as 107.81% for Litecoin, for instance). As a matter of comparison, the most volatile of the

4 coinmetrics.io/community-network-data

5 A real estate investment trust ('REIT') is a company that owns, operates, or finances income-producing real estate. The FTSE NAREIT All Equity REITs Index is tracking the performance of all traded equity REITs (therefore, excluding mortgage REITs). The returns of the index are retrieved from www.reit.com/data-research/reit-indexes/ftse-nareit-us-real-estate-index-historical-values-returns.

6 The returns of the two corporate bond indices, as well as the return of the 10-year Treasury bond and the T-bill rate, are obtained from the Federal Reserve Economic Data (FRED) repository maintained by the Federal Reserve of Saint Louis, fred.stlouisfed.org

Table 2.1 ***Summary Statistics***

	Mean	Median	Maximum	Minimum	Std. Dev.	Skewness	Kurtosis	Jarque-Bera
	Panel A: Cryptocurrencies							
Bitcoin	18.4	6.88	465.59	−41.62	61.59	4.68	30.82	4306.51
Litecoin	20.65	−5.65	735.23	−66.89	107.81	4.83	29.7	2419.55
Ripple	11.22	−0.44	161.71	−42.65	40.39	1.73	6.56	74
	Panel B: Other assets							
S&P 500 Index	1.17	1.65	12.89	−12.2	3.9	−0.32	4.49	13.09
AAA Corporate Bonds	0.44	0.33	5.15	−3.43	1.44	0.24	3.49	2.32
BBB Corporate Bonds	0.51	0.47	6.29	−10.3	1.69	−1.87	16.35	961.13
Dow Jones Precious Metals Index	0.15	0.71	37.98	−26.49	10.25	0.76	5.1	33.55
10-year Treasury Bond	0.27	0.14	2.7	−2.39	0.92	0.33	3.41	2.96
Nareit Index	0.84	1.03	14.28	−18.68	4.49	−0.55	5.67	41.63

Panel C: Correlation Matrix

	Bitcoin	Litecoin	Ripple	S&P 500 Index	Aaa Corporate Bonds	Bbb Corporate Bonds	Dow Jones Precious Metals Bond	10-year Treasury Index	Nareit Index
Bitcoin	1								
Litecoin	0.62	1							
Ripple	0.37	0.66	1						
S&P 500 Index	0.27	0.13	0.05	1					
Aaa Corporate Bonds	0.19	0.07	0.12	0.05	1				
Bbb Corporate Bonds	0.29	0.13	0.09	0.54	0.67	1			
Dow Jones Precious Metals Index	−0.08	−0.03	−0.1	0.27	0.02	0.16	1		
10-year Treasury Bond	−0.08	−0.08	−0.03	−0.43	0.7	0.13	−0.12	1	
Nareit Index	0.21	0.04	−0.01	0.68	0.49	0.73	0.18	0.04	1

The statistics are based on monthly returns for a sample period January 2011–December 2020 with the exception of what concerns Litecoin and Ripple. The statistics for Litecoin and Ripple are for the period January 2015–December 2020. Sample correlations are computed on the common sample period (January 2015–December 2020).

traditional asset classes is the precious metal index with a monthly volatility of 10.25%, while the returns of the equity show a volatility of 3.9% per month. Interestingly, all the cryptocurrencies display a positive skewness (larger than four in the case of Bitcoin and Litecoin) in contrast with the traditional asset classes, whose returns tend to show small or negative skewness. Unsurprisingly, cryptocurrency returns are also characterised by fat tails (with massive kurtosis in the order of 30.82 for the Bitcoin, to make an example). The normality assumption is rejected for most of the assets (as indicated by the Jarque–Bera test) with the exception of AAA corporate bonds and 10-year Treasury bonds.

Importantly, all the cryptocurrencies are mildly or negatively correlated with traditional asset classes. Interestingly, while they are often deemed to be similar to commodities (see, e.g., Dyhrberg (2016) and Guesmi et al. (2019)), cryptocurrencies show small and negative pairwise correlation coefficients with the precious metal index (−0.08 in the case of Bitcoin, −0.03 for the Litecoin, and −0.10 for the Ripple). Notably, the Ripple seems not to be strongly correlated with Bitcoin and Litecoin, and it is also less volatile and less positively skewed than the other two crypto-assets. This is not entirely surprising as it is based on a different protocol compared to the other two cryptocurrencies: instead of blockchain mining, Ripple uses a consensus mechanism to confirm transactions, which implies that Ripple transactions use less energy, are confirmed more rapidly, and include lower transaction costs than Bitcoin (or Litecoin) ones, see, for example, Joo et al. (2019) and Rosner and Kang (2016).

2.3 Methodology

To forecast the excess returns of cryptocurrencies (as well as the traditional asset classes that compose the asset menu of our investor), we use both individual predictive regression and combination methods (similar to Rapach et al., 2010). As a first step, we estimate

$$r_{t+1,j} = \alpha_j + \beta_j x_{t,i} + \epsilon_{t+1} \tag{2.1}$$

where $r_{t+1,j}$ is the excess return of the asset j and $x_{t,i}$ is the predictive variable i with $i = 1, 2, \ldots, K$. Henceforth, the forecast for the excess return of the asset j at time $t + 1$ is given by

$$\widehat{r}_{t+1,j} = \widehat{\alpha}_{m,j} + \widehat{\beta}_{m,j} x_{t,i} \tag{2.2}$$

where $\widehat{\alpha}_{m,j}$ and $\widehat{\beta}_{m,j}$ are estimated using the first m observations.[7]

In the second step, we combine the forecasts from each of the K individual models using the simple pooling model,

$$\widehat{r}^{c}_{t+1,j} = \sum_{i=1}^{K} \pi_{t,i} \widehat{r}^{i}_{t+1,j} \tag{2.3}$$

where $\widehat{r}^{i}_{t+1,j}$ is the forecast of the excess return at time $t+1$ under the model i and $\pi_{t,i}$ is the weight assigned to model i based on the information available at time t. We use both simple averaging weighting schemes (taking the mean or the median forecast) and more sophisticated ones as the discounted mean square prediction error suggested by Stock and Watson (2004), where the combining weights are a function of the historical forecasting performance of the individual models over a holdout OOS period (equal to two years of data in our case). The weight assigned to forecast j at time t is

$$\pi_{t,i} = \phi^{-1}_{i,t} / \sum_{s=1}^{K} \phi^{-1}_{s,t} \tag{2.4}$$

where

$$\phi^{-1}_{i,t} = \sum_{s=m}^{t-1} \theta^{t-1-s} (r_{s+1,j} - \widehat{r}_{s+1,j})^2 \tag{2.5}$$

and θ is a discount factor that we set alternatively equal to 1 (no discounting) and to 0.9 (similar to Rapach et al., 2010). The statistical accuracy of each of the individual predictive models, as well as the forecast combinations, is measured using the OOS R-square (Campbell and Thompson, 2008) computed as

$$R^2_{OOS} = 1 - \frac{\sum_{t+1}^{T} (r_{t+1,j} - \widehat{r}_{t+1,j})^2}{\sum_{t+1}^{T} (r_{t+1,j} - \overline{r}_{t+1,j})^2} \tag{2.6}$$

[7] We use an expanding window approach; the first in-sample estimation is obtained using five years of data (60 monthly observations) when Litecoin and Ripple are excluded and three years of data (36 monthly observation) when they are included.

where $\bar{r}_{t+1,j}$ is the historical mean, which we use as a benchmark. Therefore, the OOS R-square is positive when the predictive regression outperforms the historical mean benchmark, and negative otherwise.

In our predictive exercises, we employ two sets of predictors: the eight factors of Ludvigson and Ng (2009) and a pool of cryptocurrency-specific variables (similar to Bianchi et al. (2020), and Liu and Tsyvinski (2021)).[8] More precisely, the cryptocurrency-specific predictors are: the crypto's own 1-month lagged return, the crypto-specific momentum (computed as the last 3-month cumulative performance), the growth rate in the volume of Google searches for the word 'Bitcoin' (see, e.g., Dastgir et al., 2019), the returns of the FTSE China Electricity Index and the Dow Jones Electricity Index and of the major manufacturers of either GPU mining chips (Nvidia Corporation and Advanced Micro Devices, Inc., AMD for short) or ASIC mining chips (Taiwan Semiconductor Manufacturing Company, Limited and Advanced Semiconductor Engineering, Inc., TSMC for short).[9]

2.4 Are Cryptocurrency Returns Predictable?

Table 2.2 shows the results of the OOS predictive exercise presented in Section 2.3; the initial in-sample period is 2011–2015. We report the OOS R-square (computed as in Equation 2.6) for individual predictive regressions (including those based on crypto-specific variables) and for forecast combinations. For what concerns the Bitcoin, we base our forecast combinations either on the Ludvigson and Ng's (henceforth, LN) factors only or on all the predictive variables, with the aim of assessing the value of adding the crypto-specific variables to the set of predictors.

[8] Ludvigson and Ng (2009) estimate the principal components of 132 economic series and derive eight factors, which we shall call F1–F8, that are deemed to capture more than 50% of the variability of the series. Although the economic interpretation of the factors is not trivial, Ludvigson and Ng (2009) relate F1 to cyclical variation in real factors (such as employment and production) and F2 to interest rate spreads; F3 and F4 are called inflation factors, while F8 is deemed to be the stock market factor. The data are retrieved from www.sydneyludvigson.com/data-and-appendixes.

[9] The rationale for including the returns of the electricity sector and of the major producers of mining chips is that those represent the core productive factors for the mining activity, see, e.g., Danielius et al. (2019) and Liu and Tsyvinski (2021) for a technical background.

Table 2.2 *Recursive Out-of-Sample Realised Forecasting Performances of Alternative Models (2011–2020)*

	Bitcoin	S&P 500 Index	Dow Jones Precious Metals Index	10-year Treasury Bond	Nareit Index	Aaa Corporate Bonds	Bbb Corporate Bonds
	Panel A: Ludvigson & Ng Predictors						
F1	−3.78	−0.57	−11.16	−1.07	−0.65	−2.52	−1
F2	2.13	−1.81	−3.18	−8.34	−1.58	−5.5	−1.83
F3	0.28	0.91	−5.52	−1.29	−3.58	−1.53	−0.35
F4	9.51	−1.52	21.25	−8.12	2.11	−1.61	−1.99
F5	−12.51	3.92	−1.53	−1.89	−0.41	−2.79	−0.46
F6	−41.32	4.12	−1.78	−17.25	−1.73	−9.86	−6.58
F7	−9	−2.29	6.62	−4.52	−7.1	−2.96	−0.84
F8	−38.75	−0.68	−7.58	−0.84	1.14	−0.76	−1.47
	Panel B: Forecast Combinations						
FC Mean	4.63	0.56	4.33	−2.96	−0.88	−2.55	−1.21
FC Median	4.14	−0.05	1.2	−1.4	−0.26	−1.41	−0.55
FC DMSPE theta = 1	5.39	0.58	5.04	−2.92	−0.85	−2.53	−1.2
FC DMSPE theta = 0.9	5.72	0.58	4.14	−2.84	−0.83	−2.5	−1.19

Table 2.2 *(cont.)*

	Bitcoin	S&P 500 Index	Dow Jones Precious Metals Index	10-year Treasury Bond	Nareit Index	Aaa Corporate Bonds	Bbb Corporate Bonds
	Panel C: Crypto-specific predictors						
Bitcoin (Lag)	12.7			Bitcoin			
3 Month MOM Bitcoin	5.75	FC mean (LN +Crypto)		5.7			
Google SV	−0.69	FC median (LN +Crypto)		4.04			
ADM	−4.03	FC DMSPE theta = 1 (LN +Crypto)		5.72			
NVDA	−1.37	FC DMSPE theta = 0.9 (LN +Crypto)		5.88			
TSM	−21.61						
FTSE China Electricity	1.87						
DJ U.S. Electricity Index	1.64						

The table assesses the predictability of Bitcoin and traditional asset (excess) returns for the sample period 2011–2020. The OOS period is 2018–2020. The table reports the OOS R-squares yielded by eight variables summarising macroeconomic information (see Ludvigson and Ng, 2009) (Panel A), by their forecast combinations (Panel B), and by cryptocurrency-specific predictors, as well as their combinations (Panel C).

Several remarks are in order. First, consistently with what has been argued by Rapach et al. (2010), forecast combinations perform better than most of the individual predictors for most of the asset classes. While the evidence in favour of predictability (as measured by the OOS R-square) is in general very limited, for three out of the seven asset classes (namely, Bitcoin, equity, and precious metals), forecast combinations yield positive OOS R-squares; in contrast, most of the individual predictive regressions fail to outperform the historical mean benchmark. For instance, in the case of cryptocurrencies, using individual factors often yields negative OOS R-squares (of as much as −41.32% and −38.75% for regressions based on F6 and F8, respectively). A notable exception is represented by the predictive regression based on F4 (which, according to Ludvigson and Ng (2009), is a factor linked to inflation). Indeed, in this case, the OOS R-square is equal to 9.51%. Even more impressively, when F4 is used to forecast the excess returns of the precious metals index, the OOS R-square is a striking 21.25%.

Second, among the crypto-specific factors, the Bitcoin lagged return and the 3-month time series momentum are the only predictors that considerably outperform the benchmark model, originating R-squares of 12.70% and 5.75%, respectively. In contrast, when crypto-specific factors are added to the set of predictors in forecast combination schemes, the difference is negligible. Indeed, the best combination scheme (the DMSPE with $\theta = 0.9$) yields an OOS R-square of 5.75% when crypto-specific predictors are excluded, which increases to 5.88% when they are included. This fact reconciles our findings with those in Bianchi et al. (2020), as they use an essentially identical sample but look for predictability ignoring the power of combination and only within a specific set of crypto-specific and financial predictors featured in earlier literature, ignoring the information in macroeconomic time series.

Table 2.3 shows the results for an OOS recursive predictive exercise when also Litecoin and Ripple are included in the asset menu. Because the time series for these two cryptocurrencies are shorter, we reproduce the overall results for all the assets for the shorter period 2015–2020 (with the first three years of data used to initialise the recursive estimation of the coefficients) for comparability. In this shorter OOS period, cryptocurrencies are hardly predictable also when forecast combinations are employed. For instance, in the case of Bitcoin,

Table 2.3 *Recursive Out-of-Sample Realised Forecasting Performances of Alternative Models (2015–2020)*

	Bitcoin	Litecoin	Ripple	S&P 500 Index	Dow Jones Precious Metals Index	10-year Treasury Bond	Nareit Index	Aaa Corporate Bonds	Bbb Corporate Bonds
	Panel A: Ludvigson & Ng Predictors								
F1	−14.75	−17.92	−76.4	−1.5	−11.69	−4.68	−4.03	−4.37	−1.42
F2	−4.01	−8.75	−8.4	−0.6	−3.04	−1.08	−1.69	−3.44	−1.36
F3	−0.47	2.2	3.76	−1.04	−4.9	−1.29	−0.15	−0.61	0.53
F4	−4.15	−4.77	0.58	−3.49	8.23	−3.04	−2.06	−1.59	−2.26
F5	−3.15	−4.52	−13.19	7.75	−2.59	−5.31	−6.18	−7.18	−3.18
F6	−3.04	−4.37	−3.39	2.62	−5.26	−2.35	−4.7	−7.98	−5.07
F7	−2.12	−2.33	−16.8	3.11	4.06	−2.17	−1.19	−2.9	−1.31
F8	−5.43	−5.13	−30.86	−2.19	−4.19	−0.43	−2.06	−2.07	−2.09
	Panel B: Forecast Combinations								
FC Mean	−3.67	−3.49	−7.84	1.75	9.87	0	−1.4	−2.32	−1.04
FC Median	−1.39	−1.58	−4.28	0.78	−0.99	0.09	−1.25	−0.93	−0.24

	Panel C: Crypto-specific predictors						
Bitcoin (Lag)	2.67				Bitcoin	Litecoin	Ripple
Litecoin (Lag)		0.73		FC mean (LN + krypto)	−2.99	−3.7	−21.4
Ripple (Lag)			−3.65	FC median (LN + krypto)	−0.31	−1.18	−1.73
3 Month MOM Bitcoin	−13.31						
3 Month MOM Litecoin		−14.72					
3 Month MOM Ripple			−91.41				
Google SV	−16.74	−43.86	−222.38				
ADM	−5.14	−3	−0.83				
NVDA	−3.57	−5.95	−42.16				
TSM	−2.63	−3.7	−28.14				
FTSE China Electricity	−0.68	1.51	−0.94				
DJ U.S. Electricity Index	−1.82	2.64	1.87				

The table assesses the predictability of Bitcoin, Litecoin, Ripple, and traditional asset (excess) returns for the sample period 2015–2020. The OOS period is 2018–2020. The Table reports the OOS R-squares yielded by eight variables summarising macroeconomic information (see Ludvigson and Ng, 2010) (Panel A), by their forecast combinations (Panel B), and by cryptocurrency-specific predictors, as well as their combinations (Panel C).

the mean forecast combination yields an OOS R-square of −3.67% when only the LN factors are employed and of −2.99% when also crypto-specific variables are added to the set of the predictors. Even weaker evidence of predictability can be found when Litecoin and Ripple are considered. In this case, the OOS R-squares range from −3.49% to −21.40% when forecast combinations are employed, and can be as large (but negative) as −76.40% when individual predictors are considered.

Interestingly, the lagged return displays evidence of predictive power for both Bitcoin and Litecoin, in line with earlier literature that has shown that cryptocurrencies can be predicted using technical analysis (see, e.g., Gerritsen et al. (2020) and Grobys et al. (2020)).[10] Notably, in this shorter OOS period (2018–2020), which is characterised for more than one-third of its length by the COVID-19 pandemic crisis, most of the asset classes turn out to be rather unpredictable. The only exceptions are equity and precious metals. In the former case, several individual factors, as well as the mean forecast combination, deliver positive R-squares. In this case, most of the predictability is associated with F4, the factor linked to inflation.

Overall, it seems that cryptocurrency return predictability is mostly associated with crypto-specific variables that are connected to sentiment (like lagged return and momentum), while forecast combinations help when a longer sample period is considered. Notably, on the longer sample period, the inflation factor seems to show some predictive power for Bitcoin returns. This is interesting as practitioners (and some researchers) have suggested that Bitcoin is a viable hedge against future, expected inflation. For instance, in May 2020, Bloomberg News reported that hedge fund manager Paul Tudor Jones responded to concerns about the expansionary policy by many of the world's central banks during the COVID-19 pandemic by purchasing Bitcoin. Blau et al. (2021) use a vector autoregressive process to show that changes in Bitcoin Granger-cause changes in the forward inflation rate so that Bitcoin may be as a hedge against future inflation shocks as changes in the price of Bitcoin tend to lead to changes in the expected inflation. However, our results show that also the level of the inflation

[10] Liu (2019) has examined the predictive ability of technical, moving average-style indicators for excess Bitcoin returns and also experimented with averaging the resulting forecasts yielding positive OOS R-squares.

factor is able to predict future Bitcoin returns, possibly as a reflection of the fact that inflation is persistent and investors seem to be tapping the hedging power of Bitcoin already (see also Li and Wang, 2017).

2.5 The Economic Value of Cryptocurrencies for a Mean–Variance Investor

We are especially interested in understanding whether adding cryptocurrencies to the asset menu (eventually exploiting its predictability) may generate a risk-adjusted additional performance to a risk averse investor. To this purpose, we implement a recursive mean–variance allocation strategy where the asset menu either consists of traditional asset classes only or it also includes cryptocurrencies. More precisely, each month the investor chooses her portfolio weights according to the classical formula

$$\omega^* = \frac{1}{\gamma}\widehat{\Sigma}_{t+1}^{-1}\widehat{r}_{t+1} \tag{2.7}$$

where $\widehat{r}_{t+1}$ is the vector containing the predictions for the (excess) returns of the risky assets according to each of the different forecasting models described in Section 2.4 and $\widehat{\Sigma}_{t+1}$ is the historical covariance matrix of asset excess returns. The investor allocates $1 - 1'\omega^*$ in the risk-free asset; moreover, short selling of the risky assets is not allowed and the weight of each asset is capped at 150%.

To evaluate the performance of the alternative portfolios, we compute the mean return (and standard deviation), the SR, and the realised utility level from each predictive model as

$$CER = \widehat{\mu}_P - \frac{1}{2}\gamma\widehat{\sigma}_P^2 \tag{2.8}$$

where $\widehat{\mu}_P$ and $\widehat{\sigma}_P^2$ are the sample mean and variance of the ex-post, realised returns over the OOS period from the optimal $t+1$ portfolio formed by exploiting each predictive model (or the historical mean benchmark).

Table 2.4 reports the results for our longest sample, when only Bitcoin is included in the asset menu in addition to the traditional asset classes. The results concern different levels of risk aversion ($\gamma = 2, 5, 10$). The table allows us to comment on two facts: first, by comparing the performance of the asset allocations that exploit forecast combinations with those that use the historical mean, we

Table 2.4 ***Realised Performance of Recursive Mean–Variance Asset Allocations (2011–2020)***

	With Bitcoin					Without Bitcoin					With – without	
	Mean	St. Dev.	SR	CER	ΔCER	Mean	St. Dev.	SR	CER	ΔCER	ΔSR	ΔCER
	$\gamma = 2$											
FC Mean	4.48	12.97	0.34	2.8	1.21	3.78	11.93	0.32	**2.36**	**0.88**	0.03	0.44
FC Median	3.84	10.9	**0.35**	2.7	1.07	3.18	**9.36**	**0.34**	2.3	0.83	0.01	0.35
FC DMSPE theta = 1	**4.57**	**13.37**	0.34	2.8	1.19	**3.82**	12.44	0.31	2.27	0.8	0.03	0.5
FC DMSPE theta = 0.9	4.49	12.93	0.35	**2.8**	**1.24**	3.76	11.98	0.31	2.32	0.85	0.03	0.5
Historical mean	3.1	12.3	0.25	1.6	–	2.58	10.51	0.24	1.48	–	0.01	0.11
	$\gamma = 5$											
FC Mean	3.4	10.02	0.34	0.9	0.98	3.07	9.68	0.32	0.73	0.85	0.03	0.16
FC Median	3.3	**9.55**	0.34	**1**	**1.11**	2.98	**9.08**	**0.33**	**0.92**	**1.05**	0.01	0.1
FC DMSPE theta = 1	**3.42**	10.14	0.34	0.9	0.94	**3.08**	9.83	0.31	0.67	0.8	0.03	0.18
FC DMSPE theta = 0.9	3.41	10.01	0.34	0.9	0.99	3.06	9.72	0.31	0.7	0.83	0.03	0.2
Historical mean	2.67	10.52	0.25	−0.1	–	2.44	10.13	0.24	−0.13	–	0.01	0.03
	$\gamma = 10$											
FC Mean	2.93	9.37	0.31	−1.5	0.46	2.78	9.14	0.3	−1.4	0.55	0.01	−0.07
FC Median	**2.96**	**9.05**	**0.33**	**−1.1**	**0.79**	2.72	**8.89**	0.31	**−1.23**	**0.72**	0.02	0.09
FC DMSPE theta = 1	2.94	9.4	0.31	−1.5	0.45	**2.8**	9.16	0.3	−1.39	0.56	0.01	−0.08
FC DMSPE theta = 0.9	2.96	9.32	0.32	−1.4	0.54	2.8	9.11	**0.31**	−1.35	0.6	0.01	−0.04
Historical mean	2.68	9.59	0.28	−1.9	–	2.46	9.39	0.26	−1.95	–	0.02	0.02

	Weights ($\gamma = 2$)							
	FC Mean	FC Median	DMSPE theta = 1	Hist. mean	FC Mean	FC Median	DMSPE theta = 1	Hist. mean
Bitcoin	13.16	13.94	13.02	15	–	–	–	–
S&P 500 Index	150	150	150	150	150	150	150	150
DJ Precious Metals	6.01	0.95	8.11	0	5.83	0.86	8.12	0
10-year Treasury Bond	108.2	122.46	112	150	145.83	145.83	145.83	150
Nareit Index	–	–	–	–	–	–	–	–
Aaa Corporate Bonds	150	150	149.4	150	147.77	149.62	145.83	150
Bbb Corporate Bonds	15.45	49.3	17.8	54	21.66	54.94	23.04	61.59

The table shows the mean realised return, standard deviation, SR, and CER obtained by a mean–variance investor exploiting either different forecast combination methods or the historical mean when the Bitcoin is included in the asset menu and when it is excluded. We assume three different coefficients of risk aversion, that is, $\gamma = 2, 5, 10$. ΔCER is either the utility gain when predictability is exploited (vs. using the historical mean benchmark) or the utility gain (loss) from having the Bitcoin in the asset menu (in the last column of the table). ΔSR is the gain (loss) in the SR from having access to Bitcoin. The bottom panel displays the average weights assigned to each asset class when $\gamma = 2$.

can disentangle the benefits of exploiting predictability obtained from pooled models. Second, by comparing the results in the left panel with those in the right panel, we can compute the realised gains of including Bitcoin in the investable set.

For what concerns the value of predictability, we conclude that the optimised portfolios based on the predictive models always outperform those based on the historical mean benchmark, irrespective of the level of risk aversion and whether cryptocurrencies are available to investors. For instance, in the case of $\gamma = 2$, when digital currencies are available, an investor with access to forecast combinations will earn a per month return of 4.57–3.84%, implying SRs of 0.34–0.35 (per month, which compounds to approximately 1.21 on an annual basis). In contrast, an investor relying on the naive historical mean model will earn a return of 3.10% per month with an SR of 0.25. In addition, an investor with access to the pooled predictive model will realise a utility gain of approximately 1.24% per month (14.90% on an annualised basis). This corresponds to the maximum fee that the investor may be willing to pay to have access to forecast combinations, which represents a hard-to-dismiss estimate.

Comparing the results on the left and the right panels of Table 2.4, we conclude that an investor may benefit from the inclusion of cryptocurrencies in their portfolio, irrespective of the predictive model they select. The last two columns of the table report the difference in SR and certainty equivalent returns (CER) when cryptocurrencies are accessible to the investor. While the investor generally benefits from the inclusion of Bitcoin in their optimal portfolio, these gains tend to be larger when predictability is exploited (δCER is equal to approximately 6% on an annualised basis when a sophisticated DMSPE forecast combination model is employed). In contrast, when the investor relies on the historical mean, the utility gain is fairly small (around 1.32% on an annualised basis).

Finally, in the bottom panel of Table 2.4, we show the average weights assigned to each asset by an investor characterised by $\gamma = 2$ in the presence versus in the absence of Bitcoin as part of the asset menu. Notably, the investor ought to allocate on average 13–14% of their wealth in Bitcoin. When Bitcoin is not accessible, they increase their exposure to high-yield corporate bonds and government bonds. The fact that bonds and Bitcoin may be substitutes speaks of the safety characterisation of digital currency as an asset class, see, for example, Shahzad et al. (2019).

Table 2.5 shows the same results for the shorter, 2015–2020 sample. In this case, also Litecoin and Ripple are part of the asset menu. In this shorter sample, while the evidence in favour of the power of forecast combination schemes remains present (even if milder and limited to investors with a high level of risk aversion, i.e., $\gamma = 10$), the support for the inclusion of cryptocurrencies in the asset allocation fades away. In fact, an investor with access to cryptocurrencies will experience a utility loss of as much as −45% on an annualised basis. Interestingly, while Bitcoin and Litecoin massively enter the asset allocation (with a weight of as much as 50% for Bitcoin and 16% for Litecoin), the weight assigned to the Ripple is rather modest (2–4%). When cryptocurrencies are not available, the investor increases their exposure to real estate instead, also reflecting the low volatility of REIT returns in the aftermath of the financial crisis.

It must be considered that the shorter sample is characterised for approximately one-third by the COVID crisis. Therefore, the results presented in Table 2.5 represent some preliminary evidence against the claim that cryptocurrencies may represent a safe haven in times of crisis, even if and when they remain predictable (see, e.g., Caferra and Vidal-Tomás, 2021).

2.6 Conclusion

In this chapter, we have re-examined with updated data that also include the first part of the pandemic shock (with reference to 2020 data), the evidence that cryptocurrencies may represent a viable, investable asset useful in standard portfolio problems when asset returns are predictable. In particular, we study whether a mix of macroeconomic factors (diffusion indices) and crypto-specific predictors (momentum, social media attention, proxies of mining costs, etc.) can be combined to produce accurate and economically valuable pooled forecasts.

With reference to Bitcoin data and a relatively long 10-year sample of weekly data, we uncover that crypto returns are predictable OOS, at least in relative terms versus a benchmark sample mean; moreover, when the crypto-asset is made available to a mean–variance optimising investor, it generates considerable risk-adjusted OOS realised

Table 2.5 ***Realised Performance of Recursive Mean–Variance Asset Allocations (2015–2020)***

	With crypto					Without crypto					With – without	
	Mean	St. Dev.	SR	CER	ΔCER	Mean	St. Dev.	SR	CER	ΔCER	ΔSR	ΔCER
	$\gamma = 2$											
FC Mean	**5.84**	26.64	**0.22**	−1.26	−0.06	2.87	11.66	0.25	1.51	0.65	−0.03	−2.77
FC Median	3.44	23.18	0.15	−1.93	−0.74	**3.57**	13	**0.27**	**1.88**	**1.02**	−0.13	−3.82
Historical mean	3.43	**21.51**	0.16	**−1.2**	–	2	**10.68**	0.19	0.86	–	−0.03	−2.06
	$\gamma = 5$											
FC Mean	**3.81**	14.73	**0.26**	−1.62	−0.21	**2.49**	**8.19**	**0.3**	**0.81**	**0.89**	−0.04	−2.43
FC Median	2.5	12.75	0.2	−1.56	−0.16	2.32	9.07	0.25	0.26	0.34	−0.06	−1.83
Historical mean	2.33	**12.22**	0.19	**−1.41**	–	1.84	8.75	0.21	−0.1	–	−0.02	−1.33
	$\gamma = 10$											
FC Mean	**2.83**	10.49	**0.27**	−2.68	0.01	**2.17**	**7.21**	**0.3**	**−0.4**	**1.15**	−0.03	−2.24
FC Median	2.02	9.63	0.21	**−2.61**	**0.07**	1.83	8.06	0.23	−1.4	0.17	−0.02	−1.2
Historical mean	1.84	**9.51**	0.19	−2.69	–	1.68	8.08	0.21	−1.6	–	−0.01	−1.1

	Weights (γ =2)					
	FC Mean	FC Median	Hist. mean	FC Mean	FC Median	Hist. mean
Bitcoin	56.24	57.61	50.28	–	–	–
Litecoin	16.72	16.53	15.97	–	–	–
Ripple	3.5	2.17	1.93	–	–	–
S&P 500 Index	149.5	150	150	3.43	3.94	8.08
DJ Precious Metals	46.34	25.64	21.58	118.78	141.67	150
10-year Treasury Bond	145.83	150	150	34.3	38.09	15.08
Nareit Index	13.35	7.68	–	129.17	133.33	150
Aaa Corporate Bonds	82.27	66.88	46.34	24.92	–	0.16
Bbb Corporate Bonds	38.32	19.41	5.92	41.67	33.33	50.64

The table shows the mean realised return, standard deviation, SR, and CER obtained by a mean–variance investor exploiting either different forecast combination methods or the historical mean when cryptocurrencies (Bitcoin, Litecoin, and Ripple) are included in the asset menu and when they are excluded. We assume three different coefficients of risk aversion, that is, $\gamma = 2, 5, 10$. ΔCER is either the utility gain when predictability is exploited (vs. using the historical mean benchmark) or the utility gain (loss) from having the cryptocurrencies in the asset menu (in the last column of the table). ΔSR is the gain (loss) in the SR from having access to the cryptocurrencies. The bottom panel displays the average weights assigned to each asset class when $\gamma = 2$.

performance gains irrespective of the assumed risk aversion of the investor under analysis. The results on the predictability of cryptocurrencies are robust to a generalisation to Litecoin and Ripple, although on a shorter 2015–2020 sample. However, results turn mixed and come to depend on the assumed risk aversion, when we investigate the power of forecast combinations to generate economic value from the entire pool of cryptocurrencies. In spite of their stellar, realised mean returns during 2020, these results call into question the naive notion that the attractiveness of cryptocurrencies may simply derive from short-term spurts of growth in cryptocurrency prices. Yet, our evidence that at least Bitcoin may give a first-order contribution to portfolio diversification stands and will need further scrutiny before calling Bitcoin or any other companion digital currency a new asset class.

In the future, as more data becomes available, this work should be extended to include additional cryptocurrencies in our back-test. In fact, several new digital currencies have been launched in recent years, and some would deserve consideration. Among many, a notable example is Hbar by Hedera. This crypto was launched in August 2018, and has actively traded at least since late 2020. Over the sample period of January 2021–May 2022, Hbar has delivered an average annualised return of approximately 60% with a volatility of 147%, yielding an annualised SR of approximately 0.4. Because it was engineered on the Byzantine fault-tolerant algorithm, Hbar represents a response to the quest for faster and less energy-consuming block-chain transactions. In fact, it is characterised by an average time-to-consensus of 5.64 seconds, and it only requires 0.000003 average kWh per transaction (see hedera.com). This is a huge reduction in energy consumption, compared, for instance, to Bitcoin's average of 478.27 kWh per transaction in 2020 (see, e.g., De Vries et al., 2022). Even though the future belongs to these new digital assets also from an asset allocation perspective, longer time series and fresh calculations will be needed to establish this point, even though an initial SR of 0.4 or more seems promising.

Bibliography

Baur, D. G., Hong, K., and Lee, A. D. (2018). Bitcoin: Medium of exchange or speculative assets? *Journal of International Financial Markets, Institutions and Money*, 54:177–189.

Bekemeier, F. (2021). The institutionalization of crypto assets and decentralized financial markets. *Available at SSRN 3899162*.

Bianchi, D., Guidolin, M., and Pedio, M. (2020). Dissecting time-varying risk exposures in cryptocurrency markets. *BAFFI CAREFIN Centre Research Paper*, (2020–143).

Bianchi, D., Guidolin, M., and Pedio, M. (2022). The dynamics of returns predictability in cryptocurrency markets. *The European Journal of Finance*, 29(3):1–29.

Blau, B. M., Griffith, T. G., and Whitby, R. J. (2021). Inflation and Bitcoin: A descriptive time-series analysis. *Economics Letters*, 203:109848.

Bouri, E., Molnar, P., Azzi, G., Roubaud, D., and Hagfors, L. (2017). On the hedge and safe haven properties of Bitcoin: Is it really more than a diversifier? *Finance Research Letters*, 20:192–198.

Briere, M., Oosterlinck, K., and Szafarz, A. (2015). Virtual currency, tangible return: Portfolio diversification with bitcoin. *Journal of Asset Management*, 16:365–373.

Caferra, R. and Vidal-Tomás, D. (2021). Who raised from the abyss? A comparison between cryptocurrency and stock market dynamics during the covid-19 pandemic. *Finance Research Letters*, forthcoming: 101954.

Campbell, J. Y. and Thompson, S. B. (2008). Predicting excess stock returns out of sample: Can anything beat the historical average? *Review of Financial Studies*, 21(4):1509–1531.

Chuen, D. L. K., Guo, L., and Wang, Y. (2018). Cryptocurrency: A new investment opportunity? *Journal of Alternative Investments*, 20:16–40.

Ciaian, P. and Rajcaniova, M. (2019). Virtual relationships: Short and long-run evidence from Bitcoin and altcoin markets. *Journal of International Financial Markets, Institutions and Money*, 52:173–195.

Corbet, S., Larkin, C., Lucey, B., Meegan, A., and Yarovaya, L. (2018). Exploring the dynamic relationships between cryptocurrencies and other financial assets. *Economics Letters*, 165:28–34.

Danielius, P., Savenas, T., and Masteika, S. (2019). Study of factors related to grin cryptocurrency mining efficiency with GPUs. In *International Conference on Business Information Systems*, 267–273. Springer.

Dastgir, S., Demir, E., Downing, G., Gozgor, G., and Lau, C. (2019). The causal relationship between Bitcoin attention and Bitcoin returns: Evidence from the Copula-based Granger causality test. *Finance Research Letters*, 28:160–164.

De Vries, A., Gallersdörfer, U., Klaaßen, L., and Stoll, C. (2022). Revisiting Bitcoin's carbon footprint. *Joule*, 6(3):498–502.

Dyhrberg, A. H. (2016). Hedging capabilities of Bitcoin. Is it the virtual gold? *Finance Research Letters*, 16:139–144.

Gerritsen, D., Bouri, E., Ramezanifar, E., and Roubaud, D. (2020). The profitability of technical trading rules in the Bitcoin market. *Finance Research Letters*, 34:101263.

Grobys, K., Ahmed, S., and Sapkota, N. (2020). Technical trading rules in the cryptocurrency market. *Finance Research Letters*, 32:101396.

Guesmi, K., Saadi, S., Abid, I., and Ftiti, Z. (2019). Portfolio diversification with virtual currency: Evidence from Bitcoin. *International Review of Financial Analysis*, 63:431–437.

Joo, M., Nishikawa, Y., and Dandapani, K. (2019). Cryptocurrency, a successful application of blockchain technology. *Managerial Finance*, 46:715–733.

Kandel, S. and Stambaugh, R. (1996). On the predictability of stock returns: An asset-allocation perspective. *Journal of Finance*, 51:385–424.

Li, X. and Wang, C. (2017). The technology and economic determinants of cryptocurrency exchange rates: The case of Bitcoin. *Decision Support Systems*, 95:49–60.

Liu, L. (2019). Are Bitcoin returns predictable?: Evidence from technical indicators. *Physica A: Statistical Mechanics and its Applications*, 533:121950.

Liu, Y. and Tsyvinski, A. (2021). Risks and returns of cryptocurrency. *Review of Financial Studies*, 34(6):2689–2727.

Liu, Y., Tsyvinski, A., and Wu, X. (2019). Common risk factors in cryptocurrency. Technical report, National Bureau of Economic Research.

Ludvigson, S. C. and Ng, S. (2009). Macro factors in bond risk premia. *Review of Financial Studies*, 22(12):5027–5067.

Panagiotidis, T., Stengos, T., and Vravosinos, O. (2019). The effects of markets, uncertainty and search intensity on Bitcoin returns. *International Review of Financial Analysis*, 63:220–242.

Rapach, D. E., Strauss, J. K., and Zhou, G. (2010). Out-of-sample equity premium prediction: Combination forecasts and links to the real economy. *Review of Financial Studies*, 23(2):821–862.

Rosner, M. and Kang, A. (2016). Understanding and regulating twenty-first century payment systems: The Ripple case study. *Michigan Law Review*, 114:649–681.

Shahzad, S., Bouri, E., Roubaud, D., Kristoufek, L., and Lucey, B. (2019). Is Bitcoin a better safe-haven investment than gold and commodities? *International Review of Financial Analysis*, 63:322–330.

Smales, L. (2019). Bitcoin as a safe haven: Is it even worth considering? *Finance Research Letters*, 30:385–393.

Stock, J. H. and Watson, M. W. (2004). Combination forecasts of output growth in a seven-country data set. *Journal of Forecasting*, 23(6):405–430.

Symitsi, E. and Chalvatzis, K. (2019). The economic value of Bitcoin: A portfolio analysis of currencies, gold, oil and stocks. *Research in International Business and Finance*, 48:97–110.

Welch, I. and Goyal, A. (2008). A comprehensive look at the empirical performance of equity premium prediction. *The Review of Financial Studies*, 21(4):1455–1508.

Xiao, H. and Sun, Y. (2020). Forecasting the returns of cryptocurrency: A model averaging approach. *Journal of Risk and Financial Management*, 13:378.

Yermack, D. (2015). Is Bitcoin a real currency? An economic appraisal. In *Handbook of Digital Currency*, 31–43, Elsevier.

3 *DeFi versus TradFi*
Valuation Using Multiples and Discounted Cash Flows

TENG ANDREA XU, JIAHUA XU, AND KRISTOF LOMMERS

3.1 Introduction

Decentralised finance (DeFi) provides financial services such as loans or asset exchange leveraging distributed ledger technologies (DLTs). Towards the end of summer 2020, the total market cap of decentralised autonomous organisation (DAO) tokens in DeFi grew up to 154 billion USD from 1.8 billion USD as of March 2020 (Xu and Xu, 2022). The Total Value Locked (TVL), that is, the net worth of all assets locked in smart contracts, reached its peak for many DeFi protocols in that period (Figure 3.1).

Since that 'DeFi Summer', DAO tokens connected to decentralised financial services have enjoyed a large growth of interest both within the crypto community and beyond, despite the continuous debate surrounding whether DeFi is just a fad, or is to stay and co-exist with Traditional Finance (TradFi) (Qin et al., 2021). This interest was mainly driven from DeFi's *permissionless* (Werner et al., 2021) and *composable* nature (Qin et al., 2021).

The growth of interest has brought more users in the protocols with (i) higher on-chain transaction volume and (ii) higher off-chain trading volume. Similarly, entrepreneurs and hedge funds have decided to invest into digital assets, such as Grayscale and BlackRock, to cite a few. However, as a myriad of DeFi projects provide similar financial services, it is hard to reason why an investor should prefer one over the other. In classical finance, investors use valuation theory (Damodaran, 2007) for their decision-making process in asset selection.

On the one hand, the necessity for fundamental analysis is the fact that market prices often do not reflect the true underlying value of an asset. Fundamental analyses look into firms' financial statements and estimate a *fair* share price based on the firm's performance. On the other hand, comparable analysis assumes that, on average, the market

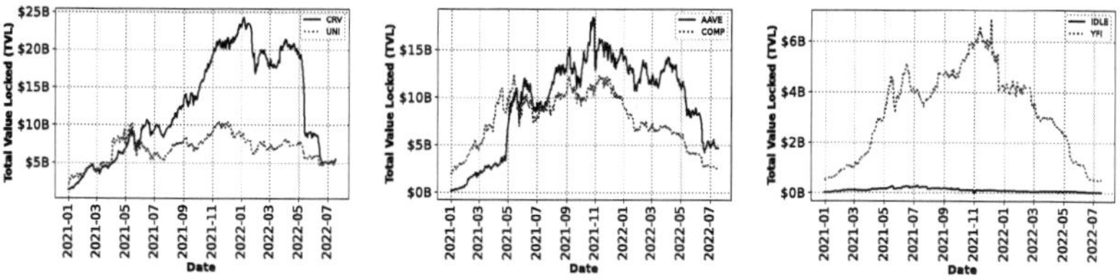

(a) DEXs (b) PLFs (c) Yield aggregators

Figure 3.1 Historical TVL for different DeFi.

prices reflect investors' beliefs (Damodaran, 2007). Comparable analysis will still look at financial fundamentals, but instead of estimating a theoretical value, it will use firms' fundamental value ratios, that is, 'multiples' to compare them and thus spot comparatively undervalued/overvalued assets. Naturally, comparable analysis is only applicable to firms within a similar segment.

In this study, we apply both intrinsic and relative valuation methods to selected DAO tokens in DeFi as well as stocks in TradFi. Our contributions can be summarised as follows:

1. First, we apply empirically fundamental and comparable analyses to DeFi DAO tokens. Surprisingly, although DeFi tokens are in a bear market for more than 1 year thus far, they remain overvalued compared to their theoretical fair value.
2. Second, we compare multiples between DeFi and TradFi. This comparison shows that DeFi tokens multiples exceed their TradFi counterparties by several times, demonstrating the general overvaluation of the former.
3. Finally, all analyses use publicly available data,[1] and the steps to reproduce the results are well-described.[2] Thus, to the best of our knowledge, we are the first to provide a clear framework and steps to value DAO tokens and compare them with stocks of traditional publicly traded firms.

This chapter is organised as follows: in Section 3.2, we provide a theoretical background. Section 3.3 provides a description of our data

[1] TokenTerminal provides a free premium account for three days upon registration.

[2] The code is publicly available at github.com/tengandreaxu/defi-value-investing

set and technical details about the approaches used. Section 3.4 shows our findings. Finally, Section 3.5 concludes.

3.2 Literature

To date, various valuation models have been developed from the literature (Damodaran, 2007, 2012):

Intrinsic The theoretical value is a function of dividends, earnings, assets, liabilities, and so on. The theoretical value can be estimated through different approaches: discounted cash flow (DCF), Gordon Growth Model (GGM) (Gordon, 1959), and the Modigliani–Miller (MM) theorem (Modigliani and Miller, 1958).

Relative This technique looks into *multiples* (Liu et al., 2002; Schreiner, 2009) such as the Price to Sales (P/S) ratio.

We focus on DeFi categories that have received major interest from the literature, that is, decentralised exchanges (DEXs) (Xu et al., 2022), protocols for loanable funds (PLFs) (Gudgeon et al., 2020), and yield aggregators (Cousaert et al., 2022). As Damodaran (2007) reports, the majority of valuation approaches rely on DCF and multiples.

3.3 Methodology

We apply both fundamental and comparable analyses to a set of DAO tokens in DeFi and stocks in TradFi. For DeFi, we focus on DEXs, PLFs, and yield aggregators, the three major DeFi classes. The three analogous TradFi sectors that we consider are exchanges, banks, and asset managers, respectively. The set of token assets and firms grouped by their respective industry/financial service is shown in Table 3.1.

Data

We use Token Terminal[3] for aggregated and processed financial metrics of tokens. In particular, we collect tokens' off-chain and on-chain *daily* measures, for example, circulating market cap, price, TVL, and protocol revenues. Protocol revenue, in this case, is defined as the

[3] docs.tokenterminal.com

Table 3.1 ***DeFi DAO protocols and publicly traded companies universe examined.***

DeFi	**DEXs**	**PLFs**	**Yield aggregators**
	Uniswap (UNI)	Aave (AAVE)	Yearn Finance (YFI)
	Curve (CRV)	Compound (COMP)	Idle Finance (IDLE)
TradFi	**Exchanges**	**Banks**	**Asset managers**
	Chicago Board Options Exchange (CBOE)	Citigroup (C)	Berkshire Hathaway (BRK.B)
	Nasdaq (NDAQ)	Bank of America (BAC)	Morgan Stanley (MS)
	Intercontinental Exchange (ICE)	Wells Fargo & Co. (WFC)	BlackRock (BLK)

amount of revenue that is distributed to token holders (Token Terminal, 2022). We compare tokens' fundamentals with publicly traded companies' balance sheets in the same industry. For companies' quarterly fundamental information, we use common financial data sources such as Center for Research in Security Prices (CRSP) and Compustat, well-known databases in empirical asset pricing works, such as Kelly and Pruitt (2013), Welch and Goyal (2008), to name a few. Similar to tokens' metrics, we are interested in companies' market cap, share price, total revenue, net assets, and pre-tax income (WRDS, 2022c). Note that for firm's and bank's total revenue, we use the Quarterly Total Revenue (WRDS, 2022d) and Quarterly Total Current Operating Revenue (WRDS, 2022e), respectively. Finally, we obtain the firm's quarter net asset value by subtracting from the firm's quarter total asset value (WRDS, 2022a) the firm's quarter total debt (WRDS, 2022b).

Fundamental Analysis

We apply the DCF approach for the fundamental analysis. Equation 3.1 shows how DCF values firms according to their future cash flows discounted by a discount factor:

$$NPV = \sum_{t=0}^{n} \frac{CASH_t}{(1+r)^t} + \frac{TerminalValue}{(1+r)^{t+1}}, \tag{3.1}$$

where the discount factor r is usually identified as the weighted average cost of capital (WACC). For tokens, *CASH* is equivalent to the yearly protocol revenue, while for publicly traded firms, it corresponds to the pre-tax income. In this work, we will estimate a fair revenue growth of 5% for the next 5 years. The WACC is defined as

$$WACC = \left(\frac{E}{E+D} \times R_e\right) + \left(\frac{D}{E+D} \times R_d \times (1 - TaxRate)\right), \tag{3.2}$$

where E is total equities, D liabilities, R_e the cost of capital, and R_d the cost of debt.

For publicly traded firms, we estimate the cost of capital by multiplying the industry average β – retrieved from Damodaran (2022c) – with the historical market returns set to 10%. The historical market return is coherent with the last 20 years' S&P 500 average annual return (9.87%) (Damodaran, 2022a). The cost of debt – the interest rate that companies have to pay on their debt – is retrieved directly from the firm's 10-K filing from the SEC Edgar database[4]. Specifically, we use the companies' debt interest rate for senior structured notes stated in the 'Financial Statements and Supplementary Data' section. Finally, the average corporate tax rate by industry is used (Damodaran, 2022b). By plugging these numbers into Equation 3.2, we obtain the firm's WACC. By contrary, we cannot use the same analysis to estimate WACC for DeFi tokens, as they achieve greater economy of scale and do not face corporate taxes. However, DeFi tokens face higher risk, therefore, we discount their value by a higher factor – a value typically used in the literature: 25% (Lord, 2022). Next, *TerminalValue* is simply defined as

$$TerminalValue = \sum_{i=1}^{\infty} \frac{CASH(1+g)^n}{(1+r)^n} = \frac{CASH(1+g)}{(r-g)}, \tag{3.3}$$

where g is the perpetual growth rate, that is, the constant rate that a company is expected to grow indefinitely. Commonly, g should be

[4] www.sec.gov/edgar/searchedgar/companysearch.html

Table 3.2 *Variables used to compute firms' DCF.*

	β	*MarketReturn*	R_d	R_e	*TaxRate*	*WACC*
BAC	1.12	10%	2.85%	11.20%	14.69%	10.59%
BLK	1.05	10%	2.10%	10.50%	13.37%	10.46%
BRK.B	1.05	10%	3.30%	10.50%	13.37%	10.47%
C	1.12	10%	2.88%	11.20%	14.69%	10.08%
CBOE	1.05	10%	2.63%	10.50%	13.37%	10.47%
ICE	1.12	10%	3.00%	10.50%	13.37%	10.42%
MS	1.12	10%	2.90%	10.50%	13.37%	9.20%
NDAQ	1.12	10%	3.75%	10.50%	13.37%	10.28%
WFC	1.05	10%	2.37%	11.20%	14.69%	10.97%

We set *MarketReturn* to the average yearly market return: 10%. We use Damodaran's industry β and *TaxRate* (Damodaran, 2022c, b). The cost of debt R_d was retrieved from the firms' 10-K document. The cost of capital R_e is the product of β and *MarketReturn*. Finally, we compute *WACC* with Equation 3.2.

in line with the nominal Gross Domestic Product (GDP) growth rate (Steiger, 2010). We thus take the average yearly GDP from 1990 to 2021 to proxy the perpetual growth rate: 2.39% (Statista, 2022). To conclude our assumptions, we estimate workforce expenses of 20% and 30% of the total income for DeFi DAO tokens and publicly traded firms respectively. In Section 3.4, we show our estimations of growth for the next five years together with historical balance sheets. In these historical balance sheets, we report the Compound Quarterly Growth Rate (CQGR), defined as:

$$CQGR = \left(\frac{V_{end}}{V_{start}}\right)^{\frac{1}{q}} - 1, \tag{3.4}$$

where q denotes the number of quarters between *start* and *end*. As the data for DeFi is limited due to its short history, the analysis starts from the last quarter of 2020 for both DeFi and TradFi.

Comparable Analysis

We use multiples to compare valuation between DeFi and TradFi. Specifically, the DeFi protocol/company's value is proxied by the token/stock' market cap. A firm's value is usually a function of the capacity of generating cash flow and risk, as reported in Damodaran (2007). Therefore, we identify the following:

For DeFi – *revenue protocol*, as the protocol's total revenue. Since, TokenTerminal provides *daily* observations, we simply sum up the daily revenue values within a quarter.
– *treasury*, as the net asset owned by the underlying protocol, which in turn is collectively owned by protocol token holders.

For TradFi – *revtq*, as WRDS (2022d) reports, this value is the firm's quarterly total revenue.
– *atq* and *dlcq*, respectively, the firm's quarterly total assets and total liabilities (WRDS, 2022a, b). Therefore, the net assets owned by the firm is the difference between the two numbers.

Hence, we end up with two multiples:

1. The *Market Cap/Revenue* multiple: this ratio shows us how the underlying value changes with respect to its own income.
2. The *Market Cap/Net Assets* multiple: similarly, this ratio shows us the change of value with respect to the net assets owned by the underlying firm/protocol.

We show and discuss the results in the Section 3.4.

3.4 Results

Fundamental Analysis: Historical Balance Sheets

In this section, we show the historical earnings for both DAO tokens and publicly traded firms. Due to DAO tokens' fairly recent phenomena, the historical data tables shown in Tables 3.3 and 3.4 start from Q4 2020. The tables show the underlying earnings from Q4 2020 to Q2 2022. In the last column, we compute and show the CQGR defined in Equation 3.4. The earnings, shown in USD millions, were steadily increasing for most DeFi tokens until 2021's last quarter. However, with the recent bearish period within the crypto ecosystem, the slope has turned negative. Fears for inflation within risk markets, regulatory uncertainty, numerous attacks, and hacks caused increasing diffidence and uncertainty in crypto-assets (see Shanaev

Table 3.3 *DAOs' historical balance sheets*

	2020	2021				2022		CQGR
	Q4	Q1	Q2	Q3	Q4	Q1	Q2	%
Uniswap								
Earnings ($M)	*NA*	25.7	46.9	30.8	46.8	31.1	23.2	*−0.02%*
% growth	*NA*	*NA*	*82.33%*	*−34.33%*	*52.13%*	*−33.5%*	*−25.48%*	
Curve								
Earnings ($M)	*NA*	*NA*	*NA*	6.34	19.8	18.5	12.2	*0.24%*
% growth	*NA*	*NA*	*NA*	*NA*	*213.04%*	*−6.78%*	*−34.21%*	
Compound								
Earnings ($M)	*NA*	10.6	10.9	9.0	10.0	4.8	1.8	*−0.30%*
% growth	*NA*	*NA*	*2.50%*	*−16.91%*	*11.14%*	*−51.89%*	*−62.69%*	
AAVE								
Earnings ($M)	*NA*	1.2	5.5	9.3	12.7	6.5	6.0	*0.37%*
% growth	*NA*	*NA*	*355.22%*	*68.66%*	*35.94%*	*−48.84%*	*−8.08%*	
Yearn Finance								
Earnings ($M)	*NA*	*NA*	22.3	23.1	26.2	14.0	6.9	*−0.25%*
% growth	*NA*	*NA*	*NA*	*3.66%*	*12.98%*	*−46.55%*	*−50.29%*	
Idle Finance								
Earnings ($M)	*NA*	*NA*	0.3	0.2	0.2	0.1	0.05	*−0.37%*
% growth	*NA*	*NA*	*NA*	*−36.96%*	*−24.12%*	*−59.15%*	*−20.77%*	

Table 3.4 ***Firms' historical earnings***

	2020	2021				2022		CQGR
	Q4	Q1	Q2	Q3	Q4	Q1	Q2	%
ICE								
Earnings ($M)	583.0	674.0	833.0	1932.0	824.0	2109.0	832.0	*6.11*
% growth	*NA*	*15.61%*	*23.59%*	*131.93%*	*−57.35%*	*155.95%*	*−60.55%*	
NDAQ								
Earnings ($M)	356.0	267.0	395.0	454.0	371.0	314.0	374.0	*0.83*
% growth	*NA*	*−25.0%*	*47.94%*	*14.94%*	*−18.28%*	*−15.36%*	*19.11%*	
CBOE								
Earnings ($M)	163.4	122.9	192.9	179.2	173.8	210.2	224.9	*5.47*
% growth	*NA*	*−24.79%*	*56.96%*	*−7.1%*	*−3.01%*	*20.94%*	*6.99%*	
C								
Earnings ($M)	5,441.0	10,309.0	7,348.0	5,862.0	3,950.0	5,266.0	5,971.0	*6.07*
% growth	*37.61%*	*89.47%*	*−28.72%*	*−20.22%*	*−32.62%*	*33.32%*	*13.39%*	
BAC								
Earnings ($M)	4,546.0	6,119.0	9,166.0	8,042.0	8,950.0	7,818.0	7,879.0	9.6
% growth	*NA*	*34.6%*	*49.8%*	*−12.26%*	*11.29%*	*−12.65%*	*0.78%*	

WFC								
Earnings ($M)	3,866.0	5,591.0	8,189.0	6,926.0	8,110.0	4,509.0	3,565.0	*1.03%*
% growth	*16.52%*	*44.62%*	*46.47%*	*−15.42%*	*17.1%*	*−44.4%*	*−20.94%*	
BRK.B								
Earnings ($M)	37,930.0	45,403.0	14,528.0	35,721.0	12,484.0	48,953.0	6,812.0	*−24.89%*
% growth	*NA*	*19.7%*	*−68.0%*	*145.88%*	*−65.05%*	*292.13%*	*−86.08%*	
MS								
Earnings ($M)	4,430.0	5,344.0	4,566.0	4,874.0	4,884.0	4,588.0	3,319.0	*−0.7%*
% growth	*27.04%*	*20.63%*	*−14.56%*	*6.75%*	*0.21%*	*−6.06%*	*−27.66%*	
BLK								
Earnings ($M)	2,167.0	1,591.0	2,201.0	2,271.0	2,110.0	1,626.0	1,321.0	*−5.62%*
% growth	*9.39%*	*−26.58%*	*38.34%*	*3.18%*	*−7.09%*	*−22.94%*	*−18.76%*	

et al. (2020) and Hu et al. (2020)). This has caused investors to re-evaluate expectations and reprice the risk of DAO tokens. We can see that moving from 2022's first quarter to the second quarter, the growth is negative for all crypto-assets. By contrary, publicly traded companies have experienced mixed results. In fact, even though the COVID-19 crisis has increased volatility in the stock market, the 2022 decline seen for DeFi tokens is less steep for publicly traded firms. Unfortunately, the CQGR numbers do not tell us much as we are considering different periods for DeFi and TradFi assets.

Fundamental Analysis: DCF Estimation

Following the historical balance sheets, we show the results of the DCF estimation with assumptions that are described in Table 3.3. Surprisingly, the projections show that a number of DeFi tokens are relatively *hyped*. As shown in Tables 3.5 and 3.6, UNI, AAVE, and COMP exhibit overvaluation with prices at least fivefold of their theoretical level. By contrast, Table 3.7 shows that yield aggregators are undervalued relative to their fundamentals. Yield aggregators use smart contracts that implement algorithmic investment strategies with their earnings mostly coming from performance fees of their vaults (Xu and Xu, 2022). In this context, a vault is another name for a smart contract which allocates locked assets and algorithmically takes portfolio management decisions. It is interesting to see how both DeFi and TradFi asset management protocols and firms are undervalued compared to their theoretical valuations. For valuation of public firms shown in Tables 3.8–3.10, apparently overpriced relative to their fundamentals, NDAQ and BLK have experienced a recent downwards correction from the market (Bloomberg, 2022; Financial Times, 2022). It is interesting to point out that albeit tokens' overvaluation, hedge funds, such as BlackRock or Grayscale, and banks, JP Morgan or Citigroup, for example, are investing in crypto-assets.

Comparable Analysis

In this section, we discuss the results of our comparable analysis. In the comparable analysis, we define multiples and compare different assets of the same kind: exchanges, banking, and asset managers. Due to their nascency, DeFi protocols have fewer data points than their

Table 3.5 *DEXs' NPV estimation using DCF*

	2022	2023	2024	2025	2026	2027
Uniswap						
Revenue ($M)	108.68	114.12	119.82	125.81	132.10	138.71
Workforce expenses ($M)	21.73	22.82	23.96	25.16	26.42	27.74
Net income ($M)	86.95	91.3	95.86	100.65	105.69	110.97
PV cashflows ($M)	86.95	73.04	61.35	51.54	43.29	36.36
PV terminal value ($M)						131.47
Total PV ($M)	484.26					
Total PV / UNI supply ($)	1.06					
UNI market price ($)	5.00					
Curve						
Revenue ($M)	61.31	64.37	67.59	70.97	74.52	78.25
Workforce expenses ($M)	12.26	12.87	13.51	14.19	14.90	15.65
Net income ($M)	49.05	51.5	54.08	56.78	59.62	62.6
PV cashflows ($M)	49.05	41.2	34.61	29.07	24.42	20.51
PV terminal value ($M)						74.31
Total PV ($M)	273.18					
Total PV / CRV supply ($)	0.70					
CRV market price ($)	0.69					

Note: market prices are retrieved on 30 June 2022. The annual growth rate for revenue and workforce expenses equals 5% and 20%, respectively.

Table 3.6 *PLFs' NPV estimation using DCF*

	2022	2023	2024	2025	2026	2027
Compound						
Revenue ($M)	13.25	13.91	14.6	15.33	16.1	16.91
Workforce expenses ($M)	2.65	2.78	2.92	3.07	3.22	3.38
Net income ($M)	10.6	11.13	11.68	12.27	12.88	13.52
PV cashflows ($M)	10.6	8.9	7.48	6.28	5.28	4.43
PV terminal value ($M)						16.06
Total PV ($M)	59.02					
Total PV / COMP supply ($)	8.59					
COMP market price ($)	47.48					
AAVE						
Revenue ($M)	24.93	26.18	27.48	28.86	30.3	31.82
Workforce expenses ($M)	4.99	5.24	5.5	5.77	6.06	6.36
Net income ($M)	19.94	20.94	21.99	23.09	24.24	25.45
PV cashflows ($M)	19.94	16.75	14.07	11.82	9.93	8.34
PV terminal value ($M)						30.22
Total PV ($M)	111.07					
Total PV / AAVE supply ($)	8.01					
AAVE market price ($)	57.00					

Note: market prices are retrieved on 30 June 2022. The annual growth rate for revenue and workforce expenses equals 5% and 20%, respectively.

Table 3.7 ***Yield aggregators' NPV evaluation using DCF***

	2022	2023	2024	2025	2026	2027
Yearn Finance						
Revenue ($M)	41.87	43.96	46.16	48.47	50.9	53.44
Workforce expenses ($M)	8.37	8.79	9.23	9.69	10.18	10.69
Net income ($M)	33.5	35.17	36.93	38.78	40.72	42.75
PV cashflows ($M)	33.5	28.14	23.64	19.85	16.68	14.01
PV terminal value ($M)						50.75
Total PV ($M)	186.56					
Total PV / YFI supply ($)	5,902.42					
YFI market price ($)	5,419.10					
Idle Finance						
Revenue ($M)	0.25	0.26	0.27	0.28	0.3	0.31
Workforce expenses ($M)	0.05	0.05	0.05	0.06	0.06	0.06
Net income ($M)	0.2	0.21	0.22	0.23	0.24	0.25
PV cashflows ($M)	0.2	0.16	0.14	0.12	0.1	0.08
PV terminal value ($M)						0.30
Total PV ($M)	1.10					
Total PV / IDLE supply ($)	0.41					
IDLE market price ($)	0.23					

Note: market prices are retrieved on 30 June 2022. The annual growth rate for revenue and workforce expenses equals 5% and 20%, respectively.

Table 3.8 *CEXs' NPV evaluation using DCF*

	2022	2023	2024	2025	2026	2027
Intercontinental Exchange						
Revenue ($M)	5,882.0	6,176.1	6,484.9	6,809.15	7,149.61	7,507.09
Workforce expenses ($M)	1,764.6	1,852.83	1,945.47	2,042.74	2,144.88	2,252.13
Net income ($M)	4,117.4	4,323.27	4,539.43	4,766.4	5,004.73	5,254.96
PV cashflows ($M)	4,117.4	3,915.12	3,722.77	3,539.88	3,365.97	3,200.61
PV terminal value ($M)						40,667.48
Total PV ($M)	62,529.23					
Total PV / ICE supply ($)	111.86					
ICE market price ($)	94.04					
Nasdaq						
Revenue ($M)	1,376.0	1,444.8	1,517.04	1,592.89	1,672.54	1,756.16
Workforce expenses ($M)	412.8	433.44	455.11	477.87	501.76	526.85
Net income ($M)	963.2	1,011.36	1,061.93	1,115.02	1,170.78	1,229.31
PV cashflows ($M)	963.2	917.06	873.14	831.32	791.5	753.59
PV terminal value ($M)						9,720.70
Total PV ($M)	14,850.51					
Total PV / NDAQ supply ($)	90.28					
NDAQ market price ($)	152.54					

Chicago Board of Trade						
Revenue ($M)	870.2	913.71	959.4	1,007.36	1,057.73	1,110.62
Workforce expenses ($M)	261.06	274.11	287.82	302.21	317.32	333.19
Net income ($M)	609.14	639.6	671.58	705.16	740.41	777.43
PV cashflows ($M)	609.14	578.98	550.32	523.07	497.17	472.56
PV terminal value ($M)						5,976.65
Total PV ($M)	9,207.89					
Total PV / CBOE supply ($)	86.71					
CBOE market price ($)	113.19					

Note: market prices are retrieved on 30 June 2022. The annual growth rate for revenue and workforce expenses equals 5% and 30%, respectively.

Table 3.9 *Banks' NPV evaluation using DCF*

	2022	2023	2024	2025	2026	2027
Citigroup						
Revenue ($M)	522,474.0	23,597.7	24,777.58	26,016.46	27,317.29	28,683.15
Workforce expenses ($M)	16,742.2	7,079.31	7,433.28	7,804.94	8,195.19	8,604.95
Net income ($M)	15,731.8	16,518.39	17,344.31	18,211.53	19,122.1	20,078.21
PV cashflows ($M)	15,731.8	15,006.1	14,313.88	13,653.59	13,023.76	12,422.99
PV terminal value ($M)						163,802.15
Total PV ($M)	247,954.28					
Total PV / C supply ($)	128.02					
C market price ($)	46.02					
Bank of America						
Revenue ($M)	31,394.0	32,963.7	34,611.88	36,342.48	38,159.6	40,067.58
Workforce expenses ($M)	9,418.2	9,889.11	10,383.56	10,902.74	11,447.88	12,020.28
Net income ($M)	21,975.8	23,074.59	24,228.32	25,439.74	26,711.72	28,047.31
PV cashflows ($M)	21,975.8	20,864.52	19,809.44	18,807.71	17,856.64	16,953.66
PV terminal value ($M)						211,690.06
Total PV ($M)	327,957.84					
Total PV / BAC supply ($)	40.68					
BAC market price ($)	31.15					

Well Fargo & Co.						
Revenue ($M)	16,148.0	16,955.4	17,803.17	18,693.33	19,628.0	20,609.4
Workforce expenses ($M)	4,844.4	5,086.62	5,340.95	5,608.0	5,888.4	6,182.82
Net income ($M)	11,303.6	11,868.78	12,462.22	13,085.33	13,739.6	14,426.58
PV cashflows ($M)	11,303.6	10,695.06	10,119.27	9,574.49	9,059.03	8,571.33
PV terminal value ($M)						102,944.03
Total PV ($M)	162,266.81					
Total PV / WFC supply ($)	42.78					
WFC market price ($)	39.17					

Note: market prices are retrieved on 30 June 2022. The annual growth rate for revenue and workforce expenses equals 5% and 30%, respectively.

Table 3.10 *Asset management firms' NPV evaluation using DCF*

	2022	2023	2024	2025	2026	2027
Berkshire Hathaway						
Revenue ($M)	111,530.0	117,106.5	122,961.82	129,109.92	135,565.41	142,343.68
Workforce expenses ($M)	33,459.0	35,131.95	36,888.55	38,732.98	40,669.62	42,703.1
Net income ($M)	78,071.0	81,974.55	86,073.28	90,376.94	94,895.79	99,640.58
PV cashflows ($M)	78,071.0	74,205.71	70,531.78	67,039.76	63,720.62	60,565.82
PV terminal value ($M)						765,995.62
Total PV ($M)	1,180,130.30					
Total PV / BRK.B supply ($)	535.06					
BRK.B market price ($)	273.02					
Morgan Stanley						
Revenue ($M)	15,814.0	16,604.7	17,434.94	18,306.68	19,222.02	20,183.12
Workforce expenses ($M)	4,744.2	4,981.41	5,230.48	5,492.0	5,766.6	6,054.94
Net income ($M)	11,069.8	11,623.29	12,204.45	12,814.68	13,455.41	14,128.18
PV cashflows ($M)	11,069.8	10,644.02	10,234.61	9,840.96	9,462.44	9,098.48
PV terminal value ($M)						132,466.85
Total PV ($M)	192,817.15					
Total PV / MS supply ($)	111.91					
MS market price ($)	76.10					

BlackRock						
Revenue ($M)	5,894.0	6,188.7	6,498.14	6,823.04	7,164.19	7,522.4
Workforce expenses ($M)	41,768.2	1,856.61	1,949.44	2,046.91	2,149.26	2,256.72
Net income ($M)	4,125.8	4,332.09	4,548.7	4,776.13	5,014.94	5,265.68
PV cashflows ($M)	4,125.8	3,921.81	3,727.91	3,543.59	3,368.39	3,201.84
PV terminal value ($M)						40,528.04
Total PV ($M)	62,417.382					
Total PV / BLK supply ($)	413.45					
BLK market price ($)	609.04					

Note: market prices are retrieved on 30 June 2022. The annual growth rate for revenue and workforce expenses equals 5% and 30%, respectively.

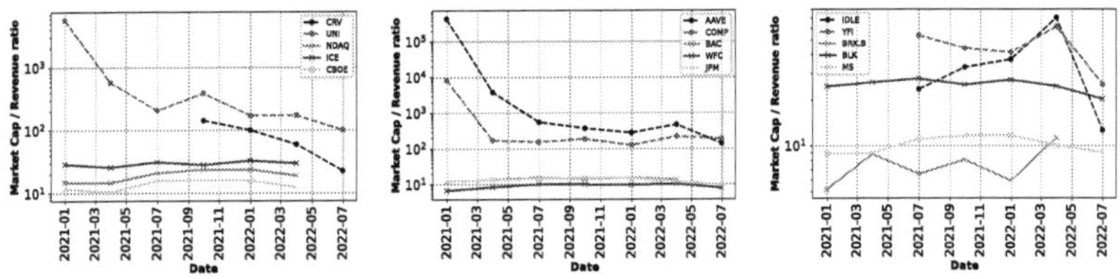

(a) DEXs and exchanges (b) PLFs and banks (c) Yield aggregators and asset managers

Figure 3.2 The historical (log) Market Cap/Revenue ratio.

TradFi counterparties. We show that the multiples change over time starting from Q1 2021 to Q2 2022.

Figure 3.2 shows the *Market Cap/Revenue* ratio for (a) exchanges, (b) banks, and (c) asset managers. We merge both DeFi and TradFi assets. These figures show that DeFi assets were relatively overvalued with respect to their TradFi counterparties, and have been only recently converging to a more fair price. In fact, in Q2 2022, we can see DeFi converging to TradFi multiple values. This could be explained by the slump in the crypto market where high growth expectations have been adjusted towards more realistic levels. Due to the large price increases in crypto tokens and high growth in DeFi protocol usage, aggressive (growth) expectations were priced in. The crypto market slump and sluggish recovery caused a reassessment of the aggressive growth expectations and the subsequent revaluation of DeFi tokens. As previously discussed, comparable analysis assumes that market prices reflect investors' expectations on average. Therefore, by comparing similar assets' multiples, the empirical observations can reveal undervalued and/or overvalued assets. For example, by looking at Figure 3.2a, Uniswap during 2021 was overvalued compared to its TradFi counterparties and only recently its price has been converging to a 'fair' price.

Similarly, Figure 3.3 shows the *Market Cap/Net Assets* ratio for the same set of financial services and assets from Figure 3.2. Net assets are represented by the protocol treasury value for DeFi and equal the difference between total assets and total liabilities for TradFi. We generally observe overvaluation for DeFi tokens which is, differently from the latest multiples, not disappearing with the recent market slump. It should be noted that this behaviour is mixed between different DeFi tokens. First, in Figure 3.3a, we can see that Uniswap is 'fairly' valued with respect to its TradFi equivalents. This could be explained

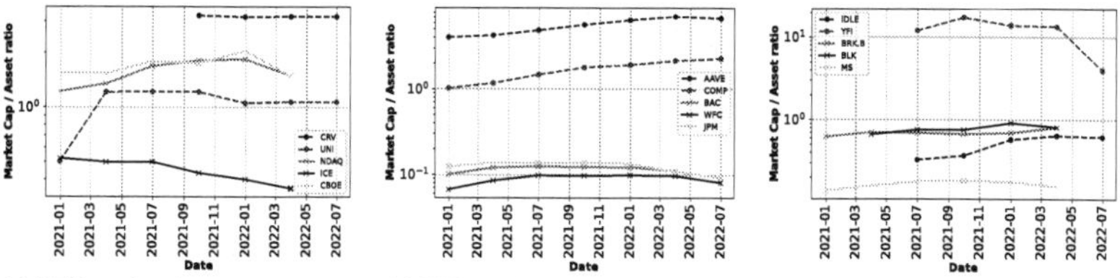

(a) DEXs and exchanges (b) PLFs and banks (c) Yield aggregators and asset managers

Figure 3.3 Historical (log) *Market Cap/Net Asset* ratio.

by Uniswap retaining 430M UNI tokens in its own treasury that can be distributed to the community in the future (Uniswap, 2022). To date, these tokens have a value of \$3B, and Uniswap's market cap is around \$5B. This relatively large treasury size makes Uniswap the 'richest' DeFi protocol with the highest treasury value (Mihal, 2022). Compared to Uniswap, other protocols' treasury values have been driven by crypto-assets that users pay as fees for using the DeFi service (Xu and Xu, 2022). Therefore, moving to Figure 3.3b, we can observe that – since the slopes are positive – the recent market cap crash was lower than their treasury loss. Finally, Figure 3.3c shows an overpriced YFI consistent with Figure 3.2c. Interestingly, Idle Finance's *Market Cap/Net Assets* ratio is comparable to TradFi Hedge Funds.

3.5 Conclusion

In this study, we apply conventional valuation analysis on DeFi tokens and provide a comparison with the valuation of stocks of publicly listed firms within similar categories. Specifically, we analyse DEXs, PLFs, and yield aggregators, which are also compared with exchanges, banks, and asset managers, respectively.

The results show that DeFi tokens have been rather overpriced relative to the equity of financial services firms. More specifically, DeFi assets were overvalued with respect to their TradFi counterparties and have been only recently converging to a more fair price. We believe high growth expectations in DeFi have been adjusted towards more realistic levels in line with TradFi.

Despite the large growth in DeFi tokens and cryptocurrencies in general, little research has been conducted on the valuation of these. Research on digital assets and DeFi tokens valuation is still in an early stage, and we contribute by providing a framework to think about fundamental valuation in DeFi. Future research could build upon our approach by further developing fundamental measures and frameworks specific to DeFi.

Bibliography

Bloomberg (2022). Your evening briefing: How BlackRock lost $1.7 trillion in six months. www.bloomberg.com.

Cousaert, S., Xu, J., and Matsui, T. (2022). Sok: Yield aggregators in defi. In *2022 IEEE International Conference on Blockchain and Cryptocurrency (ICBC)*, 1–14. IEEE.

Damodaran, A. (2007). *Valuation approaches and metrics: A survey of the theory and evidence*. Now Publishers Inc.

Damodaran, A. (2012). *Investment valuation: Tools and techniques for determining the value of any asset*, volume 666. John Wiley & Sons.

Damodaran, A. (2022a). Historical returns on stocks, bonds and bills: 1928–2021. pages.stern.nyu.edu.

Damodaran, A. (2022b). Tax rate by sector. pages.stern.nyu.edu/adamodar.

Damodaran, A. (2022c). Total betas by sector. pages.stern.nyu.edu/adamodar.

Financial Times (2022). Nasdaq closes down 5% in sharpest fall since 2020. www.ft.com.

Gordon, M. J. (1959). Dividends, earnings, and stock prices. *The Review of Economics and Statistics*, 41(2): 99–105.

Gudgeon, L., Werner, S., Perez, D., and Knottenbelt, W. J. (2020). Defi protocols for loanable funds: Interest rates, liquidity and market efficiency. In *Proceedings of the 2nd ACM Conference on Advances in Financial Technologies*, 92–112.

Hu, J., Luo, Q., and Zhang, J. (2020). The fluctuations of Bitcoin price during the hacks. *International Journal of Applied Research in Management and Economics*, 3(1):10–20.

Kelly, B. and Pruitt, S. (2013). Market expectations in the cross-section of present values. *The Journal of Finance*, 68(5):1721–1756.

Liu, J., Nissim, D., and Thomas, J. (2002). Equity valuation using multiples. *Journal of Accounting Research*, 40(1):135–172.

Lord, F. (2022). MakerDAO Valuation. messari.io.

Mihal, D. (2022). DAO are the new companies. What's on their balance sheets? openorgs.info.

Modigliani, F. and Miller, M. H. (1958). The cost of capital, corporation finance and the theory of investment. *The American* Economic Review, 48(3):261–297.

Qin, K., Zhou, L., Afonin, Y., Lazzaretti, L., and Gervais, A. (2021). Cefi vs. DeFi – comparing centralized to decentralized finance. *arXiv preprint arXiv:2106.08157*.

Schreiner, A. (2009). *Equity valuation using multiples: An empirical investigation*. Springer Science & Business Media.

Shanaev, S., Sharma, S., Ghimire, B., and Shuraeva, A. (2020). Taming the blockchain beast? Regulatory implications for the cryptocurrency market. *Research in International Business and Finance*, 51:101080.

Statista (2022). Annual growth of the real gross domestic product (GDP) of the United States from 1990 to 2021. *www.statista.com*.

Steiger, F. (2010). The validity of company valuation using discounted cash flow methods. *arXiv preprint arXiv:1003.4881*.

Token Terminal (2022). Our metrics. tokenterminal.com.

Uniswap (2022). Introducing UNI. uniswap.org.

Welch, I. and Goyal, A. (2008). A comprehensive look at the empirical performance of equity premium prediction. *The Review of Financial Studies*, 21(4):1455–1508.

Werner, S. M., Perez, D., Gudgeon, L., Klages-Mundt, A., Harz, D., and Knottenbelt, W. J. (2022). SoK: Decentralized Finance (DeFi). *The 4th ACM Conference on Advances in Financial Technologies*, 30–46. https://doi.org/10.1145/3558535.3559780.

WRDS (2022a). Assets – Total. wrds-www.wharton.upenn.edu.

WRDS (2022b). Debt in current liabilities – total. wrds-www.wharton .upenn.edu.

WRDS (2022c). Pretax – Income. wrds-www.wharton.upenn.edu.

WRDS (2022d). Revenue – Total. wrds-www.wharton.upenn.edu.

WRDS (2022e). Total current operating revenue. wrds-www.wharton .upenn.edu.

Xu, J., Paruch, K., Cousaert, S., and Feng, Y. (2023). SoK: Decentralized Exchanges (DEX) with Automated Market Maker (AMM) Protocols. *ACM Computing Surveys*, 55(11), 1–50. https://doi.org/10.1145/3570639.

Xu, T. A. and Xu, J. (2023). A Short Survey on Business Models of Decentralized Finance (DeFi) Protocols. *International Conference on Financial Cryptography and Data Security (FC)*, 197–206. https://doi.org/10.1007/978-3-031-32415-4_13.

PART II

Digital Assets and Decentralised Finance

4 *The Suitability of Securities Token Offerings, Cryptocurrencies, and Crypto-Related Assets for Pension Investments*

JOHN A. TURNER*

The US Securities and Exchange Commission (SEC) recently noted that the total value of cryptocurrency is roughly $1.6 trillion (Goldberg and Rickard, 2021). This valuation encompasses a variety of tokens, including 77 tokens each valued at $1 billion or more. These tokens include popular consensus layer tokens such as Bitcoin, Ethereum, XRP, Litecoin, HBAR, as well as application layer tokens such as Dai and Uniswap. In addition, there are approximately 1,600 tokens valued at $1 million or more. Bitcoin alone in 2021 was worth more than $1 trillion on several occasions. Seven billionaires on the Fortune list of the 400 wealthiest people in the US made their fortunes through crypto-related assets (Ehrlick and Bambysheva, 2021).

This chapter considers securities token offerings, cryptocurrencies such as Bitcoin, and crypto-related assets such as crypto exchanges and crypto security firms as possible investments for pension plans and pension participants. Relatively little money has been invested in cryptocurrency and crypto-related assets in pension plans, but that amount is growing. Because pension investing is done to provide retirement income, highly risky investments generally would not be suitable for this purpose. While many of the financial products developed in this area have thus far not incorporated characteristics that would qualify them for consideration for investments for pensions, it is nonetheless worth understanding recent developments because some offer potential for future investments.

* I have received valuable comments from Heinz-Dietrich Steinmeyer, Kamila Bielawska, Eskil Wadsenjo, Marek Szczepanski, Jacques-André Schneider, Humberto Godinez, Paul Roels, Markus Roth, Sally Shen, Susan Thorp, Niko Väänänen, Stephan Neetens, and the editors of this volume.

We begin the chapter by discussing the current use of cryptocurrencies and crypto-related assets by pension funds and pension participants in a number of different countries. Then, we evaluate the suitability of cryptocurrency and crypto-related assets for pension plans.

4.1 Crypto Investing for Pension Funds and Participants

Liew and Hewlett (2017), using standard portfolio analysis, investigate whether Bitcoin should be included in pension portfolios. They find that it provides unique diversification benefits and has a relatively high Sharpe ratio (ratio of return to risk). The optimal allocation to Bitcoin they find to be 1.3% of the portfolio. Just like for any asset, investing in multiple cryptocurrencies whose returns are not correlated provides diversification. Their analysis is based on historical data on risk and return for cryptocurrencies.

4.2 Defined Benefit Pension Funds

The next two sections survey pension investments in crypto-related assets. This section surveys such pension investments in defined benefit plans, which are traditional pension plans sponsored by employers that typically provide benefits as annuities. The following section investigates crypto pension investments in defined contribution plans, which are individual account plans. These plans take two forms. They can be sponsored by employers for their employees, such as 401(k) plans in the US, or they can be established independently of the worker's employer, such as individual retirement accounts (IRAs) in the US.

South Korea

As of 2018, the South Korean National Pension Fund, the third-largest pension fund globally, invests in four cryptocurrency exchanges through two venture capital funds (Helms, 2018). The exchanges are Upbit, Korbit, Bithumb, and Coinplug. Bithumb is a South Korean cryptocurrency exchange. Cryptocurrencies are bought and sold on cryptocurrency exchanges. Thus, this investment is not in cryptocurrencies, but rather in their exchanges.

United States

In 2019 in Virginia, the $4.2 billion Fairfax County Employees' Retirement System and the $1.5 billion Fairfax County Police Officers Retirement System became the first known US public pension plans to invest in blockchain technology firms and cryptocurrencies. Both pension plans invested less than 1% of their assets in this area. Both plans invested in the Morgan Creek Blockchain Opportunities Fund, managed by Morgan Creek Digital Assets, a subsidiary of Morgan Creek Capital Management LLC (Morgan Creek Capital Management, 2019).

In 2021, the Houston Firefighters' Relief and Retirement Fund invested $25 million in the Bitcoin and Ether cryptocurrencies through digital assets manager and Stone Ridge Asset Management subsidiary NYDIG. It became the first US. pension fund investing directly in cryptocurrencies. The investment has been made through a customised private fund that NYDIG manages. The investment is roughly 0.5 percent of the Firefighters' Fund investment portfolio (Comtois, 2021). Explaining reasons for the purchase, the Fund's chief investment officer Ajit Singh said the investment expressed their belief in 'the disruptive potential' of cryptocurrencies. He added, 'As more and more institutional adoptions happen, there will be more and more dynamics that develop for supply and demand'. 'It has a low correlation to every other asset class'. 'It became an asset class we could not ignore anymore' (Bitcoin Exchange Guide, 2021).

Concerning the private sector defined benefit pensions, the question arises whether the prudent person rule relating to investments would be satisfied for cryptocurrency. This issue has not yet been addressed by the regulators or the courts.

Canada

The Caisse de dépôt et placement du Québec (CDPQ) has participated in a US $400-million investment, or about 0.2% of its assets, in Celsius Network, a cryptocurrency interest and lending platform. The Caisse is an institutional investor that manages several public and parapublic pension plans and insurance programmes in Quebec. Celsius Network specialises in deposits and loans of cryptocurrencies, such as Bitcoin or Ethereum. The company lends deposited cryptocurrencies to institutional investors. It states that 80% of the proceeds from these exchanges are returned to depositors in the form of interest. More than 1 million customers are registered on its platform, according to the company, which says it has total assets of US $25 billion (CTV News, 2021).

The Ontario Teachers' Pension Plan Board, via its Teachers' Innovation Platform (TIP), in 2021 invested in FTX, which is a cryptocurrency exchange that has its global headquarters in the Bahamas. FTX was established in 2019 and was worth $25 billion but in 2022 declared bankruptcy. TIP focuses on growth equity and venture capital investments in companies, such as FTX, that are using technology to shape future markets (Ontario Teachers' Pension Plan, 2021).

Germany

Germany permits crypto-assets as alternative investments (AIF), at least for certain pension funds with less strict rules – pensionsfonds. These investments are accepted if the market value can be fixed. Pensionsfonds (pension funds – the English name of a type of pension in Germany) are separate legal entities that provide company pension plans for one or several employers. Insurance law regulates them. Pension funds can be set up by a single company, a financial services provider, or by an industry-wide pension scheme sponsored by the employers' association and the unions (Pension Funds Online, 2021). As of 2021, it appears that no funds have been invested in crypto-related assets.

4.3 Individual Pension Funds – Defined Contribution Plans

Individual account pension plans can be provided by employers, or in some countries, they can be established by employees independently of an employer. In individual account pension plans that are established by employers, generally the employer selects the investments or the employee chooses from a menu of investments selected by the employer or plan sponsor. Sometimes, the employee is allowed to choose from a much wider range of investments not selected by the employer but available in financial markets.

When employers select the investments or select the menu of investments that employees choose from, generally they have a fiduciary duty to select investments that satisfy the prudent person principle. In those circumstances, employers may be reluctant to choose cryptocurrencies because cryptocurrencies often have prices that vary considerably, and it is difficult to determine their intrinsic value as an investment.

Australia

Investment in cryptocurrency is allowed for self-managed superannuation funds (SMSFs) (Australian Tax Office, 2018). SMSFs are small (fewer than four participants) and each participant is a fund trustee, but these funds hold about one-third of superannuation assets because they are favoured by wealthier people. Australians call them 'Do-it-yourself' superannuation funds. SMSFs are compliance regulated, not prudentially regulated as are large funds. Cryptocurrencies are not treated as money under tax law but as capital gains tax assets. Some crypto investing is being done in these funds. However, pension contributions and benefit payments must be made in cash, rather than cryptocurrencies. Also, cryptocurrencies must be purchased through exchanges and cannot be purchased from family members.

For the large fund sector, prudentially regulated by the Australian Prudential Regulation Authority, investing in crypto-assets is also allowed. It is being done by some funds via venture capital allocations, where they allocate money to a venture capital fund and that fund in turn invests in cryptocurrency or crypto-related assets, such as blockchain. One large fund has commented that it would consider the environmental impact of cryptocurrencies when deciding whether to invest (Waters, 2021).

New Zealand

KiwiSaver is a voluntary, work-based retirement savings programme. Independent KiwiSaver providers run the savings plans. Workers choose one of them to manage their savings (KiwiSaver, 2021). In 2021, the KiwiSaver Growth Strategy fund, which is part of New Zealand's national KiwiSaver programme, invested 5% of its funds into Bitcoin (Chawaga, 2021).

Also in 2021, the Pathfinder KiwiSaver fund invested half a percent of its portfolio in cryptocurrency retail platform, Easy Crypto. Easy Crypto seeks to be a global marketplace for crypto-assets. John Berry, Chief Executive of Pathfinder KiwiSaver, explains, 'While we are not ready to invest in cryptocurrency itself, this investment is into crypto infrastructure. The Easy Crypto platform is helping to solve a global problem, providing a secure trading foundation. The positive social impact of this aligns with our wider ESG strategy'. Further, he states, 'There are still some issues to be resolved around the energy needs of currencies like Bitcoin and the anonymity that crypto provides. But these concerns need to be balanced against potential positives for an ethical investor from decentralised finance (DeFi). This is much more than just trading cryptocurrency'. Pathfinder is New Zealand's first dedicated ethical fund manager and is a leader in environmental, social, and governance (ESG) investing (Scoop Business, 2021).

Finland

Finland does not prohibit pensions investing in crypto-related assets. However, as of 2021, it is believed that no Finnish pension funds have made such an investment.

Switzerland

Cryptocurrencies are under the regulatory category of alternative investments, which are allowed but only through diversified collective investment vehicles (e.g., exchange traded funds (ETFs) or mutual funds), diversified certificates, or diversified structured products. Because of the volatility of these assets and the difficulty of valuing them, few people have invested their pension funds in them.

United Kingdom

Workers cannot invest in cryptocurrencies through self-invested personal pensions, but they can invest in crypto infrastructure, such as crypto mining companies and crypto exchanges (Smith, 2021).

Canada

Employers who use Wealthsimple Work for their group retirement plans can let their employees put up to 3% of their money into Bitcoin and Ethereum ETFs. Wealthsimple is the largest robo-advisor in Canada. The allocation will be automatically adjusted, and Wealthsimple will decide the Bitcoin and Ethereum weights.

'If crypto prices skyrocket, retirement portfolios will automatically rebalance and reallocate your gains into more stable investments like stocks and bonds', Wealthsimple CIO Ben Reeves, told Yahoo Finance Canada. 'On the other hand, if the crypto price falls, we will not sell other assets to buy crypto. We would only allocate deposits in proportion to the target allocation'.

Wealthsimple Work will use an algorithm to decide the best ETFs based on factors such as trading spreads and management fees (Bains, 2021).

United States

Some 401(k) participants in plans that offer self-directed brokerage accounts may be able to invest in cryptocurrencies through those accounts (Hagen, 2021). Current US pension law does not prohibit holding cryptocurrencies in 401(k) plans. One hurdle this approach faces is that plan sponsors have been sued by participants for offering investment options that were viewed as overly risky or high-fee options (Turner, 2021). However, most federal courts that have considered the issue have agreed that investments selected by 401(k) participants through individual brokerage windows are not subject to Employee Retirement Income Security Act (ERISA)'s fiduciary duties placed on employers (Goldberg and Rickard, 2021). The pension regulatory agency at the Department of Labor has expressed the opinion that indirect exposure to Bitcoin, such as investing in Tesla, which permits payment in Bitcoin for cars, is different from investing directly in Bitcoin, but so far no direct regulatory action has been taken (Correia, 2021).

In 2021, it became possible to invest in cryptocurrencies through a 401(k) plan that has the self-directed 401(k) feature, which allows participants to direct the investment of their account in a wide range of assets. ForUsAll, a retirement investment platform for small business, began offering its Alt 401(k) plan, allowing investments of up to 5% of a portfolio in cryptocurrencies. This plan allows employers to offer a 401(k) plan that permits participants to invest in cryptocurrencies, using what is called a self-directed cryptocurrency window. Participants can buy and sell cryptocurrencies like any other asset in their pension portfolio without needing electronic wallets or digital keys (Anderson, 2021).

Coinbase partnered with ForUsAll to allow cryptocurrency investing in 401(k) plans. Coinbase is a platform that allows users to invest in cryptocurrency. ForUsAll manages over $1.7 billion in assets for over 70,000 employees. Employees who sign up for the plan will be able to transfer up to 5% of their account balances to a self-directed cryptocurrency window that will use Coinbase's trading platform and give them access to about 50 cryptocurrencies (Expat, 2021).

As well as investments in cryptocurrencies by individual investors and by pension funds, in the United States, people having self-directed IRAs can invest in cryptocurrency through their IRAs. IRAs are individual accounts that can be established by individuals independently of an employer. As of 2019, workers had invested $300 million in Bitcoin in IRAs (del Castillo, 2021). The SEC (2018) warns that, 'Fraudsters may use the allure associated with Initial Coin Offeringss (ICOs) and other digital assets to entice self-directed IRA investors with the promise of high returns. While digital assets may provide fair and lawful investment opportunities, they may also be conducted without SEC registration or a valid exemption from registration and may not provide complete or accurate information to aid investors in making informed decisions. In addition, many of the trading platforms for these digital assets refer to themselves as "exchanges", which may give investors the misimpression that they are regulated by the SEC'.

Having transferred capital into a self-directed IRA, the IRA holder must then set up a 'wallet' for use by their new IRA. A wallet is the cryptocurrency equivalent of a safe deposit box that holds the information necessary to buy, sell, and use the Bitcoins. Wallets are provided by many vendors and offer varying degrees of security (Ellis, 2021).

Before the person establishes a wallet for his IRA, he or she needs to contact their self-directed IRA custodian to determine their preferred strategy. Some custodians allow IRA holders to establish a wallet directly in the name of their IRA. Others require the person to take the intermediary step of establishing a limited liability company (LLC) within their IRA to hold their Bitcoin wallet. The IRA holder would be charged a few hundred dollars each year to maintain proper government registration of the LLC (Ellis, 2021).

The direct style is simpler and may become the standard in the future. As for now, a few Bitcoin-oriented IRA providers allow direct ownership by an IRA, but most of them are expensive, frequently charging commissions of up to 15% or more of the IRA balance (Ellis, 2021).

One commentator has provided the following advice concerning investing in a self-directed IRA so as to invest in cryptocurrency and other alternative investments. 'For nontraditional investments, you'll need to open a self-directed IRA, a type of account specifically designed to invest in alternative investments, such as cryptocurrencies, real estate and precious metals. (Major IRA providers, such as Fidelity, Vanguard and Schwab, place restrictions on their customers' investments.) Fees may be higher than you'd pay for a traditional IRA, and self-directed IRAs have occasionally been hijacked by financial outlaws to steer investors into fraudulent investments. Before investing in a self-directed IRA, check with your state securities regulator and the Securities and Exchange Commission to see whether the provider or custodian has been the subject of any enforcement actions. Avoid unsolicited offers to invest in a self-directed IRA, particularly if the promoter urges you to transfer money from a traditional IRA or 401(k) plan' (Block, 2021).

4.4 Countries Where Crypto Investing in Pensions Is Not Permitted[1]

Some countries have policies that prohibit crypto investing in pensions. China has prohibited all crypto transactions. Poland and Sweden do not permit investing in cryptocurrencies or crypto-related assets in pensions. Belgium relies on the prudent person rule concerning the suitability of investments. It thus does not explicitly prohibit investing in crypto-related assets. However, it does not permit pension investing in crypto-related assets because those assets are not sold in regulated markets.

The European Insurance and Occupational Pensions Authority (EIOPA) is an independent advisory body to the European Commission, the European Parliament, and the Council of the European Union. It provides evidence-based advice to help shape informed policies and laws at the EU and national level. EIOPA (2021) writes, 'There are many different types of crypto assets, but the majority of them remain unregulated in the EU. To address this gap the European Commission has published a legislative proposal for a regulation on markets in crypto assets (MiCA) which is being discussed by the European Parliament and the Council'. MiCA is Europe's Markets in Crypto-Assets Regulation. The proposed regulation does not apply

[1] I have received help with this section from members of the European Network for Research on Supplementary Pensions (ENRSP), who are acknowledged in the acknowledgement footnote for this chapter.

to the blockchain or distributed ledger technologies underlying cryptocurrencies. It does not apply to digital currencies issued by states and regulated by central banks. All other cryptocurrencies that do not qualify as financial instruments, including utility tokens and payment tokens, fall within the scope of the regulation (Cengiz, 2021).

El Salvador has legalised the use of Bitcoin as a form of payment, but does not allow pension payments to be made in Bitcoin (Lee, 2021). In Mexico, investments in crypto-related assets are banned. However, despite the ban, crypto exchanges and companies operate in Mexico, but are registered elsewhere. For example, Bitso – the largest crypto exchange – is registered in Gibraltar.

4.5 Should Pension Participants Invest in Crypto-related Assets?

There is a disconnect between the advice of both leading financial economists and government regulators compared to the actions of millions of investors and the financial service providers that cater to them. The first group is generally wary of investing in cryptocurrencies because of their high degree of volatility and because there is no way to rationally determine the value of these assets. Further, the free entry into the provision of cryptocurrencies suggests that their value will fall over time. In addition, the environmental cost due to the energy consumption related to them is a factor that makes them unattractive. Bitcoin has been available for more than a decade, and other than for illegal activities, arguably it has found little practical use. In part because of the large number of pension lawsuits in the US related to plan investment options (Turner, 2021) and in part because of the riskiness of some cryptocurrencies as an investment, plan sponsors would be placing themselves at risk of being sued (Lawton, 2021).

The opposing viewpoint is that cryptocurrencies are no longer a new idea. Millions of investors have invested billions of dollars in them. Indeed, in the financial market, cryptocurrencies are gaining acceptance not only among investors but also among the financial service providers who cater to these investors.

Freer (2021) makes the point that most pension plans have indirect exposure to cryptocurrencies. For example, Tesla and other companies hold cryptocurrencies. Thus, any pension plan that invests in a company that holds cryptocurrencies has indirect exposure.

4.6 The Psychology of Cryptocurrency Investing

Shiller (2017), a Nobel Prize winner in economics based on his work on financial asset pricing, argues that cryptocurrencies have neither fundamental value as an investment asset nor central bank association as a medium of exchange. Thus, he argues that buying cryptocurrencies is not investing but speculation similar to gambling. In particular, he writes, 'true investing requires a rational appraisal of an asset's value and that is simply not possible at present with Bitcoin.... It is that no one can attach objective probabilities to the various possible outcomes of the current Bitcoin enthusiasm'. Because cryptocurrencies have no backing in productive assets, and unlike gold have no intrinsic value, it is unclear that in the long term, they will have value as investible assets.

Part of the psychology of individuals investing in cryptocurrency may be due to the psychological phenomenon called FOMO, which stands for fear of missing out (Torpey, 2019). Some people may invest in them because other people seem to be making a lot of money, but without considering the merit of the investment. The US SEC (Securities and Exchange Commission, 2018), commenting on the psychology of some Bitcoin investors, writes, 'A new product, technology, or innovation – such as Bitcoin – has the potential to give rise both to frauds and high-risk investment opportunities. Potential investors can be easily enticed with the promise of high returns in a new investment space and also may be less sceptical when assessing something novel, new and cutting-edge'.

Shiller (2017) refers to Keynes' (1936) theory of animal spirits as a possible explanation for the apparently irrational enthusiasm for Bitcoin among some investors. Keynes argued that sometimes in stock markets, people invest out of emotion and are guided by what they think other people will do. Animal spirits describe the psychological and emotional factors that cause investors to take action when faced with high levels of volatility in the capital markets (Tardi, 2019). Thus, that explanation, like the FOMO explanation, hypothesises that people base their investment decisions on what they think other people are thinking or doing rather than on an assessment of the fundamental merits of the investment.

Some predictions project substantial increases in future Bitcoin prices. For example, one venture capitalist predicts that it will increase to $250,000 by the beginning of 2023 (Bambrough, 2020), while others warn of the possibility of losing everything (Shiller, 2017).

An important issue for investors is what determines the value of Bitcoin. A study by Jeremy Schneider compared the price of Bitcoin to the number of Google searches for buying Bitcoin and found that when searches went up, the price of Bitcoin went up (Salisbury, 2021). Dhawan and Putniņš (2020) find that a small percentage of cryptocurrencies are subject to currency manipulation in schemes called pump and dump. The currency manipulator purchases a cryptocurrency, and then publicly announces that it is launching a pump and dump scheme. In the pump part of the scheme, the manipulator encourages other investors to purchase the cryptocurrency, which some do on the strategy that they can buy before the scheme has had much effect and sell before it collapses, providing a profit. The manipulator then dumps its coins by selling off, causing a crash from the cryptocurrency's artificial high. While the manipulator generally profits, the other participants tend to not get out quickly enough, and many end up with losses. The participants tend to be characterised by overconfidence and a gambling mentality.

The Basel Committee on Banking Supervision has decided that banks who hold cryptocurrencies should hold sufficient reserves to cover the situation that the cryptocurrencies become worthless. The bank placed substantially less stringent requirements on tokenised traditional assets and stablecoins because of their lower risk (Clark and Ostroff, 2021).

Crypto and Fraud

In the US in 2021, a lawsuit was initiated alleging that the executives behind the failed cryptocurrency Helbiz raised $38.6 million through the sale of its coin and promises to innovate urban transportation rentals, but reneged on the promise and declined to return the money to the original buyers (Simpson, 2021).

Cryptocurrencies have been used as required payment in ransomware attacks, such as the attack on a major oil pipeline in the US. They have also been used in money laundering and tax evasion. In fairness, it is worth noting that money laundering and tax evasion are not exclusive to cryptocurrencies; they also occur with traditional currencies.

Cryptocurrencies can be stolen, a risk of holding cryptocurrency that presumably adversely affects its demand. In 2016, almost 120,000 Bitcoins worth around $78 million were stolen from Hong Kong-based Bitfinex, then one of the most popular cryptocurrency exchanges, which resulted in a 20% drop in the value of the cryptocurrency at that time (Hickey, 2017). Hackers have successfully penetrated blockchains in a few circumstances – nearly $2 billion worth of cryptocurrency was stolen between the beginning of 2017 and March 2019 (Iacurci, 2019). Just like other companies operating online, cryptocurrency exchanges can be hacked.

Outright thefts, as well as scams and other misappropriation of funds from cryptocurrency users and exchanges, resulted in losses of approximately $4.26 billion through the first half of 2019. Insider thefts were by far the largest source of losses to investors and exchange users. An example is the Ponzi plan QuadrigaCX, alleged to have defrauded millions of users out of $2.9 billion in crypto-assets (Ciphertrace, 2019). North Korea's government is believed to have established an organisation to hack cryptocurrency exchanges to steal cryptocurrency. It is thought to have stolen as much as $2 billion from a mix of traditional banks and cryptocurrency exchanges, which it is using in part to fund its nuclear weapons programme (Brewster, 2019).

In the United States, Coinbase and Gemini are the two highest-profile Bitcoin exchanges. Coinbase is a digital currency brokerage exchange for the cryptocurrencies Bitcoin, Bitcoin cash, Ethereum, Ethereum classic, and Litecoin with fiat currencies in 32 countries, and Bitcoin transactions and storage in 190 countries (Breen, 2019). Both exchanges take measures to protect Bitcoin deposits. For instance, they store only a small percentage of cryptocurrencies online, with most being held in offline storage, out of reach of any potential hacker (Deleon, 2017).

Cryptocurrency and Government The dream of the early cryptocurrency innovators was that the cryptocurrencies would be free from government interference. That dream was naïve. In the US, government regulators disagree as to the classification of Bitcoin as an asset. The Commodity Futures Trading Commission classifies it as a commodity, the Internal Revenue Service (IRS) considers it property, and the SEC has decided to approach it on a case-by-case basis (Burniske and White, 2017).

China, the US, and other countries are considering developing their own cryptocurrencies. If they do so, which seems likely, that would reduce the demand for, and price of, the other cryptocurrencies (Lawton, 2021).

4.7 Conclusions

Fintech is rapidly developing, and this development may provide investment opportunities for pension plans and participants. Some countries prohibit pensions and pension participants investing in cryptocurrency or crypto-related assets. Other countries permit investments in crypto-related assets but not in cryptocurrency, while yet other countries permit investments in both. When permitted, generally, the percent of the portfolio invested is less than 1%, with some pensions allowing up to 3% but rarely as high as 5%.

A central issue with cryptocurrencies is the fundamental conflict between their use as a medium of exchange and an investible asset. Thus, if they develop in the future in a way that fulfils their promise as a medium of exchange, it is likely that they would be a poor investment. In the future, some cryptocurrencies may develop as mediums of exchange, while others develop as investment assets. However, because cryptocurrencies have no backing in productive assets, and unlike gold or art they have no intrinsic value, it is unclear that in the long term they will have value as investible assets. For this reason, it would be a highly risky decision for pensions to invest in them. Their high volatility is a related issue.

Bibliography

Anderson, B. (2021). New 'Alt 401(k)' to provide retirement plan cryptocurrency access.

Australian Tax Office (2018). SMSF investing in cryptocurrencies.

Bains, J. (2021). A canadian company is bringing crypto investing to workplace retirement plans. *Yahoo! Sports*.

Bambrough, B. (2020). A multi-millionaire venture capitalist made a massive bet on Bitcoin. *Forbes*.

Bitcoin Exchange Guide (2021). $5.5 billion AUM pension fund buys Bitcoin and Ether because they can't 'ignore' it any more. *Bitcoin Exchange Guide*.

Block, S. (2021). Nontraditional options let IRA investors crank up the risk. *Kiplinger.*

Breen, O. (2019). Schwab dismisses crypto currencies as 'speculative' and too insignificant for its RIA platform as rivals stake out turf for the coming boom... or is that bust? *RIABiz.*

Brewster, T. (2019). Apple Mac hack warning: North Korea uses fake cryptocurrency companies to break into macOS. *Forbes.*

Burniske, C. and White, A. (2017). Bitcoin: Ringing the bell for a new asset class. *Ark Invest.*

Cengiz, F. (2021). What the EU's new MiCA regulation could mean for cryptocurrencies. *LSE Blog.*

Chawaga, P. (2021). New Zealand retirement fund invests in Bitcoin. *Bitcoin Magazine.*

Ciphertrace (2019). Q2 2019 Cryptocurrency anti-money laundering report.

Clark, S. and Ostroff, C. (2021). Bitcoin, other crypto assets targeted for strict banking regulation. *The Wall Street Journal.*

Comtois, J. (2021). Houston firefighters invests $25 million in cryptocurrency. *Pensions & Investments.*

Correia, M. (2021). DOL: Cybersecurity of retirement accounts to remain a top priority. *Pensions & Investments.*

CTV News (2021). The Caisse invests in a cryptocurrency lender targeted by market authorities in the United States.

del Castillo, M. (2021). Police pension backs Morgan Creek's $40 million blockchain venture capital fund. *Forbes.*

Deleon, N. (2017). How safe is Bitcoin, really? *Consumer Reports.*

Dhawan, A. and Putniņš, T. (2020). A new wolf in town? Pump-and-dump manipulation in cryptocurrency markets.

Ehrlick, S. and Bambysheva, N. (2021). Crypto confidential. *Forbes.*

Ellis, B. (2021). Bitcoin IRA investing: Three crucial first steps. *Forbes.*

European Insurance and Occupational Pensions Authority (EIOPA) (2021). Innovation: Blockchain and crypto assets. *European Insurance and Occupational Pensions Authority (EIOPA).*

Expat, I. (2021). Coinbase partners with 401(k) advisor. *Expat, Indonesia.*

Freer, M. (2021). There is a Bitcoin link in most pensions. *Jersey Evening Post.*

Goldberg, E. S. and Rickard, E. M. (2021). Department of Labor teases cryptocurrency interest.

Hagen, K. (2021). Does your 401(k) let you invest in bitcoin? *Motley Fool.*

Helms, K. (2018). South Korean national pension fund indirectly invests in crypto exchanges.

Hickey, S. (2017). Will Bitcoin ever be a safe investment or always a gamble? *The Guardian.*

Iacurci, G. (2019). Blockchain will upend the 401(k) market. *Investment News.*

Keynes, J. (1936). The general theory of employment, interest and money.

KiwiSaver (2021). How KiwiSaver works. *KiwiSaver.*

Lawton, R. (2021). Offering cryptocurrency investments in a 401k is irresponsible. *LRPC's Plan Sponsor Insight.*

Lee, K. (2021). El salvador assures: No salary or pension will be paid in Bitcoins. *D1SoftbalalNews.*

Liew, J. K.-S. and Hewlett, L. (2017). *The Case for Bitcoin for Institutional Investors: Bubble Investing or Fundamentally Sound?* Ph.D. thesis.

Morgan Creek Capital Management (2019). The digital asset index fund: An index fund built for the world's leading institutions.

Ontario Teachers' Pension Plan (2021). Teachers' innovation platform invests in FTX.

Pension Funds Online (2021). Pension system in Germany. *Pension Funds Online.*

Salisbury, I. (2021). The best time to buy Bitcoin, explained in one chart. *Money.*

Scoop Business (2021). Pathfinder KiwiSaver invests in crypto infrastructure. *Scoop Business.*

Securities and Exchange Commission (2018). Self-directed IRAs and the risk of fraud. *Securities and Exchange Commission*, 8.

Shiller, R. J. (2017). What is Bitcoin really worth? Don't even ask. *New York Times.*

Simpson, D. (2021). 2nd Circuit revives fraud suit over $38.6 Helbiz Crypto ICO. *Law360 Securities.*

Smith, A. (2021). Can i put bitcoin in my pension, SIPP or ISA in the UK?

Tardi, C. (2019). Animal Spirits. *Investopedia.*

Torpey, K. (2019). Here's the case for a $100,000 Bitcoin price by the end of 2021. *Forbes.*

Turner, J. A. (2021). Pension litigation as a way of improving pension participants' outcomes. *New York University Review of Employee Benefits and Executive Compensation.*

Waters, C. (2021). Can't be ignored': Hostplus, Square Peg open to crypto investments. *The Sydney Morning Herald.*

5 Regulatory Considerations of the Decentralised Financial System

RYOSUKE USHIDA AND SHIN'ICHIRO MATSUO

5.1 Expansion of DeFi Ecosystem

The ecosystem of decentralised finance (DeFi), which generally refers to a decentralised form of financial applications executed by smart contracts on a public blockchain, has been rapidly expanding since early 2020. In terms of Total Value Locked (TVL), which represents the total value of tokens locked in a smart contract on blockchain such as Ethereum and is often used as an indicator of DeFi market size, it has increased more than 80 times since the beginning of 2020, to about $58 billion as of the end of May 2021.[1] Many financial products are available without KYC (Know Your Customers), including crypto-assets exchange, lending, derivatives, insurance, and decentralised stablecoins.

In 2019, the Financial Stability Board (FSB) (Financial Stability Board, 2019) defined decentralised financial technology as 'Technologies that have the potential to reduce or eliminate the need for one or more intermediaries or centralised processes in the provision of financial services', and decentralised financial systems as 'new financial systems that decentralised financial technology could bring'. On the other hand, there is no widely accepted definition of DeFi, and the word seems to be used arbitrarily for marketing and other purposes. In this Section 5.1, we define DeFi as a 'financial application that could consist of a part of a decentralised financial system' based on the definition of Ushida and Angel (Ushida and Angel, 2021). While underlying blockchain platforms such as Bitcoin and Ethereum could be categorised as DeFi broadly, our analysis focuses on smart contract-based

[1] defipulse.com. Note that the actual amount of asset inflows may be overestimated, as some tokens are double-counted in TVL. When a token issued on the back of locked token is locked in another smart contract, both tokens are counted in TVL.

applications on such platforms. DeFi protocols are often developed and managed by so-called DAOs, decentralised autonomous organisations. Although the DAO is also not strictly defined, we use Chohan's (Chohan, 2017) definition: 'an organisation represented by rules encoded as a computer program that is transparent, controlled by the organisation members and not influenced by a centralised entity'. Typical DAOs include The DAO (2016), MakerDAO,[2] and KyberDAO.[3]

As mentioned in the FSB report (Financial Stability Board, 2019), even regulatory authorities have expectations for decentralised financial technology, as it may contribute to the financial system stability and diversification of financial services. For example, reduced reliance on intermediaries could mitigate solvency and liquidity risks, and increased transparency in financial transactions could help to reduce uncertainty. It also has the potential to achieve better availability and resilience to cyber threats if the architecture is appropriately designed and integrated into the financial system. Furthermore, it could help financially excluded people to access financial services that meet their desperate needs, such as micropayment.

On the other hand, there are some risks that decentralised financial technology may pose. The decentralised financial system is not a 'trustless' system, but instead creates new concentration risks due to the centralised aspect described in the following section. Such characteristics may result in negative impacts on financial stability. In addition, regulatory concerns such as anti-money laundering/countering the financing of terrorism (AML/CFT) and consumer protection arise from the unique nature of blockchain-based systems such as anonymity/pseudonymity, openness, and global nature.

Security risk is another major issue. DeFi has seen many security incidents since 2020. According to CipherTrace,[4] most crypto-assets hacks in 2020 were related to DeFi ($129 million in value). Though the most significant incident of 2020 is the $281 million hack of KuCoin, a centralised exchange, it also involved DeFi as the

[2] makerdao.com
[3] kyber.org
[4] ciphertrace.com/2020-year-end-cryptocurrency-crime-and-anti-money-laundering-report

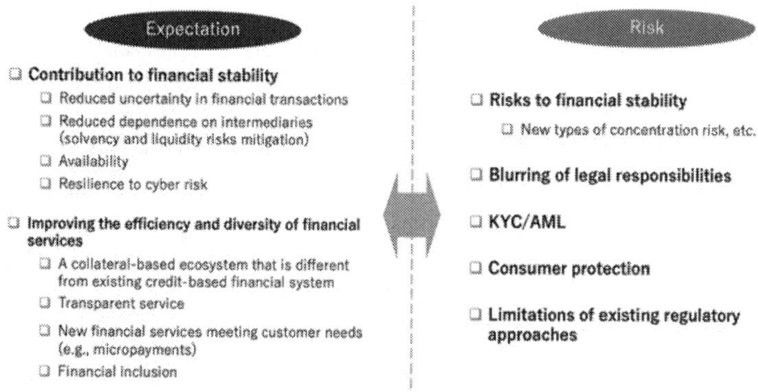

Figure 5.1 Expectations and risks from regulatory[5]

Date	protocol	Classification	Estimated damage	Overview
2020.2.14/18	bZx	Lending / Derivatives	$1 million (Total of two incidents)	Flash loan attack exploiting Protocol vulnerability
2020.4.19	Lendf.me	lending	$25 million	Reentrancy attack exploiting vulnerability in token standard (ERC-777)
2020.10.26	Harvest Finance	yield farming aggregator	$24 million	Flash loan attack exploiting Protocol vulnerability
2020.11.16	Origin Protocol	Sharing Economy marketplace	$7.7 million	Flash loan attack exploiting Protocol vulnerability
2020.11.21	Pickle Finance	lending	$19.7 million	Hacking into control contracts (Pickle Jar)
2020.12.14	Nexus Mutual	insurance	$8 million	Unauthorized access to CEO's computer that generates fake signature
2020.12.28	Cover Protocol	insurance	$3 million	Exploiting a protocol bug to cast a large number of governance tokens

Figure 5.2 Series of incidents in DeFi space[6]

criminal attempted to launder illegally acquired crypto-assets through Uniswap.[7]

As the ecosystem grows, financial regulators in many jurisdictions pay increasing attention to this domain and combat unfavourable transactions/applications relying on traditional enforcement regimes (e.g., Financial Action Task Force (FATF) travel rule).

[5] Source: www.fsa.go.jp/en/policy/bgin/20201020_Fintech_Association_presentation_EN.pdf
[6] Source: created by authors based on various sources.
[7] uniswap.org

Degree of Decentralisation →

		Traditional centralised finance	Private chains (e.g., security tokens, private digital currencies)	Partially decentralised finance (e.g. DeFi, Stablecoin)	Fully decentralised finance (e.g., Bitcoin)
Characteristics	Permission	Permissioned		Permissionless (partially permissioned)	permissioned
	programmability	Small	Medium	High	High
	Transaction entities	Individuals/corporations		Individuals/corporations /Machines (IoT devices, etc.)/DAO	
	Role of Intermediary	Large	Medium to small	Small	minimum
Legislation	Legal language	Natural language		Natural Language / Machine Language (Smart Contracts)	Machine Language (Smart Contracts)
Monitoring	Data acquisition	API			
		-	Supervisory Node	Supervisory node / General node	general node
	Data storage	Cloud	Cloud/Distributed database		
	Data processing	RPA, AI			
		-	Smart Contracts		
Enforcement	Enforcement method	Analog (Enforcement officer's discretionary basis)	Analog/Automatic enforcement of regulation	Analog/Automatic enforcement of regulation	Automatic enforcement of regulation

Figure 5.3 Regulatory considerations by the category of financial system

5.2 Regulatory Considerations by the Category of Financial System

In discussing the regulatory issues in the decentralised financial system, it is crucial to analyse the differences from traditional centralised financial systems in terms of technologies, governance, and use cases. In addition, since a decentralised financial system is a broad concept and has various types of applications, including crypto-assets such as Bitcoin, DeFi, stablecoins, and security tokens provided on the permissioned blockchain, we classified the decentralised financial systems into three categories as shown in Figure 5.3.

Category 2: Partially Decentralised Finance

Partially DeFi is a financial system provided on a permissionless blockchain with a significant degree of centralised aspects. Typical examples are centralised stablecoins such as Tether and many of the existing DeFi projects. In considering the enforceability of the conventional regulatory approach, it would be helpful to focus on the centralised aspect of the system. The regulatory issues based on the centralised element are discussed in detail in Section 5.3.

Category 3: Fully Decentralised Finance

Fully DeFi is a financial system that minimises centralised points such as Bitcoin, a financial system with the highest degree of decentralisation compared to the other methods. While there are various arguments about the centralisation of Bitcoin, such as the concentration of miners, it has different regulatory implications in that it does not have a specific Single Point of Failure, and decision-making is highly decentralised based on the off-chain consensus. Therefore, in Section 5.5, we analyse the regulatory challenges of a financial system in this category.

It should be noted that the objectives of the financial regulation remain the same for all types of financial systems. Financial regulators generally have three regulatory goals: financial system stability, investor protection, and financial crime prevention. These three objectives must be achieved regardless of the types of financial systems and technologies applied. In applying regulation, it is essential to understand the technical and governance characteristics of the decentralised financial system and to adopt the regulatory approach that is considered to be most effective. For example, as shown in Figure 5.3, one possible method of supervising transactions is collecting and analysing data through a node operated by a regulator, called a supervisory node.

5.3 Regulatory Considerations on Centralised Aspects of DeFi Managed by DAOs

Contrary to what the name 'DeFi' might suggest, the degree of decentralisation varies from one DeFi project to another. Many of them are pretty centralised, especially in the bootstrapping stage. For example, specific individuals or groups have the authority to change the protocol or freeze locked assets, unlike highly decentralised ecosystems such as Bitcoin. The centralised aspects of DeFi, such as admin key and large governance token holders, have significant implications on their governance mechanism and regulatory enforceability. From a regulatory viewpoint, centralised aspects could be captured by a conventional entity-based approach (e.g., enforcement action against regulated entity) and increase regulatory enforceability. In the following sections, we point out the quintessential centralised points of DeFi and analyse its regulatory considerations.

Admin Keys

Some DeFi projects have a specific party with administrative authorities to modify the protocol at its discretion via private keys, typically called 'admin keys'. The existence of such centralised functions might be accepted by its community members in its bootstrapping stage as it could help facilitate the community's growth through swift and justifiable updates by the administrators who are strongly committed to the project, such as the initial developer team. Indeed, we saw cases, such as Compound,[8] which issued governance tokens to transfer the authority from admin key holders to token holders as the community grows. On the other hand, some protocols do not have admin keys from the beginning, such as Maker and Uniswap. Taking as an example of the bZx hack explained in Figure 5.2, we can argue that the bZx developer team could fix the bug relatively quickly because they had an admin key. As such, it is not necessarily a bad thing to hold an admin key. However, many projects make only ambiguous statements about the existence and management of such private keys. These custody risks are difficult to verify even with external audits, and the ecosystem participants need to trust the key holders. It would be necessary to follow the security management standards such as ISO/TR 23576 from the operational security perspective. The administrators should strive for appropriate life cycle management of private keys and transparent information disclosure. In addition, the admin key may act as a backdoor and threaten the entire system's security.

Regulatory Considerations The admin keys and their holders could be control points for regulators, as Takanashi et al. (2020) argue that backdoor 'could facilitate nearly perfect oversight from the government within the network'. SEC (U.S. Securities and Exchange Commission, 2017) refers to the fact that eleven 'high profile' individuals are selected as holders of The DAO's Curator 'Multisig' (or 'private key') in its investigation report. The EtherDelta case[9] is another proof that regulatory bodies take the admin keys seriously to assess whether the developer is liable for the unlawful financial service provision via smart contracts. If regulators can identify the admin key holders, they might ask them to take necessary actions such as freezing stolen tokens in case of theft or money laundering. For example, when crypto-assets

[8] compound.finance

[9] SEC charged the founder of EtherDelta with operating an unregistered exchange in November 2018. SEC points out the concentration of power to the founder exampled by his exclusive access to the private key for the 'administrator account'. www.sec.gov/news/press-release/2018-258

were stolen from the hot wallet of a centralised exchange KuCoin, some ERC-20 token issuers such as USDT and Ocean (government tokens) restricted token movement by the administrator's judgement. Though it is not clear whether there was an order or request from the authorities, it is conceivable that the authorities will take similar enforcement actions against future incidents. Moreover, depending on the type of financial product offered, authorities might require the admin key holders to comply with the same regulations that existing financial institutions providing comparable services must abide by.

The authorities may decide that uncontrollable projects are unacceptable to achieve their regulatory objectives and demand that the adoption of admin keys be required at the launch of the protocol despite its enforceability. In the early 1990s, the National Security Agency (NSA) intended to force telecom companies to adopt a chip set with a backdoor called the Clipper chip so that law enforcement authorities could decode the intercepted voice and data transmissions. The attempt failed due to strong opposition from cryptographers and related groups. Still, it should be kept in mind that some authorities could have a solid motivation to have control over the protocol, as exemplified by the recent discussion on restricting end-to-end encryption. Since the admin key encompasses issues such as custody risk, as pointed out in the previous paragraph, developers and authorities should at least conduct an in-depth risk assessment analysis before making critical decisions.

Governance Token Holders

Blemus and Gregan (2019) argue that one of the purposes of distributed governance is to minimise the risk of 'tyranny of the majority'. However, regarding the degree of concentration of decision-making, governance tokens could increase the concentration of control over the protocols. Observing the DeFi ecosystem, most of the governance token is held by the developer team or early investors such as venture capital in many projects. For example, 40% of Uniswap's UNI is going to be distributed to the inner members, such as initial investors and developers.[10] Community members usually receive the token via retrospective distribution or as a reward for adding liquidity to the

[10] In the case of Uniswap, about 18% is distributed to investors, 21.2% to team members and future employees, 0.7% to team advisers, and the remaining

protocol pool. Still, many holders only hold a minority portion of the stake and play only a limited role in governance voting. As a result, large token holders occupy a dominant position in decision-making. It should also be noted that voting rights are often concentrated in specific holders through delegation function.

Regulatory Considerations One of the significant regulatory issues is the applicability of governance tokens as securities. While the holders of some governance tokens are entitled to receive a part of the fee income generated by the protocol, others have only voting rights and do not have the right to the treasury of the protocol directly. However, in many protocols, a portion of the tokens is burned as the cash flow to the protocol increases, which is equivalent to a share buyback in the case of ordinary stocks and can be considered to have the same economic function as a dividend. Collomb et al. (2019) argue that regulators should assess not only the original nature or function of the tokens being issued but also the underlying motivations of both token issuers and investors, as well as the risks that investors may incur in purchasing these tokens. Given the assumptions that token holders' primary motivation is capital and income gains that would be realised from the growth of the DeFi projects, it is conceivable that some of them are regarded as kind of securities or investment contracts, especially for those that have a specific centralised party to manage the protocol. However, it needs to be examined in the context of the legal framework of relevant jurisdictions. As an example, the SEC (U.S. Securities and Exchange Commission, 2017) has concluded that The DAO token was a security at the issuance and charged Ripple Labs Inc. and two of its executives alleging that they raised over $1.3 billion through an unregistered, ongoing digital asset securities offering.[11]

Given the similarity of the governance tokens to securities, disclosure requirements should be well considered, particularly for the minor token holder protection. Many jurisdictions have put various institutional frameworks in place in corporate governance, such as a requirement to submit statements of large-volume holdings to mitigate the dominance by extensive investor regulation to protect minority shareholders' interests. While such regulatory frameworks

60% to community members such as liquidity providers over a 4-year period. uniswap.org/blog/uni

11 www.sec.gov/news/press-release/2020-338

are not in place as of now, some projects such as Nexus Mutual implement specific voting rules to curve the strong voting power of large holders by, as an example, limiting the maximum voting rights to 5% of the total voting rights.[12] However, this kind of arrangement could also raise concerns about fairness among shareholders.

Another consideration is concerning the possibility of token-based voting mechanisms being captured by authorities. It is conceivable that the authorities could hold many tokens and intervene in the DeFi community's decision-making.

Collateral

Even if the DeFi protocol itself is highly decentralised, there are cases where assets accepted as collateral or locked in its pools are managed in a centralised manner. Maker community decided to add the USDC, custodial stablecoins backed by U.S. dollars, as one of the collateral assets in March 2020 to increase the pool's liquidity after the liquidation failure incidents.[13] As a US corporation, Circle manages the USDC. Enforcement officials may demand the company to freeze the USDC used as collateral of Dai, a stablecoin issued by Maker protocol, to stop illegal financial transactions. Also, if the Maker community could intervene in the decision via on-chain voting, the voters against the request from authorities could have legal responsibilities. If voters have no generally agreed extent of liability, the token holders might choose not to join the voting to avoid getting involved in the complicated situation.

Aggregator

The need for aggregation services is growing as the DeFi ecosystem expands. CEXaggregators enable users to access multiple liquidity pools and offer the best trading price. Yearn Finance provides lending aggregation by which the interest accrual process is optimised by shifting deposited funds automatically between lending pools such as Compound and AAVE. Yearn Finance also helps users to maximise their

[12] nexusmutual.io/pages/NexusMutualRulesV1.0.pdf
[13] forum.makerdao.com/t/proposal-for-collateral-onboarding-of-usdc/1588

profit-making via liquidity mining or yield firming. Whereas aggregators are yet another protocol like many other DeFi protocols and often do not custody the user's assets, it could be a point of centralisation when many users rely on the aggregation services and access the user-friendly front interface. The operators of the website might be deemed liable if it is evident that the aggregation protocols facilitate illegal activities.

5.4 The Future of DeFi: Further Decentralisation?

As discussed in the previous section, the degree of decentralisation of most DeFi projects at this point is not necessarily high, and the conventional entity-based regulatory approach could work to a large extent. However, the brief history of the crypto-assets ecosystem does not necessarily indicate that the current low decentralisation situation will remain in the future. When Ethereum was launched in 2015, it was not necessarily highly decentralised in terms of decision-making at first due to the strong influence of a few parities such as Vitalik Buterin and the Ethereum Foundation. However, as the community grew, various stakeholders became involved in the ecosystem, and the degree of influence of such entities decreased. In the US, Ethereum is currently treated as a commodity along with Bitcoin rather than security. The statements of high-ranking officials[14] indicate that the degree of decentralisation is an essential factor influencing regulatory categories' decisions.

Then what does the future hold for DeFi? Of course, it is difficult to foresee precisely, but it is likely that some DeFi projects will achieve further decentralisation. One of the reasons for this is the motivation to avoid regulatory capture. One of the differentiating factors among DeFi projects is the willingness of the community to comply or circumvent the existing legal framework applied to financial services in each jurisdiction. At present, it seems that the primary value proposition of many DeFi is not complying with regulatory requirements such as KYC/AML (Know Your Customer/Anti Money Laundering rules). It purportedly 'democratises' the financial services for financial inclusion while protecting users from the threat of government actions such as

[14] www.jdsupra.com/post/contentViewerEmbed.aspx?fid=b55667d0-f4e3-4d42-941d-020081243c60

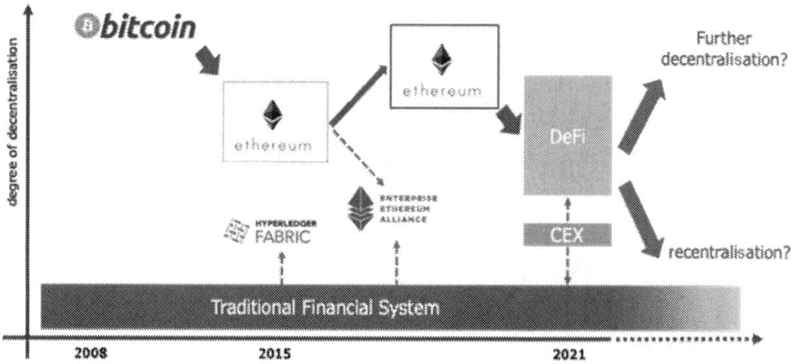

Figure 5.4 How DeFi ecosystem is likely to advance[15]

taxation and expropriation. In light of growing concerns and scrutiny from regulatory authorities, some DeFi projects might choose to further decentralise the project by, for example, dispersing the governance token ownership, anonymising the developer and community members, or voiding administrative functions to lessen the control points that regulators could capture.

On the contrary, others might choose to work closely with regulators and other stakeholders outside the blockchain ecosystem to ensure legal certainty closely. For that sake, whether it should be called 'DeFi', they could choose to increase the centralised aspects of the DeFi project to meet regulatory requirements effectively as traditional organisations usually do. One example is Nexus Mutual, a P2P discretionary mutual on Ethereum offering a blockchain-based solution to cover against smart contract failure such as 'The DAO' hack. It was established as a company limited in the UK and has received approval from the Financial Conduct Authority. KYC/AML requirements must be fulfilled to become a member of the community, and the membership gives legal rights to the assets of the mutual. Residents in some jurisdictions are not able to become members due to relevant local regulations.[16] Another eye-catching initiative is OpenLaw's LAO, a Limited liability autonomous organisation that enables its members to invest in Ethereum ventures projects and generate a profit in a

[15] Source: drive.google.com/file/d/1cirOXFbPvAOMPneBEMWIcdb1GwexDeSP
[16] nexusmutual.gitbook.io/docs/welcome/use-cases

legally compliant manner.[17] The LAO is an Limited Liability Company (LLC) set up in Delaware, and it harnesses smart contracts to handle mechanics related to voting, funding, and allocation of collected funds. It intends to ensure legal certainty, limit the members' liability, and streamline complex tax issues. A similar example is the Flamingo,[18] an NFT (non-fungible token)-focused DAO organised as a Delaware LLC that aims to explore emerging investment opportunities for ownable, blockchain-based assets.

In general, there exists a trade-off between regulatory compliance and openness of the project. In the case of the LAO, the maximum number of members is limited to 99, the minimum investment is 120 ETH, and the membership is limited to 9% or 1,080 ETH.[19] The Flamingo also limits its membership to accredited investors capped at a maximum of 100. Such limitations could curve some of the key value propositions of DeFi, such as composability upheld by its permissionless nature while paving the way to mass adoption in complying with social requirements. It should be noted that they might need to meet not only securities regulation but also other regulatory requirements regarding AML/KYC and financial stability, which could further increase compliance costs.

In addition, a certain degree of community members aspire to attain a higher degree of decentralisation, aiming to reduce single point of failure (SPoF) risk. To mitigate the SPoF risk caused by dependence on trusted parties, many communities are heading for bottom-up, decentralised governance by transferring management authority of the protocol to the DAO through on-chain voting. Given the incessant hacking incidents and increasing attention from regulatory authorities, the sound development of governance of the entire ecosystem is indispensable if they look ahead to mass adoption beyond niche use cases.

5.5 Regulatory Challenges in the Highly Decentralised Financial System

When the financial system becomes highly decentralised, as Takanashi et al. (2020) discuss, financial regulators will face enforcement challenges to achieve their goals such as financial stability, consumer

[17] medium.com/openlawofficial/the-lao-a-for-profit-limited-liability-autonomous-organization-9eae89c9669c
[18] flamingodao.xyz
[19] docs.flamingodao.xyz/membership.html

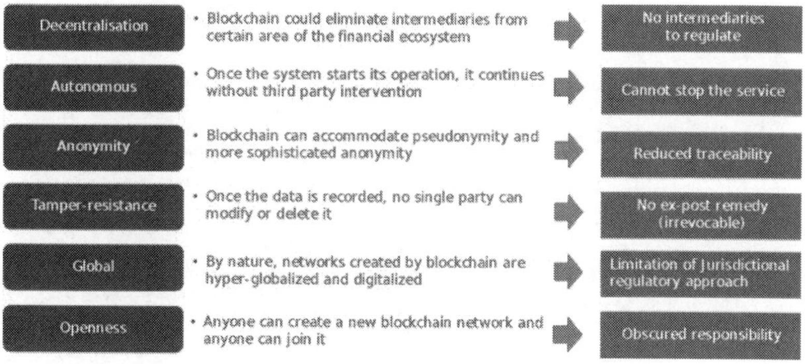

Figure 5.5 Reduced enforceability[20]

protection, and financial crime prevention. The regulatory enforceability by laws and regulations alone will reduce due to the innate characteristics of the system and the resulting challenges as described in Figure 5.5.

In particular, if a highly decentralised financial system becomes mainstream, the number of financial transactions may increase exponentially as P2P (peer-to-peer), and M2M (machine-to-machine) transactions that do not require human intervention could increase exponentially. In this case, even if the enforcement officers want to crack down on problematic transactions, enforcement methods that rely on limited human resources may find it challenging to take effective actions against a vast number of transactions. One of the solutions to this is to leverage technology, rather than relying solely on laws and regulations written in natural language, to achieve regulatory goals.

The governance issues of decentralised financial systems are attracting many researchers' attention. Some explore to build sound governance of decentralised financial systems in light of the Internet governance lessons. Filippi and Wright (2018) discuss the applicability of the four regulatory tools (i.e., Law, Market, Norm, and Architecture/Code) in cyberspace proposed by Lessig (1999) to control activities in decentralised financial systems. Takanashi et al. (2020) point out the importance of developing an architecture/code that harmonises with law/regulations, aligns with social norms, and is competitive in the market. Given the multifaceted aspects of the DeFi

[20] Source: www.fsa.go.jp/en/policy/bgin/20201020_Fintech_Association_presentation_EN.pdf

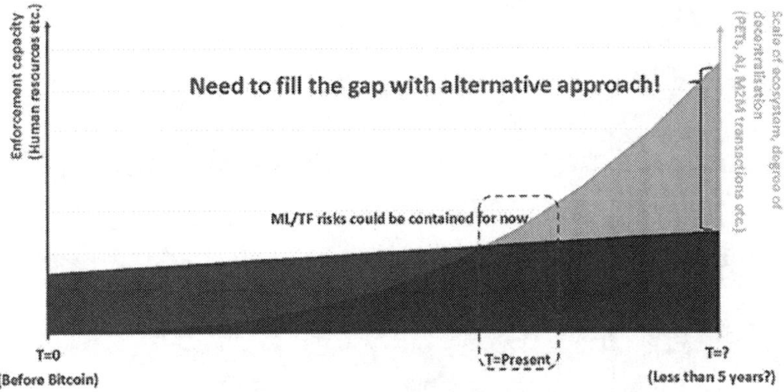

Figure 5.6 Increasing gap between ecosystem expansion and enforcement capacity[21]

projects in terms of the degree of decentralisation, the DeFi ecosystem should learn lessons from both the Internet governance as a partially decentralised system and from the corporate governance best practices to address issues stemming from the centralised characteristics that traditional organisations have been tackling to solve. Given the different degrees of decentralisation of ongoing projects, the hybrid approach might hit the target. However, it is worth mentioning that it does not mean that we should ignore the existing governance arrangement.

One notable example in this context is Hedera, which stands out for its decentralised decision-making process. The Hedera Council serves as the governing body of the network, providing distributed governance. The council consists of up to 39 leading organisations and enterprises from diverse industries and geographies, including notable entities such as Boeing, Dell, Google, IBM, and others. This composition reflects a wide range of perspectives and trusted market positions, enhancing the balanced and fair decision-making process. By adopting such an approach, Hedera achieves a higher level of decentralisation in contrast to a single foundation with limited decision-makers.

[21] Source: drive.google.com/file/d/1cirOXFbPvAOMPneBEMWIcdb1GwexDeSP

5.6 Implementation of Multi-stakeholder Approach through BGIN

By definition, crypto-assets systems based on permissionless blockchain have global nature. The software codes run independently of each nation, and no government can stop the operation of such a system. On the other hand, each nation and a group of nations acts in a national/international manner; they have mandates to protect citizens' safety and property, prevent (financial) crime, and maintain financial stability. Given the situation that program codes produced by engineers play a part of roles to form an order of financial systems, it is needed to establish a new framework to facilitate harmonisation among technology, law, economic soundness, and social norm.

In the case of the Blockchain and DeFi ecosystem, the main difficulty which prevents the harmonisation is the lack of healthy communications among stakeholders. In the DeFi ecosystem, roughly, there are four types of stakeholders; engineers, regulators, businesses and consumers sometimes do not want to talk with regulators, and both engineers and regulators do not have communication channels and common languages. Business entities wish to start their business even if technology and software codes are immature. They also want to avoid friction against regulations. On the other hand, regulators may not be able to catch up with the advanced DeFi business. Consumers need transparency for the business, but in many cases, the explanations from the business entity are just a white paper and complicated technical documents. It makes less transparency for average consumers. From above, FSB published a report, 'Decentralised financial technologies: Report on financial stability, regulatory and governance implications' in 2019 (Ushida and Angel, 2021). This report emphasises the importance of introducing multi-stakeholder dialogue in the era of DeFi. Right after the publication of the report, G20 agreed to welcome the report in its communiqué.[22] Because introducing multi-stakeholder governance may imply that governments and regulators need to give up some existing governance power, the agreement was historical to realise a healthy and productive DeFi ecosystem design.

[22] www.mofa.go.jp/policy/economy/g20_summit/osaka19/en/documents/final_g20_osaka_leaders_declaration.html

After having several multi-stakeholder workshops in geographically diversified venues, 23 global blockchain experts from engineering communities, regulators, blockchain businesses standards, internet pioneers, and academia initiated Blockchain Governance Initiative Network (BGIN) in March 2020. BGIN plays similar roles as ISOC/ICANN/IETF plays for Internet governance. Anyone can join its activities to create technical specifications and guidance, operational guidance, and other documents through a multi-stakeholder discussion process.

When writing this chapter, BGIN is working on creating several documents on key management at centralised custody and decentralised custody and regulatory consideration on DeFi. BGIN holds three general meetings per year and has already held three general meetings. At the third general meeting (Block #3) held in June/July 2021, BGIN discussed AML/KYC issues with a co-chair of the Virtual Asset Contact Group (VACG) at the FATF and discussed initiating work on Ransomware reaction process with FATF. At the same meeting, BGIN discussed another big issue on the institutionalisation of crypto-assets, which El Salvador raised to make Bitcoin a legal tender. BGIN invited, the Director del Banco Centroamericano de Integración Económica para El Salvador and an engineer from Bitcoin Beach, who promote Bitcoin in El Salvador to the panel discussion. BGIN decided to continue to work on the application of blockchain technology to realise financial inclusion.

Bibliography

Blemus, S. and Guegan, D. (2019). Initial crypto-asset offerings (ICOs), tokenization and corporate governance.

Chohan, U. W. (2017). The decentralised autonomous organization and governance issues. *Available at SSRN 3082055*.

Collomb, A., Filippi, P. D. E., and Sok, K. (2019). Blockchain technology and financial regulation: A risk-based approach to the regulation of ICOs. *European Journal of Risk Regulation*, 10(2):263–314.

Filippi, P. D. and Wright, A. (2018). Blockchain and the law: The rule of code. *Harvard University Press*.

Financial Stability Board (2019). Decentralised financial technologies: Report on financial stability, regulatory and governance implications. *Financial Stability Board*.

Lessig, L. (1999). *Code and other laws of cyberspace*. Basic Books.

Takanashi, Y., Matsuo, S., Burger, E., Sullivan, C., Miller, J., and Sato, H. (2020). Call for multi-stakeholder communication to establish a governance mechanism for the emerging blockchain-based financial ecosystem. *Stanford Journal of Blockchain Law Policy*, part 1 of 2.

U.S. Securities and Exchange Commission (2017). Report of investigation pursuant to section 21(a) of the securities exchange act of 1934: The dao.

Ushida, R. and Angel, J. (2021). Regulatory considerations on centralized aspects of DeFi managed by DAOs. In *Financial Cryptography and Data Security. FC 2021 International Workshops*, pages 21–36. Springer Berlin Heidelberg.

6 *A Hayekian View of Digital Currencies*

ANDY YEE AND NIKHIL VADGAMA

6.1 Introduction

With the advent of blockchain, a tidal wave of change is coming to the world of monetary technology. Alongside Bitcoin's spectacular rise, there has been an explosion of other cryptocurrencies, stablecoins,[1] corporate tokens, and sovereign digital currencies. In just a decade, Bitcoin's market capitalisation has grown to over USD 400 billion.[2] Including the hundreds of other cryptocurrencies that have emerged, the total market capitalisation of cryptocurrencies is over USD 1 trillion.[3] A few years ago, stablecoins were launched with the objective of minimising the price volatility of cryptocurrencies. In 2020, there were dozens of stablecoins with a total market value of USD 20 billion, facilitating hundreds of billions of dollars in transaction flow (Messari, 2020). In 2022, just Tether (USDT), USD Coin (USDC), and Binance USD (BUSD) (three popular stablecoins) comprise a market capitalisation of over USD 100 billion[4] – five times the growth since 2020. More recently, financial institutions and technology giants – the BigTechs (Frost et al., 2019) – have entered the fray, with many announcing their intention to explore or launch stablecoins in their digital networks and indeed with some abandoning their plans in 2022 showcasing the fast cycle of emergence, exploration, and abandonment. Realising that this might be the early stages of a paradigm shift, many central banks are determining whether to redesign government-issued money into digital currency.

1 Cryptocurrencies designed to minimise the volatility of the price of the stablecoin, relative to some 'stable' asset or basket of assets. A stablecoin can be pegged to a cryptocurrency, fiat money, or to exchange-traded commodities (such as precious metals or industrial metals).

2 Coinmarketcap.com retrieved 12 August 2022.

3 ibid.

4 ibid.

This chapter details new finance business models and the associated proliferation of digital currencies from the perspective of Friedrich Hayek's classic work on monetary denationalisation. It also briefly introduces the bridge between centralised finance (CeFi) and decentralised finance (DeFi). In the *Denationalisation of Money* (Hayek, 1976), Hayek argues that the state monopoly of money must be eliminated to prevent periods of inflation for the gain of governments and that there should be free competition in money issued by public and private enterprises for consumers to determine the best possible option. The emergence of Bitcoin in 2009 sparked a monetary revolution which is making Hayek's vision a reality. The proliferation of digital currencies, which offer greater convenience, resilience, and usefulness, is challenging the existing value exchange process based on fiat currency. In turn, this could stimulate central bank money to be more user-friendly in the digital world.

In this chapter, we consider the major actors in the digital currency space, and postulate possible future developments. The chapter is organised as follows. We first establish a taxonomy of digital money that captures the major categories by issuer/actor types. Next, we lay out the business models, motivations, and ideologies for each category. We then present possible futures based on the dynamics of competition and interaction between these major issuer/actor types. Thereafter, there is discussion on the bridge between CeFi and DeFi. We conclude that the rise of and competition between new digital forms of money will only accelerate, with significant implications on global monetary arrangements.

6.2 Taxonomy of Digital Money

Digital currencies can be classified into various categories subject to an evolving typology. This part briefly surveys some existing taxonomies before presenting a simplified politico-economic model that focuses on issuer types to capture their competitive dynamics.

Literature Review

According to Bech and Garratt (2017), the 'money flower' reflects what appears to be emerging in practice and classifies money according to four properties: issuer (central bank or other), form (electronic or physical), accessibility (universal or limited), and transfer mechanism (centralised or decentralised, i.e., peer-to-peer). Adrian and Griffoli (2019) further refined the 'money flower' into a complementary, branch-like framework called the 'money tree'. It highlights four attributes of means of payment: type (a claim or an object), value (fixed or variable value redemption), backstop (government or private), and technology (centralised or decentralised). Raskin et al. (2019) offered a typology of digital currency along two axes: state-sponsorship (public or private) and centralisation (formal barriers to network participation or lack thereof). Finally, Bullmann et al. (2019) introduced the "crypto cube" which identifies crypto-assets according to three criteria: the existence or absence of an issuer, the decentralisation or centralisation of responsibilities, and that which underpins the value of a crypto-asset and its stability.

A Politico-economic Model

Complex technologies such as blockchain contain a 'margin of manoeuvre'; a contested terrain in which alternative politico-economic visions compete with each other (Manski and Manski, 2018). In the case of blockchain technology, its generative nature allows a range of third parties to innovate upon it. This opens up the possibility for new actors who wish to use the technology to subvert the existing sovereign order. In monetary arrangements, this is a revolutionary era in which currencies are continually being re-invented by a diverse group of creators, ranging from the cypherpunk communities, startups, and crypto companies to social media networks, financial institutions, and governments. Furthermore, competition and alliances are formed between them in surprisingly new ways.

The taxonomies of digital money surveyed above have two attributes in common: the nature of the issuer (public, government, or private) and technology (decentralised or centralised). By adopting a simplified framework based on these attributes alone, the politico-economic interactions between the different groups of actors can be appropriately captured. Accordingly, first a dichotomy is established that comprehensively cuts the digital currency landscape: trustlessness vs trustedness. The former recognises the libertarian and decentralised origin of cryptocurrencies. The latter considers the three main groups of stablecoin issuers, corporations, and governments.

6.3 Ideologies, Business Models, and Sovereignties

Based on the simplified taxonomy, this section successively outlines four sets of digital currency players: decentralised communities, first-generation stablecoin issuers, corporations, and central banks. Together they span the full spectrum of social coordination, from the most decentralised to the most centralised. There are clear connections between this monetary landscape and Hayek's *Denationalisation of Money* (Sanz Bas, 2020). The various non-state digital currencies, which are based on voluntary mutual acceptance, challenge the prerogative of governments to be sole issuers of money through legal tenders. Furthermore, the fixed nature of the monetary rule of most digital currencies removes the political factors and arbitrary interests found in traditional monetary policy. Paradoxically, the rigidity in the monetary rules of some of these non-state digital currencies may prevent a dynamic equilibrium between supply and demand to be achieved, making it impossible for these digital currencies to achieve a stable purchasing power that Hayek advocates for. However, having non-state alternative digital currencies with predetermined or algorithmically determined supply schedules provides competitive checks to central banks. Their mere existence incentivises policymakers to behave in a more responsible manner, thereby promoting sound monetary policy (Bailey et al., 2021).

Trustless

Bitcoin represents the first example of blockchain technology which enables trustless direct exchange among network participants. Often described as having a libertarian tendency, it challenges existing institutions by removing the need for centralised intermediaries. As a form of money, Bitcoin's key innovation is simulating a bearer instrument digitally on a register that is global, decentralised, transparent, and open. Consequently, Bitcoin exhibits some unique characteristics, including an emphasis on individual sovereignty, resistance to censorship, and a monetary policy that is politically neutral, moving towards Hayek's view (Hayek, 1976).

More importantly, the blockchain and the public consensus mechanism that Bitcoin inspired have ushered in an era of decentralized computing. This is the idea that a computer application can be run simultaneously on many computers worldwide rather than just one central server, thus avoiding the necessity to trust the honesty or integrity of any one computer (Roubini, 2018). From a politico-economic perspective, this enables cryptosecession, the creation of new decentralised governance structures through blockchain applications which allows individuals and entrepreneurs to exit existing institutional hierarchies. This forms an entirely new cryptoeconomy, a non-territorial collection of governance structures in which interaction and exchange are governed through blockchain technology rather than governments and firms (Allen, 2019). Bitcoin relies on a system of financial incentives through the proof of work algorithm to verify and record transactions. Later projects make use of tokens to incentivise both economic and governance participation: economic participation in terms of an accounting system that tracks and rewards contributions, and governance participation through voting, decision-making, and the ability to propose initiatives (Swan, 2019).

Trusted

Stablecoin Issuers

Stablecoins were introduced to bring stability to the volatile market of cryptocurrencies with reference to assets such as fiat currencies or commodities. In general, three price stabilisation mechanisms are recognised: off-chain collateralised, on-chain collateralised, and non-collateralised (algorithmic)[5] (PwC and Loopring, 2019). Although the latter two designs are more innovative and decentralised, with no requirements to trust a single counterparty, they are yet to succeed in any material fashion and have indeed had some spectacular failures (Shen, 2022). Here we will focus on off-chain collateralised stablecoins, which involve a centralised issuer holding an off-chain, real-world asset. Stability is underpinned by the fact that the stablecoin can always be redeemed for the corresponding off-chain asset. Fiat-collateralised stablecoins are the simplest to understand and are where the most substantial activity is observed. The top two stablecoins by market value, namely Tether and USD Coin, are both pegged to the US dollar. With USD 20 billion in circulating supply, Tether grew more

[5] The latter two respectively rely on the over-collateralisation of on-chain assets and algorithmically adjusting the coin supply to offset changes in coin demand to achieve price stability.

than four times in 2020 and surpassed Bitcoin as the most actively traded cryptocurrency on public blockchains (Messari, 2020). In 2022 Tether's market capitalisation peaked above USD 80 billion, growing four times again since 2020.[6]

Trading represents the largest use case of stablecoins. They facilitate several key functions for traders, including price pairs in fiat terms, hedge exposure, tax efficiency, and short-term stores of value during market downturns – without bank connectivity and the associated latency of current financial market processes. Stablecoins could also potentially underpin the next generation of faster and cheaper payment rails and act as a store of value for citizens with a hyperinflationary national currency (PwC and Loopring, 2019). Stablecoins generally share similar business models and typically profit in two ways. First, stablecoin issuers charge fees to issue and redeem stablecoins, generating revenue based on fluctuations in demand. Second, issuers invest collateral in short-term and liquid securities (such as treasuries and money market funds) to generate yield (Etienne, 2019).

An emerging business model is decentralised applications (dApps) powered by programmable stablecoins, of which finance is a major area. This is in part due to blockchain technology's potential to establish new financial services infrastructure and processes. Some of the transformative characteristics of blockchain include immutable and distributed record-keeping, reduced information asymmetry, and autonomous execution capabilities, which collectively eliminate the need for a centralised enforcer of trust in the ecosystem (WEF, 2016). By way of their blockchain-native and programmable nature, stablecoins will be a crucial part of this new financial services infrastructure to govern value exchange between users and providers directly without the involvement of intermediaries and create complex financial instruments. In 2019, the European Central Bank identified more than 2,000 dApps, which are being used by over 100,000 active users on a monthly basis (Bullmann et al., 2019).

In 2020, the proliferation of stablecoins has led to a wave of innovations in DeFi, permissionless and decentralised protocols geared towards financial applications. DeFi protocols have emerged across the full spectrum of financial services, from lending (Aave,[7]

[6] Coinmarketcap.com retrieved 12 August 2022.
[7] aave.com

Compound,[8] and Maker[9]), insurance (Nexus Mutual[10]), asset management (Yearn Finance[11]), to automated market making (Uniswap[12] and Curve[13]). While DeFi tokens command in aggregate just USD 7 billion in market capitalisation, they offer a preview of what a fully decentralised and algorithmic financial system could look like and are expected to grow rapidly (Messari, 2020). The DeFi industry in general is measured with Total Value Locked (TVL). TVL represents the market capitalisation of cryptocurrency held in smart contracts of DeFi protocols (Sun, 2021). TVL has grown from approximately USD 20 billion in 2020 to peaking at USD 100 billion in 2021 and falling to approximately USD 44 billion in August 2022.[14]

Corporations

In contrast to stablecoin projects launched by dedicated companies and foundations or cryptocurrency exchanges, an emerging class of stablecoins is being created by traditional financial institutions and BigTechs (Frost et al., 2019). For these new issuers, stablecoins present an opportunity to further develop their robust ecosystem of users and services. Traditional commercial banks can rely on their large number of stable customer relationships and suite of financial services. BigTechs, apart from their established digital networks and large user base, have competitive advantages in proprietary customer data due to their non-financial services and access to advanced technologies to process big data (Financial Stability Board, 2019). At work here are two-way network effects, which compress the time-to-market of corporate stablecoins deployed on the already-existing digital networks of banks and BigTechs without having to bootstrap their own networks from scratch.

Many companies and financial institutions are evaluating the issuance of their own stablecoins. Industry verticals that are particularly active include finance, social media, and retail. Stablecoin

[8] compound.finance
[9] makerdao.com/en
[10] nexusmutual.io
[11] yearn.finance
[12] uniswap.org
[13] curve.fi
[14] Defipulse.com retrieved 12 August 2022.

projects already released by banks include JP Morgan's JPM Coin and Mizuho's J-Coin. In social media, disclosed examples include Facebook's Diem (formerly Libra), Japanese Internet giant GMO's GMO Yen, and Russian social media network VKontakte's VK Coin. In retail, Walmart has reportedly filed a patent for a stablecoin of its own (McIntosh, 2019).

Corporate stablecoins mark a transition from an interest-collecting business model to one that improves internal business processes or even underpins entirely new digital ecosystems. The former is best illustrated by JPM Coin, a pioneering blockchain settlement product primarily used for settlement and value transfer use cases. Launched by JP Morgan in February 2019, it initially targets efficiency gains and risk reduction in clearing and settlement functions, as well as cost reductions across back-office functions for institutional clients. Although JPM Coin and similar offerings by other banks are unlikely to displace publicly traded stablecoins given their closed ecosystems built on private blockchains, it is possible for them to disrupt the entire stablecoin industry as they expand their use cases through the extensive networks and asset base of financial institutions (Etienne, 2019).

Diem is a canonical example of data giants venturing into stablecoins to underpin digital ecosystems. Announced by Facebook in June 2019, it was a stablecoin backed by stable financial assets which would be incorporated into the Facebook ecosystem built around Messenger, WhatsApp, and Facebook. With billions of existing users, Diem would have had a global footprint from day one. With a low-volatility digital currency and a smart contract platform, it could have created new opportunities for financial services innovation. In the short term, it may have empowered billions of unbanked people through financial inclusion and cost savings in prominent use cases such as remittances and government welfare payments (Zetzsche et al., 2019). In the medium to long term, it could have potentially become a platform upon which new financial services providers can build innovative, decentralised applications on the Diem network (Etienne and Calvin, 2019). The Diem project was shut down in January 2022 having sold its assets to Silvergate (a crypto-focused bank) for approximately USD 200 million (Heath, 2022). Diem stated that 'despite giving us positive substantive feedback on the design of the network, it nevertheless became clear from our dialogue with federal regulators that the project could not move ahead' (Diem Association, 2022).

Central Banks

In the past century, competition for pre-eminence in the international monetary system has been confined to sovereign currencies. With the advent of digitisation and blockchain technology, however, the proliferation of decentralised and private forms of money has accentuated competition. Emerging literature has begun to investigate the implications of competing currencies, finding that a global digital currency could lead to a 'crypto-enforced monetary policy synchronisation', restricting monetary authorities from pursuing their own monetary policy or setting exchange rates (Benigno et al., 2019). With their monetary sovereignty challenged, central banks have been deliberating on a digital upgrade of fiat currencies that could allow them to compete more effectively. One possibility is central bank digital currency (CBDC), a new form of money issued digitally by the central bank and intended to serve as legal tender. A recent survey by the Bank for International Settlements (BIS) found that 80% of central banks are engaged in investigating CBDC, and half of them have progressed beyond conceptual research to running experiments, proof-of-concepts, or pilots. Their works span across CBDC for both general purpose (retail) and wholesale uses (Boar et al., 2020).

According to a survey by the International Monetary Fund (IMF), central banks perceive a range of benefits and opportunities brought by CBDC. Foremost is countering the growth of private forms of money to maintain financial integrity, financial stability, and monetary policy effectiveness. There are also opportunities for cash displacement in advanced economies and financial inclusion in emerging markets. Other benefits include broader access to central bank money, cost efficiency, better tracking of economic activities, and the modernisation of payment systems (Griffoli et al., 2018). As private stablecoin initiatives proliferate, it is only a matter of time before central banks move forward with their digital equivalents. ING chief economist Mark Cliffemight predicts that CBDCs could be deployed in just 2–3 years, pressured by launch timelines of, for example, Facebook-led Diem, adding a sense of urgency to the policy community (Palmer, 2019).

Table 6.1 *Development scenarios of digital currencies*

Time frame	Scenario	Description
Short term	Public–private partnership	Co-option of private digital currencies by regulators to help advance official and societal goals through public–private partnership.
Medium term	Geopolitical competition	Emergence of digital regional currency areas, each with their own public–private ecosystem, leading to the risks of geopolitical competition and fragmentation.
Long term	Transition to a decentralised future	Formation of a decentralised crypto-financial infrastructure as mainstream crypto literacy grows with the preceding scenarios.

6.4 Possible Futures

The public and private actors outlined in the previous section do not exist in separate vacuums but rather continuously interact with each other. Using insights from Schumpeterian evolutionary economics, either competition or partnership could emerge from the symbiotic relationships among players. This section discusses three successive development scenarios in the short, medium, and long term, namely partnership between public and private actors, competition between sovereigns, and a transition from trusted to trustless alternatives. These development scenarios are summarised in Table 6.1.

Public–Private Partnership

The massive scale of stablecoins rolled out by digital giants and financial institutions will accelerate the need for a prompt regulatory response. In this sense, Facebook's Diem is a market disruptor, as demonstrated by the high level of regulatory attention it has received. In the realm of fintech, it is an example of innovation that will move from 'too small to care' (such as niche stablecoin issuers) to 'too big to fail' in a very short time (Arner et al., 2015). Against this background, authorities around the world are working to develop regulatory frameworks for stablecoins to maintain monetary and financial stability. This includes supranational organisations such as the European Union, Financial Action Task Force, Financial Stability Board, G20, G7, and others. Individual jurisdictions such as Switzerland, the UK, and the US are also in the process of deliberating relevant legislation. The general trend is that significant stablecoin arrangements will likely be subject to formal registration or licensing regimes to address issues around financial integrity (AML/CFT), safety and efficiency, consumer and investor protection, data privacy, cybersecurity, and so on.

From a regulatory standpoint, formal endorsement by regulators will co-opt stablecoin arrangements into public–private partnership to help advance broader official or societal goals. A case in point is again Facebook's Diem. After receiving considerable scepticism from policymakers around the world, it published a revised version in April 2020 which addresses some of the above-mentioned regulatory issues. With its intention to register with the US Treasury's Financial Crimes Enforcement Network (FinCEN), the perception that Diem is another dollar-based payment system that could be used to implement US foreign policy sanctions is reinforced (Massad, 2022). The biggest change, namely the switch from a single multi-currency coin to a series of stablecoins each backed by a single sovereign currency, represents a more modest undertaking than displacing the world's major sovereign currencies as originally intended. Furthermore, Diem 2.0 suggests that the network could accommodate CBDCs if a CBDC in that currency is issued, thereby assisting central banks to build out a network for their digital currencies and bringing us to the second form of public–private partnership around CBDCs. Nevertheless, Diem will not be the avenue for public–private partnership, but there are other private stablecoin initiatives still emerging that could. Indeed, CBDCs have their own room for private partnerships as discussed below.

For hundreds of years, central banks have been providing trusted money to the public. However, they seldom manage consumer-facing digital infrastructure; such roles are assumed by commercial banks and fintech companies. For countries that decide to introduce a CBDC, they will be faced with unprecedented operational and reputational risks. To minimise the central bank's footprint and partially insulate it from general users, an indirect or hybrid CBDC could be launched together with the private sector. By adopting a public–private partnership approach, central banks can leverage the digital capabilities and distribution power of private actors to achieve scale and reach immediately (G30, 2020).

Such an approach was first formalised by the IMF as a 'synthetic CBDC', or simply 'sCBDC' (Adrian and Griffoli, 2019). This is a model in which the central bank creates tokens while outsourcing several steps to the private sector, including technology choices, interface designs, customer management, transaction monitoring, AML/CFT, and regulatory compliance. The central bank merely remains responsible for offering settlement services between trust accounts. It is a far cheaper and less risky model compared with a fully fledged version of a CBDC in which the central bank creates tokens and offers accounts directly to the public. It also preserves the comparative advantage of the private sector to innovate and interact with customers, and that of the central bank to provide trust and efficiency. There are indeed multiple CBDC architectures proposed for public–private partnerships that can be seen in the work of Arner et al. (2020).

CBDC explorations of central banks so far have focused on two-layer architectures. One example is China's soon-to-be-launched CBDC, called the e-CNY. The People's Bank of China (PBOC) has acknowledged at the outset that, given China's vast geographic and economic diversity, e-CNY is a complex project that cannot be managed by the PBOC alone. It will adopt a two-tiered model in which the e-CNY will be issued by the PBOC, but operated and exchanged by authorised operators including commercial banks and other private sector institutions. This approach allows the effective use of existing business resources and technologies in the private sector, and promotes innovation and competition through market-driven development. Furthermore, this model maintains the existing currency circulation and two-tier account structure with commercial banks, thereby avoiding banking disintermediation (G30, 2020). Similarly, the Bank of England has proposed a platform model in which private sector Payment Interface Providers (PIPs) will provide customer-facing CBDC payment services on top of the central bank's core infrastructure (Bank of England, 2020).

Geopolitical Competition

In the medium term, the launch of CBDCs will drive other central banks to reactively follow suit and launch their versions in partnership with private actors. Faster, cheaper, and easier to use, these CBDCs are a better representation of fiat currencies and the projection of geopolitical influence. The fast-tracking of China's CBDC in response to Facebook's Diem is the most high-profile example of the looming 'war of currencies' (Casey, 2019) in which countries seek to strengthen their sovereign currencies. With the e-CNY, China can increase the utility of the renminbi as a means of exchange with countries along the Belt and Road Initiative, and attempt to erode the US dollar's dominant role in international transactions (Paterson, 2020). Per Gresham's Law in reverse, good money pushes out bad. This will be especially challenging for nations that are smaller or with weaker institutional environments, as a substantial shift from local currencies to more superior CBDCs will mean a loss of control over monetary policy (Zetzsche et al., 2019).

To counter this, smaller countries could form alliances, or leverage existing ones such as the European Union or the Association of Southeast Asian Nations, and launch regionally hegemonic CBDCs. For example, France and Germany have called for the launch of a European-wide public digital currency to regain monetary sovereignty in the face of Facebook's Diem (Guarascio, 2019). In 2020, the European Central Bank advanced work on the possible issuance of a digital euro, citing the fostering of the international role of the euro and the maintenance of the strategic independence of the European Union as motivations (European Central Bank, 2020). In the US, the private sector has called for public–private partnership to pilot a digital dollar in order to future-proof the US dollar and enshrine US values in the future of money (Accenture and Digital Dollar Foundation, 2020). However, because digital networks today such as Amazon, Facebook, Alipay, and Tencent remain dominant only regionally and are not truly global, any digital currencies that central banks deploy in partnership with these networks would be confined to geographical blocks. One conceivable outcome is the emergence of digital regional currency areas, which entails the risks of geopolitical competition and fragmentation of the international monetary system (Cœuré, 2019).

It is also possible that global central banks could cooperate to reap the benefits of recent technological advances, thus avoiding regionalisation and fragmentation. For example, then Bank of England Governor Mark Carney has called for a new digital synthetic hegemonic currency, which is composed of a basket of CBDCs, to dampen the domineering influence of the US dollar on global trade and finance and support better policy outcomes (Carney, 2019). A group of seven central banks together with the BIS have also recognised the importance of interoperability between CBDCs and common standards to ensure seamless cross-border payments (Bank for International Settlements, 2020).

A Decentralised Future

In the long run, the proliferation of new forms of money – including stablecoins and corporate and central bank digital currencies – may merely act as a bridge and educational tool for the mainstream public to transition from legacy systems into a new tokenised economy (PwC and Loopring, 2019). Crypto-enthusiasts may argue that digital currencies issued by centralised entities are not indeed cryptocurrencies due to the censorship concessions made. Nevertheless, they provide a compliant and price-stable stepping stone which drives broader familiarity with blockchain technology and flattens the learning curve for everyday participants. Ironically, more collaborations between central banks and private stablecoin providers may provide a massive boost to the credibility, legitimacy, and adoption of cryptocurrencies and blockchain technology.

One central tenet of decentralised cryptocurrencies such as Bitcoin is that their independent monetary policies are free from the influence of political considerations. Many observers have associated their adoption with political uncertainty, such as the escalating US–China trade war and the currency crises in Argentina or Venezuela. Importantly, millennials, the generation born between 1981 and 1996, are expected to provide strong tailwinds for the adoption of Bitcoin. With the largest demographic in the world and their disposable income soon set to supersede all other generations, their mistrust of governments and banks makes them open to cryptocurrencies (Adamant Capital, 2019). Another important phenomenon that occurred in 2020 is institutional flows into Bitcoin, including hedge funds, asset managers, and listed corporations, as a form of ideologically driven divestment from fiat currencies. With Bitcoin's gradual recognition by regulators and large scale institutional investors, a powerful constituency is taking shape which could influence policy-making to favour censorship-resistant forms of money (Kaminska, 2020).

This paves the way to a future in which a relatively decentralised crypto-financial infrastructure with non-state monetary assets may exist alongside the existing financial system. The historical parallels are the free banking paradigms in eighteenth-century Scotland and nineteenth-century America, where private entities issued money outside of state control (Carter and Walsh, 2020). There are good reasons to believe that such paradigms may prevail again in today's digital world. An overly harsh attempt to curtail the crypto-financial ecosystem may direct the market towards decentralised solutions that are truly censorship-resistant and out of regulatory purview (Qureshi, 2020). On the other hand, state actors may find it beneficial to collaborate with the crypto-financial ecosystem. In the case of the US government, decentralised cryptocurrencies denominated in the US dollar could be used as an offensive tool to expand the reach of the official currency and codify democratic values (Electric Capital, 2020). In a Bloomberg opinion piece, Ferguson (2020) has similarly suggested that the US government 'should recognise the benefits of integrating Bitcoin into the US financial system – which, after all, was originally designed to be less centralised and more respectful of individual privacy than the system of less-free societies'.

6.5 From CeFi to DeFi

As digital currency proliferation increases, whether this is utility token, stablecoin, or legal-tender on blockchain technology as CBDC, a wider DeFi industry beyond payments is emerging. New digital currency industries include lending, exchange, insurance, asset management, and derivatives. In this section, we will explore in greater detail some of these areas, how they use digital currency, and how the centralised finance (CeFi) world could bridge into this world, particularly in the context of lending, insurance, and exchange.

Lending

Within the CeFi world, lending has often had issues with financial inclusion, pass-through issues, intermediary costs, liquidity inefficiency, and legacy infrastructure (Xu and Vadgama, 2022). DeFi seeks to improve on these problems by offering transparency – the exact processes of the smart contract are available for all to see. A user's interactions are recorded for all to view. There is democracy – a governance token is often used to determine decisions such as interest rates and collateral required. Liquidity can be optimised based on the pooling of assets and agility in terms of market feedback on supply and demand. Finally, trust – one of the central tenets in DeFi – is tackled through collateral and smart contract arrangements (Xu and Vadgama, 2022).

Lending is the largest DeFi market, with the top three lending protocols (Maker, Aave, Compound) having a TVL of USD 16.57 billion and making up over 37% of the total TVL of DeFi markets.[15] Within this market, there also exists a spectrum of centralisation of a business model, and uses of fiat and crypto assets. Figure 6.1 shows various parts of the lending industry concerning currency and centralisation.

In Figure 6.1, the CeFi world is presented as traditional central banks, commercial banks and indeed fiat-based partially decentralised business models from P2P lending. The bridge between the CeFi world and the entirely DeFi world, as exemplified by players like Maker, Aave, and Compound, can be referred to as "CeFi crypto banks". These include the likes of Salt,[16] Youhodler,[17] and Celsius.[18] These institutions provide centralised management and facilitate access to DeFi lending protocols – behaving like traditional banks with simple maturity transformation functions.

These institutions could help bridge the traditional financial services industry to digital currencies through the hook of yields available in these markets. Certainly, when yields in digital currency markets are multiples larger than those in the traditional finance sector with near-zero interest rates, there will be demand for digital currency yields.

The only barrier to the adoption would be regulation and market conditions. Certainly, regulation is becoming clearer and therefore letting players know where they stand. Market conditions will be a factor. As of August 2022, with double-digit inflation and global central banks increasing their interest rates (Elliott, 2022), the attractiveness of digital currency yields may not be as they once were. Also, fluctuating market conditions have led to a crisis in the stability of the entire crypto world. The collapse of the Terra stablecoin, UST, shows the

15 Defipulse.com retrieved 12 August 2022.
16 saltlending.com
17 www.youhodler.com
18 celsius.network

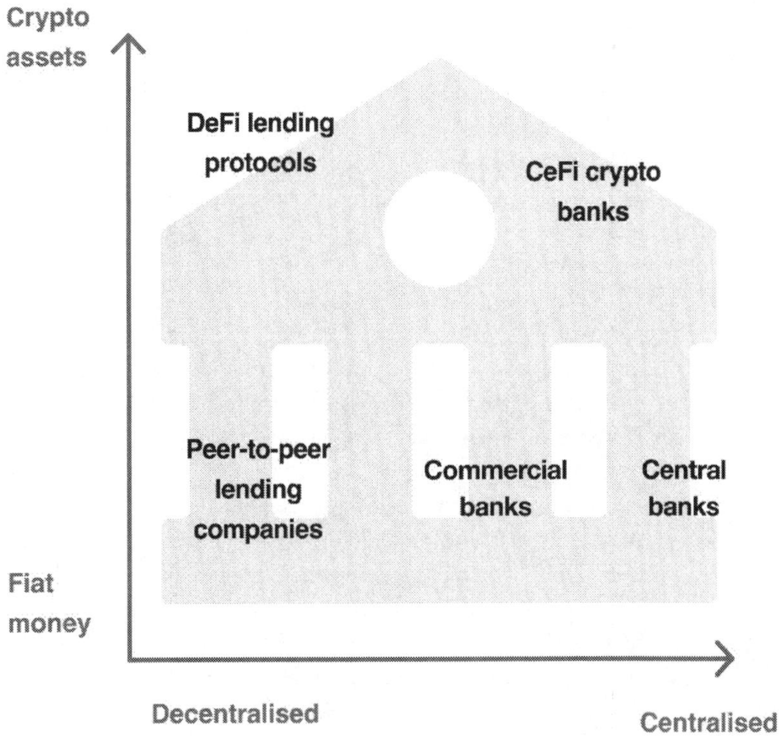

Figure 6.1 Taxonomy of lending markets (Xu and Vadgama, 2022)

fragility of these markets. UST is an algorithmic stablecoin maintaining a peg to USD 1 via a sister currency called Terra Luna. Yields on UST were as high as 20% to incentivise currency participation. Still, increasing demand and confidence in the peg were central to its equilibrium. A series of large withdrawals and a loss of confidence in the peg led this stablecoin to enter into a death spiral where the peg was broken. Over USD 60 billion of value was wiped out in a matter of days (Shen, 2022).

This further had knock-on effects on CeFi players such as Celsius. The Terra incident, extreme market conditions, and other liquidity events led to Celsius filing for bankruptcy in July 2022. Celsius was driven to the point of failure by the risk the centralised company took generating yield for its clients. Its losses are smaller than Terra's, with bankruptcy filings showing the company is around USD 1.2 billion in the red (Duggan, 2022).

Things are still at an early stage, and no doubt recent events will serve as a warning sign for further regulation in these markets and once again turn on the warning lights for traditional firms looking to move into the digital currency world. Nevertheless, traditional investment banks are entering the space (including, for example, Goldman Sachs looking to buy Celsius's assets in its bankruptcy (Wang, 2022) and Goldman Sachs also trading over-the-counter digital currency derivatives (Son, 2022)), and institutions are purchasing crypto – looking for extra yield – it is just that the velocity on the forward trajectory may temporarily decrease. Lending and banking will inevitably embrace digital currency, and many are already doing so.

Insurance

Insurance is also a market where blockchain disruption occurs – with digital currency or token-based impact being the more exotic feature. Traditional insurance products are not keeping up with expectations that they should be flexibly designed, openly auditable, and with holder and claim data being easily manageable, secure, and fit for today's modern customer (Cousaert et al., 2021). Blockchain is impacting various infrastructure-related projects embraced by traditional financial services firms, with projects such as the US's largest auto insurer utilising blockchain to settle subrogation claims (State Farm, 2021). But what about digital currency usage and this being embraced by CeFi players?

The digital currency insurance market is dominated by one player currently, Nexus Mutual. Nexus Mutual is a decentralised insurance protocol with a token called NXM. This token has various functions, including purchasing cover, participating in governance, and voting on claims. Nexus Mutual insures customers of the risks of a yield token losing its peg, hacks or halted withdrawals on exchanges, and risks of protocol failure.

As of August 2022, Nexus Mutual boasts over USD 250 million in cover with over USD 6 million annualised premiums in force. This roughly represents coverage of 0.5% of the entire DeFi market (Chen, 2022). Nexus Mutual is also interesting as it is a decentralised autonomous organisation or DAO. This DAO itself is a bridge between the CeFi and DeFi worlds. Insurance mutuals are very much from the CeFi world and now being evolved in the DeFi world.

Table 6.2 *Types of digital currency exchange*

Type of digital currency exchange	Examples
Centralised	Coinbase, Kraken, Binance, FTX
Decentralised (AMM based)	Uniswap, Sushiswap
Decentralised (Order book based)	dYdX

The Nexus Mutual DAO has also had its share of issues with claims and payouts. Nevertheless, the protocol is evolving, having learnt from its history and functioning to date (Nexus Mutual, 2022).

Blockchain technology is beginning to penetrate the traditional centralised world for insurance markets. Therefore, it will only be a matter of time before more digital currency-related insurance projects come to fruition (Cousaert et al., 2021). Digital currency-based insurance products will enhance and enrich digital currency by offering native products for financial protection on-chain.

Exchange

The exchange markets in traditional finance are highly centralised. They are optimised for speed with ancillary trust mechanisms built in place through additional clearing and settlement bodies. All these intermediaries increase fees and the time for the completion of trades.

Three types of exchanges exist within the digital currency realm, as seen in Table 6.2

Centralised exchanges take their cue from traditional finance, offering order books and off-chain settlement for trades within their environment. They often provide a diverse selection of tokens, including popular ones such as BTC, ETH, XRP, HBAR, and more. These exchanges are by far the most liquid. For example, the top three exchanges, as of August 2022, have over USD 16 billion daily volume (Coinbase,[19] Binance,[20] and FTX[21]) (compare Nasdaq daily volume at over USD 200 billion[22]). Centralised exchanges offer fast

[19] coinbase.com
[20] www.binance.com/en
[21] ftx.com/en
[22] www.nasdaqtrader.com/Trader.aspx?id=DailyMarketSummary retrieved 12 August 2022.

order book trading and a faster settlement than traditional financial exchanges as they are both exchange, counterparty and custodian. This also comes with risks as your digital currency is no longer actually your digital currency: you do not directly control the keys, a problem when exchanges collapse or are hacked (CoinSutra, 2022). Centralised exchanges typically have the friendliest interfaces for customers and are the most utilised.

In the realm of CeFi, these are the first exchanges utilised by new institutional and consumer players within the digital currency world. Indeed, they are looking to resemble traditional financial centralised exchanges with an expansion of services, including prime brokerage and now separate custody arrangements. Centralised exchanges have also gone mainstream, for example, Coinbase's IPO in 2021 (Levy, 2021). Other new exchanges are taking an institutional approach first with the appearance, facilities, licenses, and security that institutions expect to see when dealing with traditional exchanges (e.g., Archax[23]). These centralised exchanges are now also offering traditional financial products on digital currencies, creating new markets, with, for example, futures and options on digital currency created and able to be settled in digital currency itself. Some of these markets are more liquid than the underlying (e.g., HBAR on the Binance exchange). The creation of these instruments serves a very present need above and beyond speculation – one of hedging and treasury management.

Decentralised exchanges or DEXs come in two forms. The most decentralised versions are, for example, Uniswap or Sushiswap,[24] which are algorithmically enabled through smart contracts. These exchanges utilise liquidity pools of paired assets and automated market maker liquidity functions (mathematical curves) to price trades for any participant wishing to swap tokens. They are only digital currency based and, although they offer good liquidity, are mired by slow trading and settlement speed (because everything is on-chain) and a sometimes frustrating UI/UX. These protocols are evolving, and indeed Sushiswap is a clone of Uniswap and represents an evolution itself – something that both exchanges benefited from through a liquidity war over weeks in 2020 (GAINS Associates, 2020). The pace of change in the DeFi world is extremely fast, and things are evolving rapidly.

23 archax.com
24 sushi.com

DEXs serve those who wish to offer up liquidity for new digital currencies. The only requirement for listing is offering paired tokens in value for swapping. This greatly reduces the burden of listing on an exchange.

Finally, we have order book DEXs. These offer a mix of the world of centralised exchanges and decentralised exchanges. Trading and orders are facilitated by matching and market-making off-chain, while trades are settled periodically on-chain. These exchanges are again a bridge in the CeFi world, offering parts of the best of what is on and off chain.

For the future of digital currency, suitable exchange mechanisms and access to these will be paramount. Centralised exchanges will continue to lead for institutional adoption and consumer use. Traditional financial services exchanges may swallow them to offer more complete markets. DEXs will serve those looking to bring liquidity to their more niche digital currency offerings faster. Some will be utilised for those looking for on-chain security and rapid trading capability. Each of these types of exchanges will have its place. Some centralised exchanges offer DEX capabilities and even more conventional financial products in certain stocks and so on in tokenised forms.

6.6 Conclusion

It has to be caveated that the three scenarios outlined above are not mutually exclusive, nor will they follow a straightforward temporal order. Due to the preferences and trade-offs of countries, corporations, and consumers, there will be detours, and it is possible that the scenarios could co-exist. For example, nations may impose restrictions and constraints on foreign digital currencies to bolster their home currencies. Digital currencies launched by central banks and corporations may enjoy a certain degree of popularity due to better guarantees of legitimacy and consumer protection. However, the backlash over privacy and data monopolies will then drive demand for decentralised cryptocurrencies. The only thing we can be sure of is that there will be enlarged currency choice sets for citizens, and regulating them will be challenging. Certainly, new products that utilise digital currency are emerging and will support digital currency growth from CeFi to DeFi.

In the final analysis, the world of money is in an unprecedented era of innovation and competition, driven by rapid technological advances and shifting consumer behaviours. This is triggering a comprehensive rethink of global monetary arrangements. The pace of transformation will only accelerate, as major stablecoin projects such as Facebook's Diem trigger a range of similar proposals from other BigTechs or financial institutions. This will, in turn, force one or more major currency central banks to develop a CBDC, possibly in partnership with private actors (Zetzsche et al., 2019). This calls for a regulatory response to create an environment in which private and public digital currencies can thrive alongside and effectively complement each other. It is also an opportunity for central banks to improve their sovereign currencies, maintain public trust, and stay in the game in a digital and decentralised economy. As former IMF Managing Director Christine Lagarde noted in a speech at the Bank of England, 'virtual currencies might just give existing currencies and monetary policy a run for their money. The best response by central bankers is to continue running effective monetary policy while being open to fresh ideas and new demands, as economies evolve' (Lagarde, 2017). In the spirit of Hayek's monetary competition (Hayek, 1976), continued experimentation will drive us closer to a blockchain-based programmable and tokenised economy that is both fair and inclusive.

Bibliography

Accenture and Digital Dollar Foundation (2020). The digital dollar project.

Adamant Capital (2019). Bitcoin in heavy accumulation. *adamantcapitalfund.com.*

Adrian, T. and Griffoli, T. M. (2019). *The rise of digital money*. International Monetary Fund.

Allen, D. W. E. (2019). Entrepreneurial exit: developing the cryptoeconomy. In Blockchain Economics: Implications of Distributed Ledgers: Markets, Communications Networks, and Algorithmic Reality, pages 197–214. World Scientific.

Arner, D. W., Auer, R., and Frost, J. (2020). Stablecoins: Risks, potential and regulation.

Arner, D. W., Barberis, J. N., and Buckley, R. P. (2015). The evolution of fintech: A new post-crisis paradigm?

Bailey, A. M., Rettler, B., and Warmke, C. (2021). Philosophy, politics, and economics of cryptocurrency I: Money without state. *Philosophy Compass*, 16(11):e12785.

Bank for International Settlements (2020). Central bank digital currencies: foundational principles and core features.

Bank of England (2020). Central bank digital currency: opportunities, challenges and design.

Bech, M. L. and Garratt, R. (2017). Central bank cryptocurrencies. *BIS Quarterly Review, September*.

Benigno, P., Schilling, L., and Uhlig, H. (2019). World wide currency.

Boar, C., Holden, H., and Wadsworth, A. (2020). Impending arrival – a sequel to the survey on central bank digital currency. *BIS Paper*.

Bullmann, D., Klemm, J., and Pinna, A. (2019). In search for stability in crypto-assets: Are stablecoins the solution? *ECB Occasional Paper*, 230.

Carney, M. (2019). The growing challenges for monetary policy in the current international monetary and financial system – speech by Mark Carney – Bank of England.

Carter, N. and Walsh, M. (2020). Cryptodollars: The story so far.

Casey, M. (2019). Central banks, stablecoins and the looming war of currencies.

Chen, R. (2022). Nexus Mutual tracker.

CoinSutra (2022). 51 crypto exchange hacks.

Cousaert, S., Vadgama, N., and Xu, J. (2022). Token-Based Insurance Solutions on Blockchain. In *Blockchains and the Token Economy: Theory and Practice*, pages 237–260. Palgrave Macmillan. https://doi.org/10.1007/978-3-030-95108-5_9

Cœuré, B. (2019). Digital challenges to the international monetary and financial system.

Diem Association (2022). Statement by Diem CEO Stuart Levey on the sale of the Diem Group's assets to Silvergate.

Duggan, W. (2022). Crypto crash: What is Celsius? Why does it matter? *Forbes Advisor*.

Electric Capital (2020). The case for collaboration: Why the US government and crypto ecosystem must work together. *Medium*.

Elliott, L. (2022). UK inflation could reach 15% by start of 2023, experts say.

Etienne (2019). Can JPM Coin disrupt the existing stablecoin market? – Binance Research.

Etienne and Calvin (2019). First look: Libra – An in-depth review of Facebook's long-anticipated entry into cryptocurrency Binance Research.

European Central Bank (2020). Report on a digital euro.

Ferguson, N. (2020). Bitcoin and China are winning the Covid-19 monetary revolution.

Financial Stability Board (2019). Fintech and market structure in financial services: Market developments and potential financial stability implications.

Frost, J., Gambacorta, L., Huang, Y., Shin, H. S., and Zbinden, P. (2019). BigTech and the changing structure of financial intermediation. *Economic Policy*, 34(100):761–799.

G30 (2020). Digital currencies and stablecoins: Risks, opportunities, and challenges ahead.

GAINS Associates (2020). The rise, fall, and rise of Sushiswap – GAINS Associates. *Medium*.

Griffoli, T. M., Peria, M. S. M., Agur, I., Ari, A., Kiff, J., Popescu, A., and Rochon, C. (2018). Casting light on central bank digital currency. *IMF staff discussion note*, 8(18):1–39.

Guarascio, F. (2019). France, Germany blast Facebook's Libra, back public cryptocurrency. *Reuters*.

Hayek, F. A. (1976). *Denationalisation of Money: The Argument Refined.*

Heath, A. (2022). Zuckerberg's dream of launching a cryptocurrency is officially over.

Kaminska, I. (2020). 2020: The year Bitcoin went institutional.

Lagarde, C. (2017). Central banking and fintech – a brave new world?

Levy, A. (2021). Coinbase closes at $328.28 per share in Nasdaq debut, valuing crypto exchange at $85.8 billion.

Manski, S. and Manski, B. (2018). No gods, no masters, no coders? The future of sovereignty in a blockchain world. *Law and Critique*, 29(2):151–162.

Massad, T. G. (2022). Facebook's Libra 2.0.

McIntosh, R. (2019). (Crypto)currency wars: Corporate coins wage a global arms race.

Messari (2020). Crypto theses for 2021.

Nexus Mutual (2022). Proposal: Reimburse risk assessors for undue loss from claim.

Palmer, D. (2019). ING's chief economist predicts central bank digital currencies in 2–3 years.

Paterson, S. (2020). China's monetary policy and trade in an age of great power rivalry. *Hinrich Foundation*.

PwC and Loopring (2019). Emergence of stable value coins and a trust framework for fiat-backed versions.

Qureshi, H. (2020). Fighting to be stable: The evolution of stablecoins.

Raskin, M., Saleh, F., and Yermack, D. (2019). How do private digital currencies affect government policy.

Roubini, N. (2018). Exploring the cryptocurrency and blockchain ecosystem. *Testimony for the Hearing of the US Senate Committee on Banking, Housing and Community Affairs, October*.

Sanz Bas, D. (2020). Hayek and the cryptocurrency revolution.

Shen, M. (2022). How $60 billion in Terra coins went up in algorithmic smoke.

Son, H. (2022). Goldman Sachs, Galaxy Digital announce milestone over-the-counter crypto trade. *CNBC*.

State Farm (2021). Blockchain solution solves State Farm®, USAA subrogation challenge. *State Farm*.

Sun, Z. (2021). What is total value locked?

Swan, M. (2019). Blockchain economic theory: Digital asset contracting reduces debt and risk. In *Blockchain Economics: Implications of Distributed Ledgers: Markets, Communications Networks, and Algorithmic Reality*, pages 3–23. World Scientific.

Wang, T. (2022). Goldman Sachs leading investor group to buy Celsius assets: Sources.

WEF (2016). The future of financial infrastructure: An ambitious look at how blockchain can reshape financial services.

Xu, J. and Vadgama, N. (2022). From banks to DeFi: The evolution of the lending market. In *Enabling the Internet of Value*, pages 53–66. Springer.

Zetzsche, D. A., Buckley, R. P., and Arner, D. W. (2019). Regulating Libra: The transformative potential of Facebook's cryptocurrency and possible regulatory responses.

PART III

Regulations and Compliance of Digital Assets

7 *Call for a Global Crypto-assets Regulatory Framework*

Lessons from the US, Europe, and the UK

GIOVANNA MASSAROTTO

7.1 Introduction

The initial title of this chapter was 'Will the U.S. Security Law Lead Crypto-assets Regulation?', because I was quite confident it would do. Then, the exploration of this topic in different jurisdictions questioned my belief. The United States (US) was not properly leading the regulatory intervention and neither Europe nor UK, which are the jurisdictions part of my analysis. The key element that was missing in all the three regulatory frameworks was a global vision. Crypto-assets run on the Internet, which has no geographic boundaries. As a consequence, a crypto-asset regulation cannot be developed in isolation. However, there are important lessons that can be drawn from the experience of each jurisdiction singularly taken.

The chapter explores what US, EU, and UK jurisdictions have been done in the context of crypto-assets regulation towards this end. Crypto-assets can include securities, commodities, and currencies. This chapter focuses on crypto-assets as a security from a regulatory perspective. It analyses the achieved results in the three jurisdictions examined, which are useful to design a road map for future developments.

Crypto-assets are creating a plethora of new opportunities in finance, with the potential to revolutionise entirely the financial industry. Because the whole point of Bitcoin and crypto-assets is that you do not need to trust anyone, you trust the protocol, the crypto community is asking: *why should the government intervene in the first place?*

The truth is that if the slogan trust in the protocol can work for computer people; it does not apply to the general population that has no knowledge of how technologies underlying these new financial products work. Furthermore, a recent study has shown that most of the time what is written in the protocol does not reflect the reality.[1] With that in mind, the government has a great responsibility in protecting investors and financial markets overall by making protocols that govern crypto-assets more reliable and reducing the asymmetry of information between users and the protocol.

Again, blockchain is not entirely a trustless technology as the founder of Bitcoin claims.[2] Users and markets still need to trust the protocol – the technology.[3] The success of these technologies relies on network effects and decentralisation, which means that they cannot be developed in isolation. People (not only computer people) need to trust the technology to enable crypto-assets to succeed.

This is why today the letter of the law is what most of the people are looking at in the cryptospace. New rules for crypto-assets can be the real game changer for making these new investment tools mainstream. In this scenario, the US plays a critical role. Traditionally, the US is the financial industry's gatekeeper. Today, the US financial system is still the largest in the world with the US dollar the world's reserve currency. Therefore, the US is the jurisdiction that has the most to lose in a world that settles transactions using alternative unregulated crypto-assets. An understating of how the US security regulation works for crypto-assets is fundamental to appreciate the starting point of the present and future crypto-assets security regulation in the main jurisdiction. On the other hand, other jurisdictions, including Europe and the UK are setting the tone for their crypto-assets security regulation that needs to be considered with the vision of a global crypto-assets regulation.

[1] Shaanan Cohney, David Hoffman, Jeremy Sklaroff & David Wishnick, analysed 'whitepapers, and other disclosures for the fifty top-grossing ICOs of 2017' and 'how the software code controlling the projects' Initial Coin Offerings (ICO) reflected (or failed to reflect) their disclosures'. Their study 'reveals that many ICOs failed even to promise that they would protect investors against insider self-dealing. Fewer still manifested such promises in code'. Shaanan Cohney, David Hoffman, Jeremy Sklaroff & David Wishnick, Coin-Operated Capitalism, 3 Columbia L. Rev. 591 (2019).

[2] Satoshi Nakamoto, *Bitcoin: A Peer-to-Peer Electronic Cash System* (2008), bitcoin.org/bitcoin.pdf

[3] Bruce Schneir, *How Blockchain Changes the Nature of Trust, Linux Foundation Blog*(Jan, 22, 2019), linuxfoundation.org/blog/how-blockchain-changes-the-nature-of-trust

Section 7.2 introduces crypto-assets by investigating how US security regulation is affecting these assets. It envisages possible future developments in the US crypto-assets regulation looking at recent cases and statements of the US government bodies. Sections 7.3 and 7.4 explore recent studies and developments in the context of crypto-assets regulation in Europe and the UK. This comparative study enables to define the core initiatives among these three critical jurisdictions that are leading crypto-assets security regulation internationally. This chapter concludes that crypto-assets would benefit from a global regulatory framework rather than a fragmented regulation. Maybe, following the example of the UK, the US, and Europe could work together to explore not only similar rules, but also the adoption of distributed ledger technology (DLT) as a regulatory tool by providing crypto-assets a technologically managed regulatory solution. If governments trust the protocol, it is likely that the public trusts more both the protocol and the government.

7.2 US Security Regulation for Crypto-assets

Crypto-assets are digital assets recorded in distributed ledgers that adopt cryptographic techniques. Crypto-assets are mainly distinguished into cryptocurrencies and tokens, and they can serve a variety of purposes. This chapter investigates crypto-assets used as an investment tool, thus security crypto-assets/tokens. A jurisdiction to begin the investigation of how security regulation affects crypto-assets in the US. Historically the US is the financial industry's gatekeeper. The appointment of the cryptocurrencies and blockchain MIT Professor Gary Gensler as Chairman of the US Securities and Exchange Commission (SEC) shows that the Biden administration is taking the issue of crypto-assets regulation seriously. Since the beginning of his appointment, Gary Gensler emphasised the compelling requirement for protecting cryptocurrency investors, which are part of an about \$2 trillion market.[4] Gensler, for example, recognised that 'right now the exchanges trading in these crypto-assets do not have a regulatory framework, either at the SEC, or [their] sister agency, the Commodity

[4] Nikhilesh De, State of Crypto: Gary Gensler's Regulatory Clarity Sounds Awfully Familiar, COINDESK (11 May 2021) www.coindesk.com/gensler-regulatory-clarity-dcea

Futures Trading Commission'.[5] In the US, the SEC, the Commodity Futures Trading Commission (CFTC), the Office of the Comptroller of the Currency (OCC), and the Financial Crimes Enforcement Network (FINCEN) are the regulators involved with crypto-assets regulation at the federal level. Section 7.2 focuses on the SEC and CFTC's action on crypto-assets regulation relevant for this chapter. While the SEC is the regulatory agency responsible for securities markets, the CFTC regulates futures contracts including energy futures, grain futures, and interest rate futures and is considered the sister agency of the SEC.[6] Since the passage of the Dodd-Frank Act in 2010, the CFTC also regulates derivatives products such as swaps.[7]

The SEC

The SEC's main role is to protect investors and increase market efficiency in finance through the enforcement of security laws: including the Securities Act (SA) of 1933 and the Securities Exchange Act (SEA) of 1934.[8] While the SA regulates the selling of securities to the public, the SEA regulates trading securities, brokers, and exchanges – both regulations are relevant for crypto-assets. The catalyst of the SA is to eliminate the information asymmetry between investors and promoters mainly through disclosure and registration requirements. The SA determines information necessary for investors to make an informed investment decision in a public distribution, establishing the promoter's liability for material misstatements in the offering materials. Essential to making an informed investment decision is acquiring material information regarding the third party, including its background, plans, financing, and financial stake.

5 Nikhilesh De, SEC Chair Gary Gensler Recommends Congress Regulate Crypto Exchanges, COINDESK (6 May 2021) www.coindesk.com/sec-chair-gary-gensler-recommends-congress-regulate-crypto-exchanges. On 6 May 2021 Garry Gensler recognised that in the context of crypto-exchanges '[r]ight now there's not a market regulator" and thus "there's really no protection around fraud or manipulation'. Id.

6 Id.

7 The CFTC Commissioner Dawn D. Stump observed that 'treating bitcoin as a commodity, is no more surprising or unusual than, say, treating corn, oil, or copper as a commodity'. CFTC, Remarks of Commissioner Dawn D. Stump Before Texas A&M's Bitcoin Conference (16 April 2021), www.cftc.gov/PressRoom/SpeechesTestimony/opastump7

8 SEC, What We do, www.sec.gov/about/what-we-do

On the other hand, the SEA empowered the SEC to regulate all aspects of the securities markets, including regulating exchanges and brokerage firms.[9] The main way to raise capital in the context of crypto-assets is through initial coin offerings (ICOs), which are similar to initial public offerings (IPOs).[10] ICOs are specifically referred to tokens or coins' offerings and can be both public and private. As explored in the following, the SEC considered that most ICOs are securities subject to the security law.[11]

Decentralised autonomous organisation (DAO) can be built on a blockchain as a 'virtual' organisation governed by computer protocols. DAOs are also relevant in the context of security law.

Is Crypto-asset a Security?

The answer is – it depends. As the SEC specified, the term security is a broad term, which 'includes "an investment contract" as well as other instruments such as stocks, bonds, and transferable shares'.[12] Crypto-asset itself is simply code, but it might be sold as an investment contract – a security. To determine if a contract or an instrument can be qualified as a security subject to the security regulation, the SEC refers to the Howey test, which the Supreme Court defined in *SEC v. W.J. Howey Co (1946)*.[13]

According to the Howey test, an instrument/contract is a security if three elements are satisfied:

1. there is an investment of money;
2. in a common enterprise;
3. and a reasonable expectation of profits derived from efforts of others.

[9] U.S. Securities and Exchange Commission (SEC), The Laws that Govern the Securities Industry, Investor.com, www.investor.gov/introduction-investing/investing-basics/role-sec/laws-govern-securities-industry

[10] SEC, Spotlight on ICOs, www.sec.gov/ICO

[11] SEC, Release No. 81207 / 25 July 2017 Report of Investigation Pursuant to Section 21(a) of the Securities Exchange Act of 1934: *The DAO*, www.sec.gov/litigation/investreport/34-81207.pdf

[12] SEC, Framework for 'Investment Contract' Analysis of Digital Assets (modified 3 April 2019), www.sec.gov/corpfin/framework-investment-contract-analysis-digital-assets

[13] 328 U.S. 293 (1946).

Typically, crypto-assets 'are purchased or acquired in exchange for value' meeting the first element.[14] The second element requires that an enterprise is 'common', which seems to exclude crypto-asset networks that are sufficiently decentralised, such as the Bitcoin network.[15] The federal courts provide different interpretations of *common enterprise*,[16] mainly distinguishing into horizontal and vertical commonality.[17] Most courts have embraced *horizontal commonality*,[18] which refers to 'the "pooling of investors" funds as a result of which the individual investors share all the risks and benefits of the business enterprise'.[19]

In contrast, vertical commonality centres on the relationship between the promoter and investors and there is a broad and a strict interpretation of vertical commonality. In the broad vertical commonality, it is sufficient to show that the capital of investors is tied to the capital of the promoter. In strict vertical commonality, the fortunes of investors rely entirely on the efforts of the promoter.

According to the SEC, in the context of digital assets, 'a common enterprise' is typically present.[20] Though, as the SEC Director William H. Hinman noted, a common enterprise might be difficult to identify if the network underlying the asset is sufficiently decentralised, such as in the case of Bitcoins.[21] '[W]hen I look at Bitcoin today, I do not see

[14] Id.

[15] M. Todd Henderson & Max Raskin, *A regulatory Classification of Digital Assets: Toward an Operational Howey Test for cryptocurrencies, ICOs, and Other Digital Assets*, 2 Colum. Bus. L. Rev. 443, 455 (2019).

[16] *See* Benjamin Van Adrichem, Howey Should Be Distributing New Cryptocurrencies: Applying the Howey Test to Mining, Airdropping, Forking, and Initial Coin Offering, 20 Colum. Sci. & Tech L. Rev. 388, 402 (2019). The Second Circuit, for example, 'accepts horizontal commonality, has rejected broad vertical commonality, but has not rejected strict vertical commonality'. Id. See also, Adam J. Kuegler, *Cryptocurrency and the SEC: How a Piecemeal Approach to regulating New Technology Selectively Stifles Innovation*, 52(2) Conn. L. Rev. 989, 999 (2020).

[17] Kuegler, *supra* note 15 at 989.

[18] Id.

[19] Sec. & Exch. Comm'n v. ETS Payphones, Inc., 300 F.3d 1281, 1284 (11th Cir., 2002). See also, Marc G. Alcser, *Comment, The Howey Test: A Common Ground for the Common Enterprise Theory*, 29 U.C. Davis L. Rev. 1217, 1220 (Summer, 1996).

[20] SEC, Framework for 'Investment Contract' Analysis of Digital Assets, supra note 12.

[21] William Hinman, Speech: *Digital Asset Transactions: When Howey Met Gary (Plastic)*, (14 June 2018) www.sec.gov/news/speech/speech-hinman-061418

a central third party whose efforts are a key determining factor in the enterprise' – William Hinman observed. In this case, the application of the SEC's disclosure rules to the offer and resale of Bitcoins appears to be meaningless. Therefore, the level of decentralisation seems to be critical to identify the second element of the Howey test.

The third element – a reasonable expectation of profits derived from efforts of others – requires the investigation of the 'economic reality'[22] of the transaction. It needs to be investigated 'what character the instrument is given in commerce by the terms of the offer, the plan of distribution, and the economic inducements held out to the prospect'.[23] In other words, the inquired focuses on the transaction itself and how the crypto-assets are de facto offered and sold, rather than on a formal label.[24] If the purchase is driven by capital appreciation or participation in earnings resulting from the initial investment, the Supreme Court recognised that the third element is satisfied.[25] On the other hand, the element is not met if the driver of the purchase was the desire to consume or use the acquired item.[26] Differently from fruits and vegetables, which are consumed shortly after the buy and their value is known, the value of a financial product is only imprecisely known and predictable. The underlying 'good' of a financial product/security is in the earnings expectations.[27]

With respect to the 'efforts of others', Professor M. Todd Henderson and Max Raskin observed that there are no managers or entrepreneurs in sufficiently decentralised networks – the investor looks exactly in the same position as the promoter.[28] They identified a presumption of decentralisation in assets mined through a process where anyone can participate (namely an open network and process).[29] On the other hand, ICOs, presales, and their ilk should presumably meet the 'efforts of others' element of the Howey test. This is because in ICOs, presales,

[22] Tcherepnin v. Knight, 389 US 332, 336 (1967).

[23] SEC, Framework for 'Investment Contract' Analysis of Digital Assets, supra note 12.

[24] Hinman, supra note 21.

[25] United Housing Foundation, Inc. v. Forman, 421 US 837, 853 (1975).

[26] Id.

[27] See John Armour, Dan Awrey, Paul Davies, Luca Enriques, Jeffrey N. Gordon, Colin Mayer & Jennifer Payne, Principles of Financial Regulation 101 (2016).

[28] M. Todd Henderson & Max Raskin, *A regulatory Classification of Digital Assets: Toward an Operational Howey Test for Cryptocurrencies, ICOs, and Other Digital Assets*, 2 Colum. Bus. L. Rev. 443, 463 (2019).

[29] Id. at 464.

and their ilk, there is an exchange of money 'for a promise to create an asset or network that will make such an asset valuable',[30] rather than for an asset.

ICO

I believe every ICO I've seen is a security.... You can call it a coin but if it functions as a security, it is a security. (Former SEC Chairman, Jay Clayton)[31]

The former SEC Chairman Jay Clayton emphasised the main issue in the context of ICO and crypto-assets. You might change the name, but if it meets specific requirements, a crypto-asset is considered a security subject to the US security regulation.

As mentioned, ICO is the main form of funding for virtual coins or tokens (crypto-assets), which became particularly attractive for start-ups.[32] You can buy virtual tokens or coins through fiat currencies or virtual currencies. Promoters may promise profits from buying crypto-assets, or other tokens might be sold to access the platform and participate in the project or use the software. Again, if a token is offered as an investment contract, the token falls into the definition of security. Although thousands of ICOs took place, only a small fraction have complied with the security law, Gary Gensler observed.[33]

In 2018, ICOs raised about $21 billion.[34] According to a 2018 study by Satis Group, '81% of ICOs were scams',[35] making the enforcement of investors' protection regulation a compelling requirement. ICOs

30 Id.

31 Post, *Gary Gensler: Remarks at the Business of Blockchain Event*, MIT Media Lab (23 April 2018), www.media.mit.edu/posts/remarks-at-blockchain-event/ citing SEC Chairman Clayton.

32 Magnus Schückes & Tobias Gutmann, Why do Startups Pursue ICOs? The Role of Economic Drivers and Social Identity on Funding Choice, Small Business Economics (2020).

33 Gary Gensler, Cryptocurrencies: Oversight of New Assets in the Digital Age, Committee in Agriculture (Jul. 18, 2018), at 3 docs.house.govmeetings/AG/AG00/20180718/108562/HHRG-115-AG00-Wstate-GenslerG-20180718.pdf

34 Maume, Philipp and Fromberger, Mathias (2019) 'Regulation of Initial Coin Offerings: Reconciling U.S. and E.U. Securities Laws', Chicago Journal of International Law: Vol. 19: No. 2, Article 5. Available at: chicagounbound.uchicago.edu/cjil/vol19/iss2/5

35 Congressional Research Service, *Digital Assets and SEC Regulation* (30 January 2020), at 5 file:///C:/Users/GiovannaMassarotto/Downloads/833720.pdf, crsreports.congress.gov/product/pdf/R/R46208/1

are typically anticipated by a white paper[36] that describes the new blockchain-based application before the launch.[37] The future supply of tokens and its functioning is usually encoded in the software. To increase liquidity, tokens are fungible or interchangeable.

ICO's are becoming increasingly attractive for start-ups to raise capital thanks to the greater liquidity of tokens, regulatory arbitrage, and reduced transaction costs.[38] On the other hand, ICOs are risky from an investor perspective. The SEC alerted investors multiple times on the risks related to ICOs through enforcement actions[39] and informal guidelines.[40] Telegram is a symbolic example of a company that raised capital by selling about 2.9 billion of its tokens 'Grams' through two ICOs to finance its 'Telegram Open Network' (Ton Blockchain). On 11 October 2019, the SEC filed a complaint against Telegram for failing to register Grams' offers and sales.[41] On 26 June 2020, the case was settled. Telegram agreed to return more than $1.2 billion to investors.[42]

[36] Shaanan Cohney, David Hoffman, Jeremy Sklaroff & David Wishnick, analysed 'whitepapers, and other disclosures for the fifty top-grossing ICOs of 2017' and 'how the software code controlling the projects' ICO reflected (or failed to reflect) their disclosures'. Their study 'reveals that many ICOs failed even to promise that they would protect investors against insider self-dealing. Fewer still manifested such promises in code'. Shaanan Cohney, David Hoffman, Jeremy Sklaroff & David Wishnick, Coin-Operated Capitalism, 3 COLUMBIA L. REV. 591 (2019).

[37] Gary Gensler, Cryptocurrencies: Oversight of New Assets in the Digital Age, Committee in Agriculture (18 July 2018), at 7 docs.house.gov/meetings/AG/AG00/20180718/108562/HHRG-115-AG00-Wstate-GenslerG-20180718.pdf

[38] Id. at 8.

[39] Paragon Coin, Inc., Securities Act Release No. 10574, 2018 WL 6017663 (16 November 2018), www.sec.gov/litigation/admin/2018/33-10574.pdf; CarrierEQ, Inc., Securities Act Release No. 10575, 2018 WL 6017664 (16 November 2018), www.sec.gov/litigation/admin/2018/33-10575.pdf

[40] See SEC, Framework for 'Investment Contract' Analysis of Digital Assets, supra note 12; Press Release, SEC, Statement on Digital Asset Securities Issuance and Trading (16 November 2018), www.sec.gov/news/public-statement/digital-asset-securites-issuuance-and-trading; SEC, Spotlight on ICOs, www.sec.gov/ICO

[41] Press Release SEC, SEC Halts Alleged 1.7 Billion dollars Unregistered Digital Token Offering (11 October 2019), www.sec.gov/news/press-release/2019-212

[42] Press Release SEC, Telegram to Return 1.2 Billion dollars to Investors and Pay 18.5 Million dollars Penalty to Settle SEC Charges (26 June 2020), www.sec.gov/news/press-release/2020-146

In 2019, the SEC settled charges for conducting an unregistered ICO filed against the blockchain company Block.one, which agreed to pay a $24 million civil penalty. The SEC's order determined that the ICO was conducted between June 2017 and June 2018 without registering it as a security offering or seeking an exemption from the registration.[43] On 16 November 2018, the SEC settled cease and desist proceedings against Paragon Coin Inc. ('Paragon') and CarrierEQ ('Airfox'). According to the SEC, the two companies engaged in unregistered ICOs and these are 'the first cases imposing civil penalties solely for ICO securities offering registration violations',[44] in addition to ordering the two companies to return funds to investors. In *Munchee*,[45] the company agreed to end its ICO after being contacted by the SEC. Munchee created an IPhone application to review restaurant meal and started selling 'MUN tokens'. According to the SEC's order, Munchee 'conducted the offering of MUN tokens to raise about $15 million in capital so that it could improve its existing app and recruit users to eventually buy advertisements, write reviews, sell food and conduct other transactions using MUN'.[46] The SEC observed that 'no other person could make changes to the Munchee App or was working to create an "ecosystem" to create demand for MUN tokens',[47] questioning the decentralisation and 'no-security' nature of the token. Again, as the SEC Director William Hinman observed, it is clear that 'labelling an investment opportunity as a coin or token does not... remove the transaction from the securities laws',[48] particularly from the information and registration requirements.

On 3 April 2019, the SEC released a no-action letter concerning the business-travel startup TurnKey Jet Inc.'s tokens.[49] According to the

[43] SEC, Press Release, SEC Orders Blockchain Company to Pay $24 Million Penalty for Unregistered ICO (30 September 2019), www.sec.gov/news/press-release/2019-202

[44] SEC, Press Release, Two ICO Issuers Settle SEC Registration Charges, Agree to Register Tokens as Securities (16 November 2018), www.sec.gov/news/press-release/2018-264

[45] In the Matter of Munchee, Inc. Securities Act Release No. 10445 (11 December 2017) (Munchee).

[46] Id.

[47] Id. at §33.

[48] Hinman, *supra* note 21. See also, Henderson & Raskin, supra note 15, at 455.

[49] SEC, Response of the Division of Corporation Finance (3 April 2019), www.sec.gov/divisions/corpfin/cf-noaction/2019/turnkey-jet-040219-2a1.html

SEC, the company's tokens were not securities. TurnKey Jet's tokens were non-refundable and marketed in a way that underlined the functionality of the company's token.[50] In other words, they fall into the utility tokens' category.

Another interesting case in the context of ICOs concerns the Blockstack token sale, which became the first US SEC-qualified offering under Regulation A+. This implies that the public can take part of the Blockstack's network.[51] However, in contrast to an IPO, Regulation A+ has less disclosure obligations for companies along with the limit to raise up to $50 million in 12 months. The process for getting the Regulation A+ took Blockstack 10 months, as the SEC and the company needed to build a protocol for a digital-token offering under Regulation A+ from the scratch.[52] Other blockchain-based startups with assets of at least $5 million and a net worth of at least one million opted for selling their tokens under Regulation D+. This is a kind of offering limited to accredited investors, as it does not require the SEC's approval.

The DAO

Having analysed security tokens and ICOs, it is now compelling the investigation of how the US security laws affect DAOs. DAOs are 'virtual' organisations governed by computer protocols – known as *smart contracts* – built on a blockchain. On 25 July, 2017, the SEC released – *the DAO Report*[53] – warning market players that the offering and sale of digital assets through 'virtual' organisations need to comply with the federal securities laws' requirements.[54]

50 Brady Dale, The US SEC has issued a 'no-action' letter to TurnKey Jet, Inc., agreeing that tokens used by the business-travel startup are not securities. The regulatory stamp of approval is contingent upon the company using its tokens under certain conditions, Coindesk (3 April 2019), www.coindesk.com/sec-issues-first-ever-no-action-letter-clearing-ico-to-sell-tokens-under-us-law.

51 Muneeb Ali, Blockstack Token Sale Becomes the First SEC-Qualified Offering in U.S. History (10 July 2019), blog.blockstack.org/blockstack-token-sale-sec-qualified

52 Paul Vigna, SEC Clears Blockstack to Hold First Regulated Token Offering (10 July 2019), www.wsj.com/articles/sec-clears-blockstack-to-hold-first-regulated-token-offering-11562794848

53 SEC, Release No. 81207 25 July 2017 Report of Investigation Pursuant to Section 21(a) of the Securities Exchange Act of 1934: The DAO.

54 SEC, SEC Issues Investigative Report Concluding DAO Tokens, a Digital Asset, Were Securities (25 July 2017), www.sec.gov/news/press-release/2017-131

The *DAO Report* is the result of an investigation, which found that 'The DAO' was offering and selling tokens that were securities subject to security laws.[55] The DAO was the first venture capital entirely self-governed by a smart contract, which was launched in 2016 on Ethereum blockchain platform. In only a few months, the DAO raised $150 million. However, the initial enthusiasm was quickly curbed by a hacker, who drained about $50 million thanks to a bug in The DAO's smart contract.[56]

In the DAO Report, the SEC clarified that issuers of blockchain technology-based or distributed ledger securities must register offers and sales of those securities unless a valid exemption applies. The registration's requirements are critical to secure investors' protection by providing to investors proper information on the investments sold and ensuring the regulatory scrutiny over such investments. The DAO Report aims to protect investors in the specific context of 'virtual organisation', by providing useful guidelines. The former SEC's Chairman Jay Clayton observed the investors' and markets' protection come first and foremost in the SEC's enforcement action.[57]

The Ripple Case

On 22 December 2020, the SEC announced to have filed a complaint against Ripple Labs Inc. and both its CEO Bradley K. Garlinghouse and company's co-founder and chairman Christian Larsen.[58] Ripple is one of the first and most important blockchain platforms that has its own cryptocurrency – XRP.[59] According to the complaint, 'Ripple raised funds, beginning in 2013, through the sale of digital assets known as XRP in an unregistered securities offering to investors in the

[55] SEC, Report of Investigation Pursuant to Section 21(a) of the Securities Exchange Act of 1934: The DAO (25 July 2017) www.sec.gov/litigation/investreport/34-81207.pdf

[56] Adam J. Kolber, *Not-So-Smart Blockchain Contracts and Artificial Responsibility*, 21 Stan. Tech. L. Rev. 198 (2018).

[57] Press Release, SEC Issues Investigative Report Concluding DAO Tokens, a Digital Asset, Were Securities (25 July 2017), www.sec.gov/news/press-release/2017-131

[58] Press Release, SEC Charges Ripple and Two Executives with Conducting $1.3 Billion Unregistered Securities Offering (22 December 2020), www.sec.gov/news/press-release/2020-338

[59] SEC Sues Ripple Over XRP Cryptocurrency, Wall Street Journal (22 December 2021).

U.S. and worldwide'.[60] Garlinghouse and Larsen were also accused of affecting personal unregistered XRP's sales for about $600 million. Similar accusations were previously made in a class action filed before the Northern District Court of California in 2018.[61] This case is also ongoing.[62]

In summary, Ripple would have failed to register offers and sales of XRP or seeking an exemption from registration and its two key executives were sued as well. On 16 February 2021, the SEC and Ripple alleged that a settlement before trial was unlikely.[63] Ripple's CEO Garlinghouse noted that, '[t]his is about more than just Ripple. This is about more than just XRP. It really does have implications for all of crypto [..] in the United States',[64] and he is probably right.

The main Ripple's defence is that, like Bitcoin and Ether – XRP is not a security. On 6 April 2021, the Court granted Ripple access to SEC's documentation on Ether and Bitcoin with the aim to find evidence that the SEC defined XRP like Ether and Bitcoin – a non-security asset.[65] Ripple case is reinvigorating critics against the SEC for the uncertainty created in the definition of security in the context of crypto-assets.

As time goes by, the primary question remains the same – *what is the borderline between security tokens/coins and non-security tokens?* Will the Ripple case provide the guidelines that the crypto-asset market needs? As the SEC Commissioner observed, the fear of market players in the crypto-assets space 'of running afoul of the security laws

60 Id.

61 Nikhilesh De, Combined Class-Action Lawsuit Against Ripple Moves to Federal Court, Coindesk (12 November 2018), www.coindesk.com/author/nikde

62 Vladi Zakinov et al. v. Ripple Labs, Inc. Et. Al, Case No. 18-cv-06753-PJH, D.C. Nort. Cal. 2020.

63 Tanzeel Akhtar, Ripple, SEC Say Settlement Unlikely Before Trial Over Alleged Securities Violations, Coindesk (16 February 2021), www.coindesk.com/ripple-sec-say-settlement-unlikely-before-trial-over-alleged-securities-violations

64 Zack Seward, *Ripple Waiting for SEC Suit Resolution Before Going Public, Says CEO*, Coindesk (27 May 2021), www.coindesk.com/author/zseward

65 Sebastian Sinclair, Ripple Granted Access to SEC Documents on Bitcoin, Ether in Ongoing XRP Fight, Coindesk (6 April 2021), www.coindesk.com/sec-ripple-discovery-bitcoin-ether

is real'.[66] Today the SEC faces a critical task: balancing 'the need to achieve the investor protection objectives of the securities laws' with 'the need to provide the regulatory flexibility that allows innovation to flourish',[67] in the crypto-assets market.

Despite the time has passed, Howey remains the key test for identifying securities also in the context of crypto-assets.[68] But, it is unclear if this test is sufficiently assisting companies in understanding when their crypto-assets fall or do not fall within the scope of the security law. Ripple is only a symbolic example of completeness of the Howey test in the crypto-assets space. Further guidance seems to be appropriate – rather necessary – and Ripple might be the case that sets the stage for a new legal framework for crypto-assets.

The CFTC

Having analysed the role and critical actions of the SEC in the crypto-assets space, it is worth mentioning the role of the CFTC, the SEC's sister agency often cited in the context of the US crypto-assets regulation. The CFTC regulates futures contracts including energy futures, grain futures and interest rate futures. Since the passage of the Dodd-Frank Act, the CFTC regulates also swaps. The Commodity Exchange Act (CEA) provides a broad definition of commodity, which includes, for example, 'wheat, cotton, rice' and 'all services, rights, and interests. In which contracts for future delivery are presently or in the future dealt in'.[69] The CFTC does not regulate commodity markets themselves. The role of the CFTC is to investigate and prosecute civil enforcement actions in cases of fraud or manipulation related to commodity markets, such as the Bitcoin markets, as well as to regulate futures contracts.

[66] Commissioner Hester M. Peirce, Speech, Running on Empty: A Proposal to Fill the Gap Between Regulation and Decentralisation (6 February 2020), www.sec.gov/news/speech/peirce-remarks-blockress-2020-02-06

[67] Id.

[68] Michael Casey, Jonah Cane, Gary Gensler, Simon Johnson & Neha Narula, *The Impact of Blockchain Technology on Finance: A Catalyst for Change* (Geneva Report on the World Economy 21, 2018).

[69] 7 U.S. Code § 1a – Definitions (9) Commodity.

The CFTC staff recognised in an advisory letter that 'virtual currencies are unlikely any commodity that the CFTC has dealt in the past'.[70] Utility tokens (hence tokens that provide utility) are more likely to be commodities.[71] The CFTC observed that virtual currencies, such as Bitcoins, fall into the legal definition of a 'commodity'.[72] Although the CFTC is not 'in the business of regulating bitcoin transactions or the individuals or entities that buy, sell, transfer, or store bitcoin',[73] the CFTC acted against unregistered derivatives exchanges, and registered derivatives exchanges in the context of crypto-assets that violated the CFTC regulations and the CEA.[74]

In 2015, for example, the CFTC ordered Coinflip, Inc., a Bitcoin options trading platform operator, and its CEO 'to cease illegal offering bitcoin options and to cease operating a facility for trading or processing of swaps without registering'.[75] Commissioner Dan M. Berkovitz observed that DLT should not become 'an unregulated

[70] U.S. Commodity Futures Trading Commission, Advisory with respect to Virtual Currency Derivative Product Listings, CFTC Staff Advisory No. 18–14 (21 May 2018).

[71] Neil Tiwari, *The Commodification of Cryptocurrency*, 117 Mich. L. Rev. 611, 623 (2018).

[72] In re Coinflip, Inc., CFTC No. 15–29, at 3, [2015-2016 Transfer Binder] Comm. Fut. L. Rep. (CCH) par. 33,583 (17 September 2015). The CFTC Commissioner Dawn D. Stump observed that 'treating bitcoin as a commodity, is no more surprising or unusual than, say, treating corn, oil, or copper as a commodity'. Remarks of Commissioner Dawn D. Stump Before Texas A&M's Bitcoin Conference (16 April 2021), www.CFTC.gov/PressRoom/SpeechesTestimony/opastump7. See also, CFTC, Bitcoin Basics (2019), www.CFTC.gov/sites/default/files/2019-12/oceo_bitcoinbasics0218.pdf

[73] Remarks of Commissioner Dawn D. Stump Before Texas A&M's Bitcoin Conference (16 April 2021), www.CFTC.gov/PressRoom/SpeechesTestimony/opastump7

[74] Because 'well-functioning futures (and other derivatives products) rely upon a sound underlying cash market and may reference cash market indexes in their pricing'. As a consequence, 'cash [or bitcoin] market transactions can potentially be part of a scheme to manipulate prices of derivatives products that are regulated by the CFTC'. Remarks of Commissioner Dawn D. Stump Before Texas A&M's Bitcoin Conference (16 April 2021), www.CFTC.gov/PressRoom/SpeechesTestimony/opastump7

[75] CFTC Orders Bitcoin Options Trading Platform Operator and its CEO to Cease Illegally Offering Bitcoin Options and to Cease Operating a Facility for Trading or Processing of Swaps without Registering, Release Number 7231–15 (17 September 2015), www.CFTC.gov/PressRoom/PressReleases/7231-15

shadow financial market'[76] and the CFTC along with other agencies, should focus on addressing regulatory violations in these markets appropriately.[77] Crypto-assets are not exempted from registration under the CEA.[78] This is why the CFTC action is considered critical in the development of nascent financial markets, such as DeFi.

What Future for the US Crypto-assets Security Regulation?

To date, there are no specific formal rulemakings for crypto-assets; the SEC has clarified its position on crypto-assets mainly by means of enforcement actions and informal guidelines.[79] This is quite understandable given the need to provide the flexibility that these new fast-moving financial instruments need. However, the SEC's actions seem to have created uncertainty in crypto-asset markets. And the CFTC lacks powers to regulate directly 'no security' tokens, known as utility tokens.

In 2018, Gary Gensler emphasised the existing gap concerning cryptocurrencies exempted from regulation called 'crypto cash commodities', such as Bitcoin, and urged the Congress to consider filling the gap.[80] According to the same Gary Gensler, in the US, the crypto-assets space still looks pretty much like a *Wild West*.[81] However, the SEC's agenda released on 11 June 2021 did not seem to identify crypto-assets regulation among the SEC's priorities.[82]

[76] Keynote Address of Commissioner Dan M. Berkovitz Before FIA and SIFMA-AMG, Asset Management Derivatives Forum 2021 (8 June 2021), www.CFTC.gov/PressRoom/SpeechesTestimony/opaberkovitz7

[77] Prof. Kevin Werbach observed that DeFi arises multiple risks and "unique regulatory challenges that will become more serious as it grows". Kevin Werbach, DeFi is the New Frontier for FinTech Regulation, The Regulatory Review 3 (28 April 2021).

[78] Id.

[79] See Henderson & Raskin, supra note 15, at 454.

[80] Gary Gensler, Cryptocurrencies: *Oversight of New Assets in the Digital Age, Committee in Agriculture* 18 July 2018) docs.house.gov/meetings/AG/AG00/20180718/108562/HHRG-115

[81] See Gary Silverman, SEC's Gensler seeks new powers to regulate "Wild West" crypto markets, Financial Times (3 August 2021), www.ft.com/content/f0816ce3-9728-4a21-94e8-5522774be8a0

[82] Agenda Rule List – Spring 2021 Security and Exchange Commission, www.reginfo.gov/public/do/eAgendaMain?operation=OPERATION_GET_AGENCY_RULE_LIST&currentPub=true&agencyCode=&showStage=active&agencyCd=3235&csrf_token=7CE97CC2D49C9B6B70868F7B2752E582

To date, companies seem still to struggle with understanding what is forbidden and what is permitted in the crypto-assets space – the present lawsuit against Ripple is emphasising this point. According to the SEC, Bitcoin and Ethereum are not security tokens, raising the question: *Why Ripple is different?* The possible court's answer to this question will be critical, and is likely necessary to clarify what differentiates a security token from a no-security token.

Meanwhile, on 14 February 2022, the SEC settled the investigation against the crypto lending platform BlockFi, which was charged with violating provisions relating to registration under the Investment Company Act. BlockFi agreed to pay $50 million penalty and additional $50 million in fine to settle similar charges brought in 32 states and set an interesting precedent in the context of crypto lending platforms.[83] BlockFi 'offered and sold BIAs to the public' with the promise to give 'a variable monthly interest payment'.[84] Therefore, BlockFi interest accounts (BIAs) were considered securities and the company was subject to registration duties. The SEC also found a false and misleading statement. Without confirming any SEC's findings, BlockFi voluntarily agreed to cease selling BIAs in the US, as well as to a cease-and-desist order which forbid the company from violating both the registration and anti-fraud rules of the Security Act and the Investment Company Act.

In addition to the enforcement action, several legislative and executive initiatives have taken place. On 21 April, 2021 the US House passed H.R. 1602 Bill entitled 'Eliminate Barriers to Innovation Act of 2021' which requires 'to establish a digital asset working group with representative from the SEC and CFTC'[85] within 90 days. The group should include representatives from the SEC, the CFTC, and from a financial technology company, financial services institutions,

C86F1945A4A46F34426C18AF1ABE101E611318F64B67159C3A36E755 6BD0FB872C8F

[83] Press Release, BlockFi Agrees to Pay 100 million dollars in Penalties and Pursue Registration of its Crypto Lending Product (14 February 2022), www.sec.gov/news/press-release/2022-26

[84] Id.

[85] Sebastian Sinclair, US House Passes Bill to Require Financial Regulators to Set Up Digital Assets Working Group, CoinDesk (21 April 2021), www.coindesk.com/CFTC-sec-us-house-representatives

small fintech businesses, investor protection organisations, and at least one academic researcher. The aim is to ensure collaboration between the private sector and regulators on digital assets – which is good. The issue is more how long this will take. Similarly, on 9 March 2022, the US President Joseph R. Biden Jr. issued an executive order on ensuring responsible development of digital assets.[86] This order emphasises the necessity of protecting consumers, investors, and the global financial stability laying out a national policy for digital assets based on six priorities, including responsible innovation, financial stability, and consumer and investor protection.[87] To achieve these priorities, Biden's executive order calls for several reports and studies, such as the Framework for International Engagement on Digital Assets that has been released on 7 July 2022. The Secretary of the Treasury, in consultation with the Secretary of State, the Secretary of Commerce, and other relevant agencies, designed this framework emphasising the importance of international cooperation among public and private institutions and other stakeholders as the technologies underlying digital assets are typically cross-border. Key international engagements include the G7 on a broader discussion on digital payments and the creation and movement of money, the G20, the Financial Stability Board (FSB), which urged a shared understanding of global financial stability risks concerning digital markets, as well as the Financial Action Task Force (FATF) and the Egmont Group of Financial Intelligence Units (FIUs), the Organisation for Economic Cooperation and Development (OECD), other Standard-Setting Bodies (SSBs), the International Monetary Fund (IMF), and the World Bank, other Multilateral Development Banks (MDBs), and the Regional and Bilateral Engagements.[88] As outlined in Section 7.3, similar consultations have

[86] Presidential Actions, Executive Order on Ensuring Responsible Development of Digital Assets (9 March 2022), www.whitehouse.gov/briefing-room/presidential-actions/2022/03/09/executive-order-on-ensuring-responsible-development-of-digital-assets/

[87] Statements and Releases, Fact sheet: President Biden to Sign Executive Order on Ensuring Responsible Development of Digital Assets (9 March 2022), www.whitehouse.gov/briefing-room/statements-releases/2022/03/09/fact-sheet-president-biden-to-sign-executive-order-on-ensuring-responsible-innovation-in-digital-assets/

[88] Press Release, U.S. Department of the Treasury, Fact Sheet: Framework for International Engagement on Digital Assets (7 July 2022), home.treasury.gov/news/press-releases/jy0854

already taken place in Europe and the UK, which might provide useful insights to the US.

In summary, 'the incredible transformation in this space requires adaptation and creative thinking, and let's be honest, neither are among a regulator's natural tendencies',[89] CFTC Commissioner Dawn D. Stump observed. This is why the present effort to create a continuous dialogue among the public and private sectors and among different institutions to regulate digital assets makes sense in particular and should be endorsed. Maybe, the US could also look for insights in other jurisdictions, such as Europe and the UK, as well as find ways to collaborate more effectively in the definition of the principles and best rules for protecting investors in the crypto-assets space. This is all likely to assist in increasing the adaptation and creative thinking that emerging technologies require.

7.3 The European Security Laws for Crypto-assets

In the context of crypto-assets regulation, Europe is clearly not behind the scenes. Europe published a proposal for crypto-assets regulation – the Markets in Crypto-Assets (MiCA) Regulation, which is part of the Digital Finance Package. This package also includes the Digital Finance Strategy, the Retail Payments Strategy, and legislative proposals for a DLT Pilot Regime and for more *digital resilience* in the financial sector.[90] On 30 June, 2022, the Council presidency and the European Parliament provisionally agreed on the MiCA proposal.[91]

MiCA stems from major developments that occurred in the last 3 years, such as the European Banking Authority (EBA) Report of 2019[92] and the 5th Anti-Money Laundering Directive of 2018.[93] The

[89] Remarks of Commissioner Dawn D. Stump Before Texas A&M's Bitcoin Conference (16 April 2021), www.CFTC.gov/PressRoom/SpeechesTestimony/opastump7

[90] European Commission, Digital Finance Package (24 September 2020), ec.europa.eu/info/publications/200924-digital-finance-proposals_en

[91] Digital finance: agreement reached on European crypto-assets regulation (MiCA), (30 June 2022), www.consilium.europa.eu/en/press/press-releases/2022/06/30/digital-finance-agreement-reached-on-european-crypto-assets-regulation-mica/PressRelease

[92] EBA, Report with Advice for the European Commission (9 January 2019) [EBA Report].

[93] EU Directive 2018/863, 30.05.2018.

EBA evaluated the suitability and applicability of the present EU law to crypto-assets reporting that 'typically crypto-assets fall outside the scope of EU financial services regulation'.[94] Emphasis was put on the pressing need for quick intervention in such an unregulated space.

In contrast to MiCA, the DLT Pilot Regime offers a legal framework for the trading and settlement of transactions of digital securities, thus those crypto-assets that fall into the financial instruments category. It will create a testing environment that will grant provisional derogation from present rules that could limit the development of solutions for the settlement and trading in the context of crypto-assets. To operate in a DLT market infrastructure under the Pilot regime, it will be required to get permission and most provisions will be applicable from 23 March 2023.[95]

On the other hand, the 5th Anti-Money Laundering Directive required EU Member States to implement its directives by 10 January 2020, which include the extension of Anti-Money Laundering and Counter Terrorism financing rules to virtual currencies.[96] Diem's global stablecoin project, formerly Libra, also showed the importance of taking an action in the context of crypto-assets regulation.[97]

Section 7.3 starts with the investigation of the EBA Report and proceeds with the analysis of the MiCA and the DLT Pilot Regime, as they constitute the major actions in the context of the European regulatory framework for crypto-assets relevant for this chapter.

EBA Report

The EBA's warning to consumers and institutions on virtual currencies remains valid. The EBA calls on the European Commission to assess whether regulatory action is needed to achieve a common EU approach to cryptoassets. The EBA continues to monitor market developments from a

[94] EBA, EBA reports on crypto-asset (9 January 2019), www.eba.europa.eu/eba-reports-on-crypto-assets

[95] EU Regulation 2022/858, Article 19.

[96] EU Commission, Strengthened EU Rules to Prevent Money Laundering and Terrorism Financing, Fact sheet (9 July 2018).

[97] Patrick Hansen, New Crypto Rules in the European Union – Gateway for Mass Adoption, or Excessive Regulation? (12 January 2021), law.stanford.edu/2021/01/12/new-crypto-rules-in-the-eu-gateway-for-mass-adoption-or-excessive-regulation. See also, Dirk A. Zetzsche, Filippo Annunziata, Douglas W. Arner & Ross P. Buckley, The Markets in Crypto-Assets (MiCA) Regulation and the EU Digital Finance Strategy, 7 European Banking Institute 4 (2020).

prudential and consumer perspective. (The EBA's Executive Director, Adam Farkas)[98]

On 20 December 2017, the European Commission Vice President Dombrovskis asked for further work on crypto-assets. In 2018, EU Commission FinTech Action Plan and EBA FinTech Roadmap confirmed the need for work in the context of crypto-assets.[99] As a result, in 2018, EBA engaged in the assessment of the applicability and sustainability of EU financial services law to crypto-assets by preparing a report pursuant to Article 9(4) of the EBA's Founding Regulation. Article 9(4) instructs the Authority to create a Committee on financial innovation with the aim to combine all relevant competent national and supervisory authorities and coordinate the regulation and supervision of new or innovative financial actions.

The EBA highlighted the importance of conducting a case-by-case analysis on business models concerning crypto-assets to determine if it is applicable, the EU financial services law.[100] Even if the current EU financial services law is applied, this does not imply that all risks associated with crypto-assets activities are alleviated. Therefore, at its core, the report considered necessary further analysis and actions. The report noted that across the EU Member States, there are divergent approaches to the regulation of crypto-assets' activities.[101] A comprehensive costs and benefits analysis was required to identify what actions are needed to address the present concerns in the context of crypto-assets. Emphasis was put on ensuring that consumers receive appropriate disclosure and there are appropriate advertising rules to prevent misleading promotions/marketing and bothering calls.[102]

MiCA

The EBA report is the major development that led the EU Commission to release in September 2020 – MiCA.[103] The scope of MiCA

[98] EBA, Press Release, EBA Reports on Crypto-assets (9 January 2019).
[99] EBA, Report with Advice for the European Commission on crypto-assets, 5–6 (9 January 2019).
[100] Id. at 19.
[101] Id. at 18.
[102] Id. at 16.
[103] EU Commission, Proposal for Regulation on Markets in Crypto-assets, and amending Directive (EU) 2019/1937 [MiCA].

was to set the tone for global standards by shaping crypto-assets regulation worldwide.[104] In contrast to a quite fragmented (but flexible) regulatory framework in the US, MiCA sets the rules to create 'long-term legal certainty'[105] and attract crypto-assets business. MiCA is a proposal for the regulation of crypto-assets, which means that once adopted, it will be directly applicable in all European Member States.

Stakeholders have been consulted during the preparation of this proposal to consider their position in the definition of rules.[106] MiCA will not apply to crypto-assets that are already subject to EU regulation. For example, security tokens that have the same function of existing securities (e.g., bonds and stocks) are regulated as bonds, shares, or investment funds. The DLT Pilot Regime (Regulation 2022/858) published on 6 June 2022 covers those crypto-assets classified as financial instruments under MIFID II, known as 'tokenised financial instruments'.[107] While MiCA affects crypto-assets' services, such as:

1. Administration and custody
2. The operation of a trading platform
3. The exchange of crypto-assets for both fiat currency and crypto-assets

[104] Id. Article 1 (Subject matter) This Regulation lays down uniform rules for the following:

- transparency and disclosure requirements for the issuance and admission to trading of crypto-assets;
- the authorisation and supervision of crypto-asset service providers and issuers of asset-referenced tokens and issuers of electronic money tokens;
- the operation, organisation and governance of issuers of asset-referenced tokens, issuers of electronic money tokens and crypto-asset service providers;
- consumer protection rules for the issuance, trading, exchange and custody of crypto-assets;
- measures to prevent market abuse to ensure the integrity of crypto-asset markets.

[105] Patrick Hansen, New Crypto Rules in the European Union – Gateway for Mass Adoption, or Excessive Regulation? (12 January 2021), law.stanford.edu/2021/01/12/new-crypto-rules-in-the-eu-gateway-for-mass-adoption-or-excessive-regulation

[106] MiCA at 6.

[107] Regulation (EU) 2022/858 of the European Parliament and of the Council of 30 May 2022 on a pilot regime for market infrastructures based on distributed ledger technology, and amending Regulations (EU) No 600/2014 and (EU) No 909/2014 and Directive 2014/65/EU, OJ 151, 2.6.2022.

4. The placement and the execution orders for crypto-assets for third parties
5. Advice and the reception and transmission of crypto-assets' orders

MiCA requires issuers of crypto-assets to release a white paper with compulsory disclosure requirements,[108] except for small-and medium-sized enterprises (SMEs) 'where the total consideration of the offering of crypto-assets is less than €1,000,000 over a period of 12 months'.[109] Before any public offer of crypto-assets in the EU area, issuers of crypto-assets need to notify their white paper and eventual marketing communications to the Member State competent authority (e.g., BaFin in Germany) where the issuer has registered its branch or office or the token will be offered.[110] The white paper should include the description of both the issuer and the issuer's project, as well as the characteristics of the public offer, the crypto-assets rights, and obligations rights and related risks.[111] These rules are not applicable to tokens offered for free, non-fungible/unique tokens (NFTs), tokens offered to qualified investors, and when the crypto-asset is the result of mining process 'as a reward for the maintenance of the DLT or the validation of transactions'.[112]

Competent authorities (e.g., BaFin) need to have the power to prohibit or suspend public offers of crypto-assets that do not comply with the relevant requirements[113] and cooperate with each other with respect to the objects of the Regulation.[114] Competent authorities should be empowered to take appropriate administrative measures and sanctions in case of infringements of the MiCA's rules. The EBA has also the power to impose fines for specific infringements under Article 113 of MiCA.[115] On the other hand, consumers need to have the right to withdraw from the investment throughout a limited time frame from the acquisition. According to Article 12, consumers should

[108] MiCA. Article 8 (Publication of the crypto-asset white paper, and, where applicable, of the marketing communications).
[109] Id. at 9.
[110] Id. at 19.
[111] Id. Article 5. (Content and form of the crypto-asset white paper).
[112] Id. Article 4. (Offers of crypto-assets, other than asset-referenced tokens or e-money tokens, to the public, and admission of such crypto-assets to trading platform for crypto-assets.)
[113] Id. Article 82 (Powers of competent authorities).
[114] Id. Article 83 (Cooperation between competent authorities).
[115] Id. Article 113 (Fines).

have 14 days to withdraw to their investment with no costs or giving justifications. No matter what exemption is applicable, all issuers of crypto-assets,[116] excluding e-money tokens and asset-referenced tokens (which have further requirements), need to act fairly, honestly, and professionally, prevent and disclosure of conflicts of interest, and ensure that their systems and protocols comply with Union standards.[117] Exclusion of civil liability's provisions has no legal effects.[118]

MiCA also provides rules for crypto-assets services, such as custody and administration of crypto-assets on behalf of third parties. Crypto-assets services providers need to be authorised and their agreements with clients should include, for example, their responsibilities and duties.[119] Authorised trading platforms for crypto-assets need to define specific operating rules, including policies and procedures for the admission of trading of crypto-assets to the trading platform.[120] Crypto-assets service providers' advice needs to be conducted in the clients' interest by providing the necessary information.

MiCA regulates also asset-referenced tokens (ART) and E-money tokens (EMT), which are commonly known as stablecoins. This chapter does not treat stablecoins. Thus, the present analysis focuses on crypto-asset services' regulation and crypto-assets generally.

Under the provisional agreement reached on 30 June 2022 between the Council presidency and the European Parliament, MiCA will require crypto-asset service providers (CASPs) to get an authorisation to operate in Europe from national authorities, which will provide relevant information to the European Securities and Markets Authority (ESMA).[121] Credit institutions and companies, which are already authorised under MIFiD to provide financial services, do not need to

116 Issuers of crypto-assets means 'any legal person who offers to the public any type of crypto-assets'. MiCA at 18.

117 Id. Article 13. (Obligations of issuers of crypto-assets, other than asset-referenced tokens or e-money tokens.)

118 Id. Article 14 (Liability of issuers of crypto-assets, other than asset-referenced tokens or e-money tokens, for the information given in a crypto-asset white paper.)

119 Id. Article 67. (Custody and Administration of crypto-assets on behalf of third parties.)

120 Id. Article 68. (Operation of a trading platform for crypto-assets.)

121 EU Council, Digital Finance: Agreement Reached on European Crypto-Assets Regulation (MiCA), Press Release (30 June 2022), www.consilium.europa.eu/en/press/press-releases/2022/06/30/digital-finance-agreement-reached-on-european-crypto-assets-regulation-mica/

obtain another authorisation. Most of the provisions will be applicable in mid-2024.

Will Europe Set the Standards for Crypto-assets Regulation?

MiCA is certainly an interesting regulation that aims to achieve the definition of crypto-assets standards worldwide and 'put an end to the crypto wild west',[122] as the French Minister Bruno Le Maire said. However, MiCA seems to favour incumbent financial institutions, neglecting that financial start-ups constitute the backbone of the crypto-assets space. In addition, the applicability of MiCA to DeFi and decentralised token issuances (e.g., Uniswap and Maker DeFi's projects), seems to be unfeasible, due to the decentralised nature of DeFi projects. However, rules for DeFi are expected to be provided after MiCA's entry into force.[123]

MiCA clearly was designed with Libra (renamed 'Diem') stablecoin in mind,[124] and in the time frame necessary for this proposal to become law, the situation seems to have changed and be subject to continuous changes. A more flexible approach as the one that the US has adopted might be more appropriate for financial products subject to fast technological changes.[125] What will happen over the years in a dynamic market, such as the crypto-asset markets, is unclear. The EU action in the context of crypto-assets is desirable to tackle the present legal uncertainty in the crypto-asset space and ensure investors' protection. However, the EU legislator needs to consider that crypto-assets would benefit from a flexible regulatory framework to not stifle innovation, which seems to be the approach taken in the recent DLT

[122] EU Council, Digital Finance: Agreement Reached on European Crypto-Assets Regulation (MiCA), Press Release (30 June 2022), www.consilium.europa.eu/en/press/press-releases/2022/06/30/digital-finance-agreement-reached-on-european-crypto-assets-regulation-mica/

[123] Chainalysis, MiCA Licensing: The EU's New Crypto Regulations, Part 2 (19 July 2022), blog.chainalysis.com/reports/eu-cryptocurrency-regulations-july-2022-part-2

[124] See, for example, Dirk A. Zetzsche, Filippo Annunziata, Douglas W. Arner & Ross P. Buckley, *The Markets in Crypto-Assets Regulation (MICA) and the EU Digital Finance Strategy*, 16 Capital Markets L. J. 203 (2021).

[125] See Sandali Handagama, Europe's MICA Crypto Rules Are Coming Soon. Here's Why They Matter, CoinDesk (2 November 2021), www.coindesk.com/policy/2021/11/02/unpacking-europes-looming-MICA-crypto-regulation/

Pilot Regime regulation of June 2022 (Regulation 2022/858) concerning the so-called 'tokenised financial instruments'.

Regulation 2022/858 introduces three categories of DLT market infrastructures: (1) DLT Multilateral Trading Facilities; (2) DLT Trading and Settlement System; (3) DLT Settlement Systems.

The pilot would enable the European policymakers to gain experience on how crypto-assets work in concrete and identify possible adjustments to the European financial services legislation to protect investors without stifling innovation. The Pilot regime determines the requirements concerning the granting and withdrawing the permission to enter into the DLT market infrastructures, as well as the requirements related to the exemption from the European financial service legislation. The regulation also sets the supervising power of government agencies and the forms of cooperation between the DLT market infrastructures and the ESMA, and the National Competent Authorities (NCAs).[126]

7.4 UK Crypto-assets Regulation

Due to the Brexit, EU regulations, such as MiCA are not applicable in the UK. This does not mean that the UK is left to watch. It is quite the opposite. In 2018, the UK's Financial Conduct Authority (FCA), HM Treasury and Bank of England[127] constituted a Taskforce to define how and when to regulate crypto-assets.[128] Each authority engaged in activities aimed to better understand crypto-asset markets, focusing on potential risks and opportunities. However, the FCA is the critical authority in the investigation of the UK crypto-assets regulation.

As the Director of Retail and Regulatory Investigations at the FCA, Therese Chambers observed, 'the FCA is like the U.S. Commodity Futures Trading Commission (CFTC), Financial Crimes Enforcement

[126] Regulation n. 2022/858, Article 1.

[127] The FCA and the Bank of England are the main regulators of financial services in the UK. The FCA focuses on protecting consumers, markets' integrity, and booster competition in the light of consumers' interest. The Bank of England ensures the soundness and safety of companies by eliminating or lowering risks that can jeopardise the financial stability.

[128] HM Treasury, Financial Conduct Authority, Bank of England, Cryptoassets Taskforce: Final Report (Oct, 2018), assets.publishing.service.gov.uk/government/uploads/system/uploads/attachment_data/file/752070/cryptoassets_taskforce_final_report_final_web.pdf. [Final Report].

Network (FinCEN) and the Securities and Exchange Commission (SEC) combined'.[129] Therefore, Section 7.4 gives particular attention to the FCA's work in the crypto-assets space.

UK Crypto-assets Taskforce

In October 2018, the UK *Taskforce* released its final report. The report observed that the UK's Financial Authority, HM Treasury, and Bank of England engaged in a variety of activities to better understand the crypto-asset market. The government, for example, published a call for information on digital currencies, a report on 'Distributed Ledger Technologies: Beyond Blockchain' and invested £10 million to support the construction of a proof of concept of DLT for the adoption of the public sector beyond finance.[130]

On the other hand, the FCA constituted the Innovation Hub and Regulatory Sandbox to boost innovation. The Sandbox enabled businesses to test innovative products in the UK financial market in a controlled environment.[131] The aim of the sandbox was to provide 'better access to finance'[132] and assist companies in the definition of the best practice to ensure consumer protection. In addition, the FCA explored how to exploit DLT in financial services and to perform its supervisory duties (the so-called *RegTech* initiative).[133] In 2017, the FCA released

[129] FCA, Unstable coins: cryptoassets, financial regulation and preventing financial crime in the emerging market for digital assets, Speech by Therese Chambers, Director of Retail and Regulatory Investigations at the FCA, delivered at The Advancement of Digital Assets and Addressing Financial Crime Risk, New York University School of Law (6 March 2020), www.fca.org.uk/news/speeches/unstable-coins

[130] Id. at 4. 'The government has invested £ 10 million through Innovate UK and the research councils to support a diverse range of DLT projects; created a £20 million GovTech Catalyst Fund to explore technology-based solutions for public sector challenges, potentially including the use of DLT; and is considering how DLT might be deployed to support new forms of financial services infrastructure through its Shared Platforms work with Deloitte'. Id. at 47, 48.

[131] FCA, Regulatory Sandbox (11 May 2015, last updated 6 January 2021), www.fca.org.uk/firms/innovation/regulatory-sandbox.

[132] Id. Lituania also experimented a Blockchain sandbox. See Bank of Lithuania (2018) Blockchain sandbox project LBChain moving to next stage, available at: www.lb.lt/en/news/blockchainsandbox-project-lbchain-moving-to-the-next-stage

[133] Id. at 5.

a Discussion paper DP17/3 to create a dialogue on the future of DLT in finance and a Feedback Statement that sums up the feedback collected, in addition to the FCA's response.[134]

It was noted that ICOs are risky and the nature of tokens, services, projects, and companies 'can vary greatly, making overall classification of ICOs from a legal perspective more difficult'.[135] The fact that a token falls into the FCA's regulation needs to be assessed case by case looking at the characteristics of each ICO. The FCA committed to conduct further study on the ICO market to define if additional regulatory actions in this area were necessary.[136] On the other hand, the FCA's Feedback Statement highlighted the opportunities that DLT offers in the context of financial market regulation *(RegTech)*.[137]

In September 2017, the FCA's RegTech team worked with two major banks and the R3 consortium to build 'a prototype application for regulatory reporting of mortgage transaction data using the Corda DLT platform'.[138] The result of this project was interesting as the adoption of a DLT platform enabled the FCA to receive mortgage transaction reports from the two major banks in real time, showing the potential of a DLT infrastructure from a regulatory perspective.[139] However, the FCA is aware of the technical limitations of DLT's adoption, which mainly concern scalability, privacy issues, and the lack of incentives in adopting a similar solution by market players. But still the pilot is interesting and might be used to explore similar applications for crypto-assets regulation.

The Bank of England also engaged in interesting and useful activities. It constituted a Fintech Hub to analyse Fintech's policy implications, in addition to publishing Quarterly Bulletin articles related to 'Innovations in payment technologies' and 'The Economics of digital currencies'. The Bank of England also worked on a proof of concept

134 FCA, FS17/4: Distributed Ledger Technology, Feedback Statement on Discussion Paper 17/03 (last updated 15.12.2017), www.fca.org.uk/feedback/fs17-04.pdf

135 Id. at 15.

136 Id. at 16.

137 Id. at 23.

138 Final Report at 24.

139 Daniel Gozman, Jonathan Liebenau & Tomaso Aste, *A Case Study of Using Blockchain Technology in Regulatory Technology*, MIS Quarterly Executive 19 (2020).

with 18 firms to have a clearer understanding of how emerging technologies are adopted and the implications of crypto-assets' adoption on financial stability.[140]

Similar to MiCA, the UK Taskforce involved stakeholders from the crypto-asset space to include their perspective in the analysis of crypto-assets market.[141] It emerged, for example, 'the lack of regulatory clarity' and the need to introduce regulation to assist the legitimate players in the crypto-assets market. Stakeholders also emphasised the speed with which this market changes, in addition to the present technological barriers in the DLT adoption (e.g., scalability and governance).

The *Taskforce's* final report clarified that tokenisation implies an asset, which is recorded on a DLT platform, and 'represented as a token' to enhance 'trading and transfer of the asset'.[142] The tokenisation's process should not change the regulatory framework of an asset. Thus, if an asset is regulated, the same asset represented as a token would be subject to regulation.

The *Taskforce's* final report distinguished crypto-assets into three categories:

1. Crypto-assets as a mean of exchange
2. Crypto-assets as a form of investment (security tokens)
3. Crypto-assets as a form of capital raising (ICOs)

Security tokens are merely new forms of existing financial products, and they need to comply with the security regulation. For example, 'if a token is a transferable security and the tokens will either be offered to the public in the UK or admitted to trading on a regulated market, an issuer will need to publish a prospectus unless an exemption applies'.[143] However, the Taskforce observed that although security tokens fall within the present regulation, it is often difficult to define if a crypto-asset can be qualified as a security token, given the opacity and complexity of their nature.[144]

In summary, the Taskforce engaged in a variety of activities to analyse crypto-assets and regulatory interventions in the related markets.

[140] Id. at 6.
[141] Id. Annex 2, at 52.
[142] Id. at 13.
[143] FCA, Guidance on Cryptoassets, Consultation Paper CP19/3 (Jan. 2019) at 36, available at www.fca.org.uk/publication/consultation/cp19-03.pdf
[144] Id. at 20.

The Taskforce observed that there is a lot of potential in the adoption of DLT in finance, as well as several risks, such as:

- Risks of financial crimes
- Risks to consumers, who can be exposed to fraudulent activities
- Risk to market integrity and financial stability[145]

The Taskforce's report revealed the need to carefully investigate the adoption of new forms of regulation and announced the issuing of consultations on crypto-assets regulation. Meanwhile, the Taskforce alleged to continue monitoring crypto-assets market developments and supporting innovation with DLT, by also further investigating the adoption of DLT to make the work of public agencies more efficient.[146]

What Next?

After the publication of the Taskforce's final report, the Taskforce proceeded with new activities. In January 2019, for example, the FCA opened a consultation on *Guidance for cryptoassets* to increase regulatory clarity for market players active in the crypto-asset space and assist consumers in better understanding the crypto-asset market. The FCA released a Policy Statement in response to the feedback received.[147] The Final Guidance clarified that 'exchange tokens', hence crypto-assets used primary as a means of exchange,[148] and 'utility tokens' fall outside the FCA regulation.[149] The FCA also defined few factors useful to determine when a token is a specified investment, hence a security token regulated by the security law. These factors include, but are not limited to:

[145] FCA, Cryptoassets: our work (23 January 2019, last updated 16 December 2020), www.fca.org.uk/firms/cryptoassets

[146] Id. at 40.

[147] FCA, PS19/22: Guidance on Cryptoassets (23 January 2019, last update 1 August, www.fca.org.uk/publications/policy-statements/ps19-22-guidance-cryptoassets 2019).

[148] FCA, Guidance on Cryptoassets, Feedback and Final Guidance to CP 19/3, Policy Statement PS19/22 (July 2019), www.fca.org.uk/publication/policy/ps19-22.pdf

[149] Id. at 9, 36.

1. 'the contractual rights and obligations the token-holder has by virtue of holding or owning that crypto-asset';
2. 'any contractual entitlement to profit-share (like dividends), revenues, or other payment or benefit of any kind';
3. 'any contractual entitlement to ownership in, or control of, the token issuer or other relevant person (like voting rights)';
4. 'the language used in relevant documentation, like token 'whitepapers', that suggests that the tokens are intended to function as an investment';
5. 'whether the token is transferable and tradeable on crypto-assets exchanges or any other type of exchange or market';
6. 'a direct flow of payment from the issuer or other relevant party to token holders'.[150]

Companies that engage in activities in the UK, which involve a security token, or tokens that constitute e-money, should verify whether such activities demand any form of registration or authorisation. Firms that conduct regulated activities, such as, exchanges and trading platforms, custodian and wallet providers, advisers, brokers, and other intermediaries, as well as payments providers, should pay particular attention to regulation.[151]

In January 2020, the FCA was empowered to supervise how crypto-assets firms manage the risk of counter-terrorist financing and money laundering. In June 2020, the FCA reminded companies in the UK that carry out crypto-asset activities to register with the FCA by 30 June, to comply with new regulations. The registration was not necessary for those companies registered or authorised under the Financial Services and Markets Act (2000), Electronic Money Regulation (2011), or Payment Services Regulation (2017).[152] In October 2020, the FCA banned crypto derivatives products' offering to UK retailer users being such derivatives inherently risky.[153]

[150] Id. at 34.

[151] Id. at 46.

[152] FCA, FCA Reminds Cryptoasset Businesses to Register Before the end of June (22 June 2020), www.fca.org.uk/news/press-releases/fca-reminds-cryptoasset-businesses-register-end-june. "[U]ndertaking cryptoasset activity subject to the MLRs will also be required to apply for registration." Id.

[153] FCA, FCA bans the sale of crypto-derivatives to retail consumers (10 October 2020), www.fca.org.uk/news/press-releases/fca-bans-sale-crypto-derivatives-retaili-consumers

Between 2020 and 2021, the HM Treasury launched two separate consultations in response to the Treasury's March 2020 budget, which identified the need of the Treasury to take two separate actions in the context of crypto-assets. The first measure concerned 'consulting on bringing certain crypto-assets into scope of financial promotions regulation' to increase consumer protection, which resulted in the HM Treasury consultation on 'Regulatory Framework for Approval of Financial Promotions' release in July 2020.[154] The second measure was related to a broader regulatory action to crypto-assets that included stablecoins, and led to the release of the 'UK regulatory approach to crypto-assets and stablecoins' consultation in January 2021.

In summary, the UK Taskforce engaged in a variety of actions to deal with crypto-assets regulation making market players and consumers part of the regulatory process through public consultations. In the UK, this first phase of studies and analysis analysed above is likely to lead to new forms of regulation and legislation for crypto-assets. New rules for the UK crypto-assets market might include the authorities' adoption of DLT in their enforcement action.

The UK Towards a Consensus Crypto-assets Regulation

As outlined above, the UK Taskforce engaged in a variety of interesting actions aimed to find the best rules to regulate the emerging crypto-assets market and reduce the legal uncertainty that is present in the crypto-assets space. The frequent adoption of public consultations shows the key role that market players and consumers are playing in the definition of the crypto-asset market regulation. This should imply the development of rules shared with the same companies subject to regulation that benefit consumers in the end. The road towards a comprehensive set of rules for all types of crypto-assets in the UK is still long, but differently from the European legislative system, the UK legislative and regulatory' s process should be faster. Additionally, it is important to recognise the value of various initiatives aimed at leveraging the same DLT in the regulatory enforcement actions.

[154] HM Treasury, Regulatory Framework for Approval of Financial Promotions: Consultation Response (20 July 2020), www.gov.uk/government/consultations/regulatory-framework-for-approval-of-financial-promotions

In other words, despite the U.K. going through Brexit and all legal consequences that this implies, UK government agencies put a lot of effort into the definition of the best rules to employ in the emerging crypto-assets markets, which deserves attention. However, the UK cannot act in isolation to be effective in the definition of a crypto-asset regulatory framework and would benefit immensely from an increased cooperation with other countries.

7.5 Conclusion

The financial sector is going through a remarkable transformation. DLT are setting the tone for a new era in finance and the regulatory framework needs to be adapted to the new progress in technology.[155] Scams, money laundering, and tax evasion are only three symbolic examples of illegal activities that can jeopardise the development of new financial assets based on cryptographic protocols and decentralised technologies – crypto-assets. The blockchain analysis company Chainalysis observed that despite the transparent and traceable design of crypto-assets, the 'pseudonymous nature and the ease with which it allows users to instantly send funds anywhere in the world'[156] make these assets appealing to criminals. In 2014, the SEC alerted investors about the risks related to Bitcoin and other cryptocurrencies, which often used to commit frauds and 'perpetrate fraudulent schemes'.[157] This is why the government response and control over these new technological tools in finance is critical to protect investors and the financial industry overall. Fostering innovation and protecting investors in finance are complementary objectives, but the former does not guarantee the latter. In the future development of crypto-assets, an important dimension of the story is technical, the other one legal.

[155] See Werbach, supra note 76. See also, Casey, Gensler & others, supra note 67, at 32.

[156] Chainalysis, The 2021 Crypto Crime Report 4 (16 February 2021). The primary goals of cybercriminals who steal cryptocurrency, or accept it as payment for illicit goods, are to obfuscate the source of their funds and convert their cryptocurrency into cash so that it can be spent or kept in a bank.

[157] Sec, Investor Alert: Bitcoin and Other Virtual Currency-Related Investments (7 May 2014), www.sec.gov/oiea/investor-alerts-bulletins/investoralertsia_bitcoin.html

As outlined throughout the chapter, all the three jurisdictions examined here engaged in several interesting initiatives to define the best rules to regulate likely high traffic crypto-asset markets. None of these jurisdictions singularly taken provides a satisfactory solution. On the contrary, all three jurisdictions analysed in this chapter offer some useful insights for future developments in crypto-assets regulation. First and foremost, crypto-assets run on the Internet, which has no national boundaries. In addition, crypto-assets are decentralised by design. Regulators need to have a global vision in the definition of a crypto-assets regulation to be effective.

Second, the flexibility that offers a test, such as the US Howey test or the SEC guidelines, is useful in dynamic markets such as crypto-assets markets. However, clearer and more precise rules similar to those defined in Europe are likely to benefit crypto-assets markets by reducing the uncertainty of what regulatory regime is applicable. In other words, guidelines that establish clear requirements for crypto-assets, such as the release of a white paper with compulsory disclosure requirements if certain conditions are met, could represent the right way to go forward.

The UK experience with crypto-assets regulation is particularly compelling because it includes the adoption of the same DLT technologies that governments aim to oversee. Maybe, the UK experiment with a pilot blockchain project could be replicated by including the US. The adoption of DLT to regulate financial markets might be the key to ensure the necessary guidance by delivering innovation. The European DLT Pilot Regime also seems to be an interesting intervention to enable the policymakers to have a better understanding of how these markets work and enable to make adjustments to the regulatory framework through experience.

Table 7.1 summarises what has been done and can be done to improve the present crypto-assets regulation in the US, EU, and the UK by emphasising the positive effects of each crypto-asset regulatory regime.

Although the cryptocurrency community has recently celebrated the 13 anniversary of the release of the Bitcoin white paper, there is still little guidance on how government treats crypto-assets and coordination among different jurisdictions could be improved. As outlined above, regulators, firms, and investors are having a difficult time in defining

Table 7.1 ***Advancements in Cryptoasset Regulation in the US, EU, and the UK***

	Crypto-assets Security Regulation	What are the positive effects?	What can be improved?
United States	• Howey Test • No binding Guidelines • Consultations	• Flexibility	• Uncertainty about the applied regulatory framework
Europe	• MiCA • DLT Pilot Regime • Consultations	• Certainty of rules	• Incompleteness of rules • Lack of flexibility
United Kingdom	• Innovation hub and Regulatory sandbox • RegTech initiative • Multiple consultations	• Using the same technology that regulator aims to oversee • Involvement of stakeholders at initial stage	• International approach/vision

a crypto-asset as a security, a commodity, or something else, as well as establishing which body should oversee and regulate them.

The story of crypto-assets is far from being unique and can only benefit from an analysis of the experience with crypto-assets regulation in US, EU, and UK. There are multiple interesting initiatives that each jurisdiction has pursued to define the appropriate rules for crypto-assets and these jurisdictions can learn several lessons from the experience of each other.

The truth is that crypto-assets regulation cannot act in isolation and should be seen as a critical tool for crypto-assets to succeed, rather than as a brake for innovation. Therefore, it seems ineffective to define a crypto-assets regulation national in scope. On the contrary, the adoption of the same decentralised technologies that governments aim to oversee is likely to serve as a possible ideal solution for crypto-asset markets.

8 UK Anti-money Laundering Regulation of Crypto-assets

PIERRE OSTERCAMP*

8.1 Introduction

Bitcoin was first popularised in 2011 as the supposedly untraceable digital currency used on the illicit darknet marketplace 'Silk Road'.[1] Since then, Bitcoin and other crypto-assets have often been associated with crime and the laundering of its proceeds.[2] However, most crypto-assets are by nature poor choices for laundering the proceeds of crime: money laundering involves concealing the illegal origin of criminal proceeds, and crypto-asset transactions can often be traced on immutable, publicly auditable blockchains. A blockchain is a data structure where blocks of data, such as transactions, are chronologically ordered with each new block linked to the previous one.[3] Since each block is individually verified and linked to the previous one using cryptography,[4] no block can be amended or deleted without invalidating the whole chain. As such, the blockchain maintains an

* Acknowledgements: this chapter was completed during my studies at LSE and QMUL, and I am grateful to all my professors for the knowledge and enthusiasm they shared with me; in particular, Andromachi Georgosouli, Martin Lodge, Niamh Moloney, and Peter Alldridge. Thank you to my former colleagues at XReg Consulting, a regulatory consultancy specialising in crypto-assets, for giving me practical experience in crypto-asset regulation. I am also grateful to my parents and grandparents for supporting me throughout my studies. Correspondence: ostercamppierre@gmail.com

1 David Adler, 'Silk Road: The Dark Side of Cryptocurrency' (*Fordham Law School*, 2018) news.law.fordham.edu/jcfl/2018/02/21/silk-road-the-dark-side-of-cryptocurrency. Accessed 31 October 2021.

2 "Owing to their anonymity and absence of regulation, crypto-assets can facilitate the sale and purchase of illicit goods and services, and can be used to launder the proceeds of serious crime and terrorism": House of Commons Treasury Committee, 'Crypto-assets' (*House of Commons*, 2018) para 103. publications.parliament.uk/pa/cm201719/cmselect/cmtreasy/910/910.pdf. Accessed 31 October 2021.

3 Andreas Antonopoulos, *Mastering Bitcoin* (O'Reilly 2017) 211.

4 Cryptography generally refers to the art of using code to achieve secure communication, though in this context, it refers specifically to mathematical

immutable record of transactions. While transactions are associated with pseudonymous addresses,[5] the use of supplementary information and blockchain analytics can enable these addresses and transactions to be linked to criminal activity and criminals themselves.[6]

Therefore, access to information which allows pseudonymous addresses and transactions to be linked to individuals is key in identifying and prosecuting criminals using crypto-assets. Owing to this, recent applications of anti-money laundering (AML) regulation to the crypto-asset industry focus on regulating centralised crypto-asset service providers which may collect identification information from their customers. Although crypto-assets are generally designed to enable decentralised peer-to-peer (P2P) transactions and interactions which bypass intermediary services, many centralised services including crypto-asset exchanges and wallet providers are widely used. In January 2020, crypto-asset exchange providers and custodian wallet providers operating in the United Kingdom became subject to AML requirements under the amended Money Laundering, Terrorist Financing and Transfer of Funds (Information on the Payer) Regulations (MLRs) 2017.[7] Under MLRs reg 14(3)(a), a crypto-asset is 'a cryptographically secured digital representation of value or contractual rights that uses a form of distributed ledger technology and can be transferred, stored or traded electronically'. Distributed ledger technology (DLT), one form of which is a blockchain, can be broadly defined as a widely shared database.[8]

techniques in cryptography to ensure and prove the security and integrity of data.

[5] cf Antonopoulos (n 3) 55–57: Most crypto-assets including Bitcoin enable the transferring of funds to and from pseudonymous addresses following verification of users' ownership of the funds. This is done through public-key cryptography, a mathematical technique which supports cybersecurity through, for example, creating digital signatures which cannot be forged. Crypto-assets based on these systems can be transferred to pseudonymous addresses which are derived from the recipient's public key. To send transactions to another address, payers must present their public key along with a digital signature made using the associated private key to prove their ownership of the funds.

[6] David Fox, 'Cryptocurrencies in the Common Law of Property' in David Fox and Sarah Green (eds), *Cryptocurrencies in Public and Private Law* (Oxford University Press 2019) 139, 164.

[7] MLRs reg 14A.

[8] Joint Money Laundering Steering Group (JMLSG), 'Guidance for the UK Financial Sector Part I' (*JMLSG*, 2020) preface para 5.

This chapter will analyse the UK's AML regime for crypto-assets, following an extension in the regulatory framework which introduced regulatory oversight and enforcement power to a previously unregulated sector. The regime will be deemed effective to the extent that it enables authorities to identify and prosecute criminals exploiting crypto-assets for the purpose of money laundering. First, this chapter will provide an overview of the UK's AML regime with a focus on its application to crypto-assets (Section 8.2), before discussing the fundamental 'Know Your Customer' AML requirements (Section 8.3). Next, various methods of privacy enhancement will be discussed (Section 8.4), before a conclusion is drawn on the overall effectiveness and vulnerabilities of the UK's AML regime, with recommendations for its amendment.

8.2 UK AML Regime

Legislation

MLRs 2017

The MLRs subject 'relevant persons'[9] posing a risk of money laundering to various requirements including the requirement to apply customer due diligence (CDD) measures in their business operations.[10] Introduced in 2017 to transpose the EU's Fourth Money Laundering Directive[11] (4MLD) into UK legislation, the MLRs were then amended in 2019 to transpose the EU's Fifth Money Laundering Directive (5MLD)[12] which extended the EU's AML regime to bring certain crypto-asset activities and service providers within its scope. Firms and individuals are subject to the MLRs if they are a 'crypto-asset exchange provider' or a 'custodian wallet provider' as defined under reg 14A. These 'crypto-asset businesses' are required to register with and be supervised by the financial conduct authority (FCA),[13]

[9] As defined under MLRs reg 8.
[10] MLRs regs 27–38.
[11] Council Directive 2015/849/EC of 20 May 2015 on the prevention of the use of the financial system for the purposes of money laundering or terrorist financing [2015] OJ L 141/73.
[12] Council Directive 2018/843/EC of 30 May 2018 on the prevention of the use of the financial system for the purposes of money laundering or terrorist financing [2018] OJ L 156/43.
[13] MLRs reg 7(1)(a).

who must be satisfied with their AML controls as required under the MLRs for risk assessment,[14] CDD,[15] monitoring of business relationships,[16] and record-keeping,[17] as well as their suspicious activity reporting (SAR) required under the Proceeds of Crime Act (POCA) 2002 ss 330–332.[18] Indeed, the FCA announced in 2021 that many crypto-asset businesses did not meet the standards required under the MLRs, and as such, the FCA established and then extended a temporary registration regime allowing crypto-asset businesses to continue trading pending registration (if they applied prior to 16 December 2020).[19]

The MLRs 'gold-plated' 5MLD by extending the scope of AML requirements to include exchange services:

1. between crypto-assets (crypto-to-crypto exchanges); and
2. involving crypto-asset automated teller machines (ATMs).

As the definition of crypto-asset exchange provider covers the creator or issuer of crypto-assets, Initial Coin Offerings (ICOs) are within scope of the MLRs.[20] This extension of the regulatory framework beyond the EU's minimum requirements (and beyond those imposed in most other jurisdictions) is a significant strength of the UK's AML regime with respect to crypto-assets. While EU legislators had considered that the regulation of points of entry and exit into and out of the traditional financial system (on- and off-ramps) would ensure adequate AML controls, regulation of crypto-to-crypto exchange is advocated by various commentators.[21] Where crypto-to-crypto exchange

[14] MLRs reg 18.
[15] MLRs regs 27–38.
[16] MLRs regs 28, 33 and 37.
[17] MLRs regs 39–40.
[18] Therese Chambers, 'Unstable coins: cryptoassets, financial regulation and preventing financial crime in the emerging market for digital assets' (*FCA*, 2020). www.fca.org.uk/news/speeches/unstable-coins. Accessed 31 October 2021.
[19] FCA, 'Temporary Registration Regime extended for cryptoasset businesses' (*FCA*, 2021). www.fca.org.uk/news/press-releases/temporary-registration-regime-extended-cryptoasset-businesses. Accessed 31 October 2021.
[20] MLRs reg 14A(1); FCA, 'Guidance on Cryptoassets' (*FCA*, 2019) 35–36. www.fca.org.uk/publications/policy-statements/ps19-22-guidance-cryptoassets. Accessed 31 October 2021.
[21] Lars Haffke et al., 'Virtual Currencies and Anti-Money Laundering – The Shortcomings of the 5th AML Directive (EU) and How to Address Them' (2020) 21 Journal of Banking Regulation 125, 132.

services are unregulated, the detection and prevention of crypto-asset money laundering rely heavily on the AML controls implemented by the on- and off-ramp service providers. This reliance is a considerable money laundering risk because through the 'layering' of numerous unregulated crypto-to-crypto transactions, an illegal source of funds could be sufficiently concealed to prevent its detection by the time the funds arrive at an on-ramp. Moreover, the FATF found that this 'layering' technique was the primary motivation for criminal use of different types of crypto-assets, though in most cases, only one type of crypto-asset was used.[22] Nonetheless, complex sequences of transactions of even just one type of crypto-asset, potentially in conjunction with other concealment techniques, could seriously hinder efforts to identify an illegal source of funds. As such, for the UK to leave crypto-to-crypto exchanges unregulated would have posed a substantial money laundering risk, requiring stricter supervision and enforcement of AML requirements to prevent on- and off-ramp services from facilitating money laundering.

Although crypto-asset ATMs pose a significant money laundering risk by allowing individuals to obtain untraceable cash in return for traceable crypto-assets, they fall outside the scope of 5MLD. However, the UK government made the well-informed and broadly supported decision to bring them within the scope of the MLRs following an industry consultation on the UK's implementation of 5MLD.[23] Further, the associated money laundering risk is mitigated under the MLRs as crypto-asset ATM providers are required to apply CDD measures for all transactions, thus mitigating the risk of money laundering through repeated transactions just below the threshold for CDD measures (a technique known as 'smurfing').[24] Since the ease of access to ICOs facilitates their exploitation for the purpose of money laundering, their inclusion within the scope of the MLRs is another strength of

[22] FATF, '12-Month Review of the Revised FATF Standards on Virtual Assets and Virtual Asset Service Providers' (*FATF*, 2020) 6 www.fatf-gafi.org/publications/fatfrecommendations/documents/12-month-review-virtual-assets-vasps.html. Accessed 31 October 2021.

[23] HM Treasury, 'Transposition of the Fifth Money Laundering Directive: response to the consultation' (*HM Treasury*, 2019) 9 www.gov.uk/government/consultations/transposition-of-the-fifth-money-laundering-directive. Accessed 31 October 2021.

[24] ibid; MLRs reg 27(7D).

the UK's AML regime.[25] Where identification information collected by token issuers is passed on to financial intelligence units (FIUs), such as the UK's National Crime Agency (NCA), it can help them successfully trace and identify criminals.[26]

The European Commission recognised the risks associated with ICOs and crypto-to-crypto exchanges in their 2019 money laundering risk assessment, recommending that jurisdictions impose AML requirements on crypto-asset businesses undertaking these activities.[27] Until these recommendations are integrated into an EU directive or regulation, however, these risks will persist in jurisdictions which only implement the minimum requirements under 5MLD. As such, it is clear that 5MLD will not suffice to tackle money laundering using crypto-assets.[28] However, the European Commission has proposed a new AML regulation[29] with a broader scope than 5MLD, which would include crypto-to-crypto exchange.[30] Although the UK MLRs currently better address money laundering risks by extending the scope of AML requirements beyond 5MLD, the regulation remains insufficient or even inapplicable with respect to certain potentially higher-risk activities, as discussed in Section 8.4. Even where regulations are applicable, specialised technologies for enhancing privacy when using crypto-assets may facilitate money laundering and evasion of regulatory requirements.

In the US, the Financial Crimes Enforcement Network (FinCEN) regulates money services businesses (MSBs) including money

[25] cf Haffke et al. (n 21) 134; Aurelio Gurrea-Martínez and Nydia Remolina León, 'The Law and Finance of Initial Coin Offerings' in Chris Brummer (ed), *Cryptoassets: Legal, Regulatory, and Monetary Perspectives* (Oxford University Press 2019) 117, 146.

[26] cf Haffke et al. (n 21) 134.

[27] Commission, 'Report on the assessment of the risk of money laundering and terrorist financing affecting the internal market and relating to cross-border activities' COM (2019) 650 final 97–98.

[28] cf Gurrea-Martínez and León (n 25) 148.

[29] Commission, 'Proposal for a Regulation on the prevention of the use of the financial system for the purposes of money laundering or terrorist financing' COM (2021) 420 final.

[30] ibid., Recital 11; Commission, 'Proposal for a Regulation on Markets in Crypto-assets' COM (2020) 593 final. According to Recital 11, the proposed AML regulation would cover crypto-asset service providers as defined under the Commission's proposed Regulation on Markets in Crypto-assets.

transmitters,[31] that is, persons which provide 'money transmission services' or are 'engaged in the transfer of funds'.[32] FinCEN has specified that persons transacting in 'convertible virtual currencies' including crypto-assets may qualify as money transmitters and thus be required under the Bank Secrecy Act (BSA) to implement an AML program and comply with record-keeping, transaction monitoring, and reporting requirements.[33] As outlined in FinCEN's guidance on which common business models would qualify as money transmitters, the application of AML requirements to crypto-asset businesses seems to align with the approach in the UK under the MLRs.[34] Similarly, to in the UK, AML requirements apply to persons in the US providing services of crypto-asset exchange (including crypto-to-crypto exchange), custodian wallets, and crypto-asset ATMs.[35] Possible exemptions to AML requirements in the US are also similar to those in the UK crypto-asset industry, including certain P2P trading platforms and decentralised exchanges.[36] Interestingly, the US regime goes further in some areas of the crypto-asset industry, which may be seen as relative strengths compared to the UK regime as this ensures more comprehensive regulation. For example, AML requirements may apply to payment processing services, internet casinos, and providers of anonymising services such as mixers.[37]

POCA 2002 and TACT 2000

Whereas the MLRs impose AML requirements on 'relevant persons' in their business operations, POCA and the Terrorism Act (TACT) 2000 establish criminal offences for money laundering and terrorist

[31] Josias Dewey, 'USA' in Josias Dewey (ed), *Blockchain & Cryptocurrency Laws and Regulations 2022* (Global Legal Insights 2021).

[32] FinCEN, 'Application of FinCEN's Regulations to Certain Business Models Involving Convertible Virtual Currencies' (*FinCEN*, 2019) 3 www.fincen.gov/sites/default/files/2019-05/FinCEN%20Guidance%20CVC%20FINAL%20508.pdf. Accessed 31 October 2021.

[33] ibid., 12.

[34] ibid., 14–23; Michelle Gitlitz et al., 'An introduction to virtual currency money transmission regulation' in Josias Dewey (ed), *Blockchain & Cryptocurrency Laws and Regulations 2022* (Global Legal Insights 2021).

[35] ibid.

[36] ibid.

[37] ibid.

financing that are applicable to all persons and businesses.[38] As such, even individual actors and crypto-asset service providers falling outside the scope of the MLRs may be held criminally liable for money laundering under POCA and TACT. TACT contains four criminal offences relating to terrorist financing,[39] including an offence for money laundering where a person knowingly, or with reasonable grounds for suspicion, 'facilitates the retention or control by or on behalf of another person of terrorist property'.[40]

Under POCA, there are three criminal offences for interaction with criminal property, which relate to:

1. concealing;
2. arrangements; and
3. acquisition, use and possession.[41]

In addition, criminal offences apply to persons working in regulated sectors for failure to disclose information or other matters which arise in the course of business and give rise to, or provide reasonable grounds for, knowledge or suspicion of money laundering.[42] Disclosures are generally made to the company's money laundering reporting officer (MLRO), who then decides whether to submit a SAR to the NCA. Notably, failure to disclose offences can even apply to unregulated activity as long as the relevant information is obtained during the conduct of regulated sector activity.[43] Therefore, unregulated crypto-asset activity may be the subject of SARs filed by regulated entities. For example, a regulated crypto-asset exchange conducting blockchain analytics as part of its CDD process may discover suspicious transactions on the blockchain and report them to the NCA, even if these transactions were between unregulated entities such as individual users with private wallets. The broad scope of AML disclosure requirements has been blamed for the apparent over-reporting of SARs, and although the NCA has maintained that 'SARs are a critical

[38] Arun Srivastava, 'UK Part II: UK law and practice' in Arun Srivastava and others (eds), *International Guide to Money Laundering Law and Practice* (Bloomsbury 2019) 59, 63.
[39] TACT ss 16–18.
[40] TACT s 18; Terrorist property as defined under TACT s 14.
[41] POCA ss 327–329.
[42] POCA ss 330–332.
[43] POCA s 330(3).

intelligence resource for law enforcement'[44] and published guidance aimed at helping firms submit better quality SARs,[45] it appears that both low quality and over-reporting of SARs remain an issue.[46]

Guidance

FCA

When judging whether an individual committed a criminal offence under the MLRs or POCA ss 330 or 331, courts must consider whether relevant guidance was followed.[47] Similarly, under the MLRs, the designated supervisory authority (the FCA for crypto-asset businesses) must consider whether relevant guidance was followed when determining if an individual breached a relevant requirement outlined under MLRs schedule 6.[48] Also, the FCA has the power to impose directions on crypto-asset businesses in order to address non-compliance with the MLRs or otherwise prevent them from being exploited for the purpose of money laundering.[49] Six months before the amended MLRs came into force in January 2020, the FCA issued guidance on crypto-assets with a focus on defining the different types of crypto-assets (or 'tokens') and specifying which types are within the FCA's regulatory perimeter under FSMA.[50] There are two broad types of regulated tokens:

44 NCA, 'SARs Reporter Booklet' (*NCA*, 2021) 3 www.nationalcrimeagency.gov.uk/who-we-are/publications/491-sars-reporter-booklet-january-2021/file. Accessed 31 October 2021.

45 NCA, 'Guidance on submitting better quality suspicious activity reports (SARs)' (*NCA*, 2020) www.nationalcrimeagency.gov.uk/who-we-are/.publications/446-guidance-on-submitting-better-quality-sars-1/file. Accessed 31 October 2021.

46 Miriam Goldby, 'Breaches of AML reporting requirements by UK bankers: Are effective enforcement choices being made by financial regulators?' in Costanza Russo and others (eds), *Research Handbook on Law and Ethics in Banking and Finance* (Elgar 2019) 317.

47 POCA ss 330(8) and 331(7); MLRs reg 86(2)(b).

48 ibid; MLRs reg 76(6)(b).

49 MLRs reg 74C.

50 The Financial Services and Markets Act 2000 (FSMA); cf FCA (n 20). This guidance amended the crypto-asset taxonomy proposed in the Cryptoassets Taskforce Report: HM Treasury, FCA and Bank of England, 'Cryptoassets Taskforce: final report' (*Cryptoassets Taskforce*, 2018) assets.publishing.service.gov.uk/government/uploads/system/uploads/attachment_data/file/752070/cryptoassets_taskforce_final_report_final_web.pdf Accessed 31 October 2021. For a discussion of the FCA's regulatory perimeter with

1. 'security tokens' which accord rights similar to those of specified investments under RAO[51]; and
2. 'e-money tokens' which constitute e-money under the EMRs.[52]

All tokens not included in those two types are unregulated tokens, including 'exchange tokens' ('cryptocurrencies') such as Bitcoin, and 'utility tokens' such as Chainlink. However, while unregulated tokens are outside of the FCA's regulatory perimeter and are not covered by consumer protections such as the FSCS[53] and the FOS,[54] all of these tokens are within the UK's AML regime.[55] As such, the FCA supervises all crypto-asset businesses,[56] and monitors and enforces their compliance with the MLRs.[57] Compliance may be encouraged, and non-compliance punished, with recourse to (or threat of) the FCA's broad range of civil and criminal remedies including financial penalties, prosecution, and prohibition.[58]

JMLSG

Guidance issued by the Joint Money Laundering Steering Group (JMLSG), a group of UK financial services trade associations, is widely considered to be the most important AML guidance in the UK.[59] Following the introduction of the MLRs, the JMLSG updated its sector-specific guidance to cover crypto-asset businesses, including an extensive list of risk factors relating to crypto-asset activity.[60] In

respect to cryptoassets, see also Stuart Davis, Sam Maxson and Andrew Moyle, 'United Kingdom' in Josias Dewey (ed), *Blockchain & Cryptocurrency Laws and Regulations 2022* (Global Legal Insights 2021).

51 The Financial Services and Markets Act 2000 (Regulated Activities) Order 2001.

52 The Electronic Money Regulations 2011 reg 2(1); cf FCA (n 20) 14.

53 Financial Services Compensation Scheme (FSCS) www.fscs.org.uk/. Accessed 31 October 2021.

54 Financial Ombudsman Service (FOS) www.financial-ombudsman.org.uk/. Accessed 31 October 2021.

55 cf FCA (n 20) 10, 14.

56 MLRs reg 7(1)(a).

57 FCA, Enforcement Guide (*FCA*, 2020) para 19.14.2 www.handbook.fca .org.uk/handbook/EG.pdf. Accessed 31 October 2021.

58 ibid., para 19.14.3. Under FSMA s 402(1), the FCA has the power to prosecute breaches of the MLRs.

59 cf Srivastava (n 38) 115.

60 JMLSG, 'Guidance for the UK Financial Sector Part II: Sectoral Guidance' (*JMLSG*, 2020) paras 22.33, 22.34 and 22.35 secureservercdn .net/160.153.138.163/a3a.8f7.myftpupload.com/wp-content/uploads/2020/ 07/JMLSG-Guidance_Part-II_-July-2020.pdf. Accessed 31 October 2021.

addition, specific guidance is offered relating to the application of AML controls to crypto-asset activity.[61] As such, the JMLSG's guidance offers pragmatic solutions to crypto-asset businesses wishing to implement effective AML programs and is a key aspect of the UK's AML regime in supporting compliance with legislation that was not conceived with crypto-assets in mind.

FATF

The foundations of the UK's AML regime can be traced back to the recommendations of the Financial Action Task Force (FATF),[62] an international body that publishes AML standards and guidance which are widely recognised and implemented worldwide.[63] In 2015, the FATF issued its first guidance on 'virtual currencies'[64] which recommended that countries consider applying AML controls to on- and off-ramps to tackle the associated money laundering risk.[65] In 2019, the FATF updated both its standards and its guidance to clarify the scope of their application, specifying that all relevant FATF recommendations should be applied to 'virtual assets (VAs)' and 'virtual asset service providers (VASPs)'.[66] Then, in 2021, the FATF published updated guidance for VAs and VASPs, which further clarified the application of the recommendations and provided additional guidance on areas

[61] ibid., paras 22.36–22.62.

[62] FATF, 'The FATF Recommendations' (*FATF*, 2019) www.fatf-gafi.org/media/fatf/documents/recommendations/pdfs/FATF%20Recommendations%202012.pdf. Accessed 31 October 2021

[63] Elizabeth Baker and Paul Napper, 'UK Part I: UK money laundering – typological considerations' in Arun Srivastava and others (eds), *International Guide to Money Laundering Law and Practice* (Bloomsbury 2019) 1, 8; BIS, 'Annual Economic Report' (*BIS*, 2020) 83 www.bis.org/publ/arpdf/ar2020e.pdf. Accessed 31 October 2021.

[64] A 'virtual currency' was defined as 'a digital representation of value that can be digitally traded ... but does not have legal tender status': FATF, 'Virtual Currencies Key Definitions and Potential AML/CFT Risks' (*FATF*, 2014) 4. www.fatf-gafi.org/media/fatf/documents/reports/Virtual-currency-key-definitions-and-potential-aml-cft-risks.pdf. Accessed 31 October 2021.

[65] FATF, 'Guidance for a Risk-Based Approach to Virtual Currencies' (*FATF*, 2015) para 14 www.fatf-gafi.org/media/fatf/documents/reports/Guidance-RBA-Virtual-Currencies.pdf. Accessed 31 October 2021.

[66] VAs and VASPs as defined in the FATF's 2019 guidance: FATF, 'Guidance for a Risk-Based Approach to Virtual Assets and Virtual Asset Service Providers' (*FATF*, 2019) paras 5, 6, 8, 13 and 33 www.fatf-gafi.org/media/fatf/documents/recommendations/RBA-VA-VASPs.pdf. Accessed 31 October 2021.

such as the 'travel rule' (subjecting VA activities to recommendation 16 on wire transfer requirements).[67] The updated guidance specifies that VASPs and other obliged entities conducting VA activities must implement the preventive measures outlined in recommendations 10-21, including CDD measures, record keeping, and suspicious transaction reporting.[68]

Though the FATF's standards are non-binding and go further than the requirements under 5MLD, for example by including crypto-to-crypto exchange in their scope, the UK government committed to transposing the FATF standards alongside 5MLD.[69] Therefore, the UK's definitions under the MLRs of crypto-assets and crypto-asset businesses broadly align with the FATF's definitions of VAs and VASPs, and will be used interchangeably in this chapter. Further, AML requirements under the MLRs for crypto-asset businesses broadly reflect the FATF standards including the travel rule, which the Treasury proposed in 2021 to apply to crypto-asset businesses under the MLRs.[70]

8.3 Know Your Customer (KYC)

Customer Due Diligence (CDD)

KYC is Key

The Know Your Customer (KYC) process is the foundation of any effective AML regime, comprising of various CDD measures which enable the identification and management of money laundering risk. First and foremost, the KYC process involves the identification of

[67] FATF 'Updated Guidance for a Risk-Based Approach to Virtual Assets and Virtual Asset Service Providers' (*FATF*, 2021) www.fatf-gafi.org/publications/fatfrecommendations/documents/guidance-rba-virtual-assets-2021.html. Accessed 31 October 2021.

[68] ibid.

[69] cf HM Treasury (n 23) 8.

[70] HM Treasury, 'Amendments to the Money Laundering, Terrorist Financing and Transfer of Funds (Information on the Payer) Regulations 2017 Statutory Instrument 2022' (*HMT*, 2021). assets.publishing.service.gov.uk/government/uploads/system/uploads/attachment_data/file/1004603/210720_SI_Consultation_Document_final.pdf. Accessed 31 October 2021.

the customer and the verification of their identity, usually through the provision of documents and information which confirm their name and address.[71] Where crypto-assets are used for the purpose of money laundering, KYC information is often the critical element which enables the linking of criminals to their pseudonymous transaction activity. If illicit funds are identified on the blockchain and can be traced to a wallet hosted by a crypto-asset business, KYC information linked to the wallet and held by the business can permit the identification of the criminal. Indeed, this approach was taken in *AA v Persons Unknown*, where the victim of a ransomware attack enlisted the help of blockchain analytics firm Chainalysis to trace their lost Bitcoins to a wallet hosted by the crypto-asset exchange Bitfinex.[72] The victim was then granted a proprietary injunction over their lost Bitcoins, which required Bitfinex to provide the victim with the KYC information they had collected in connection to the wallet holding the victim's funds.[73] Without a connection to KYC information, making a link between a pseudonym on the blockchain and an identity is much more difficult or even impossible, as it requires the use of complicated alternative means of identification such as IP address tracing or transaction metadata analysis.

The specific CDD measures which must be applied by firms are outlined under MLRs reg 28, and include:

1. identifying the customer;
2. verifying their identity; and
3. assessing 'the purpose and intended nature of the business relationship or occasional transaction'.[74]

Further, firms must 'conduct ongoing monitoring of a business relationship', including reviewing and updating KYC information and monitoring transactions.[75] In stark contrast to the traditional financial system, the publicly auditable nature of many crypto-asset blockchains can provide a transparent audit trail which facilitates transaction monitoring. Crypto-assets can in some cases be traced throughout their

[71] MLRs reg 28(2).
[72] *AA v Persons Unknown* paras 13–15.
[73] ibid., paras 81–82.
[74] MLRs reg 28(2). Under MLRs reg 3(1), an occasional transaction 'means a transaction which is not carried out as part of a business relationship'.
[75] MLRs reg 28(11).

lifetime, allowing identification of money laundering risks even if they materialise at a later stage following concealment techniques such as 'layering'. Various blockchain analytics firms such as Coinfirm offer sophisticated transaction monitoring services which can even provide automated, real-time updates upon identification of new risks or transactions.[76] Such systems provide a major advantage over traditional monitoring programs which may be unable to trace transactions beyond their counterparty, and often rely on periodic reviews which result in delayed responses to the emergence of money laundering risks.

Identity Verification

In light of the critical importance of KYC information in tackling crypto-asset money laundering, the authenticity of this information is paramount. To ensure this, MLRs reg 28(18)(a) requires the identity of each customer to be verified on the basis of information or documents 'obtained from a reliable source which is independent of the person whose identity is being verified'. The reliability and independence of the source may be considered as verified under MLRs reg 28(19) if:

1. the information is received through an electronic identification process[77]; and
2. the process is 'secure from fraud and misuse' and can provide 'an appropriate level of assurance' of the customer's identity.

Such a strict approach to the all-important verification of KYC information is a clear strength of the UK's AML regime, though no identification system is entirely immune to fraud or misuse. For example, criminals could still complete KYC using stolen or false documents, or coerce others into allowing the criminals to use their identification documents.

Risk-based Approach

The 'appropriate level of assurance' referred to under MLRs reg 28(19)(b) alludes to the adoption of a risk-based approach (RBA) to

[76] Coinfirm, 'Monitoring of Wallets' (*Coinfirm*, 2020) www.coinfirm.com/wp-content/uploads/2020/06/case001_04.pdf. Accessed 31 October 2021.

[77] As defined under Article 3(1) of Council Regulation 2014/910/EC of 23 July 2014 on electronic identification and trust services for electronic transactions in the internal market [2014] OJ L 257/73 (eIDAS).

CDD measures, that is, where controls are proportionate to the risks identified. Under MLRs regs 28(12) and 28(16), crypto-asset businesses must adopt an RBA to the application of CDD measures and monitoring, and be able to demonstrate to the FCA that these measures are appropriate in light of the requirements under the MLRs and the money laundering risk associated with the specific circumstances.[78] Further, firms are required to conduct preliminary money laundering risk assessments of both their whole business and individual customers under MLRs regs 18(1) and 28(2)(c), respectively, which are instrumental in informing the implementation of appropriate risk-based CDD measures. Under an RBA, simplified CDD measures (SDD) may be implemented in situations which are assessed as low-risk,[79] while enhanced CDD measures (EDD) and enhanced monitoring must be applied in high-risk situations.[80] In its 2019 guidance on adopting an RBA, the FATF stated that VAs and VASPs may generally be deemed higher-risk and could warrant EDD due to the characteristics of VAs which could facilitate money laundering, and due to the challenges of the KYC process.[81]

Where appropriate, EDD measures specific to crypto-asset activity can be carried out, such as requesting information on the history of the customer's transaction activity and tracking their IP address.[82] Strict EDD measures such as these may be valuable in enabling crypto-asset businesses to identify and report suspicious activity, potentially resulting in the detection and prevention of money laundering. Tech-savvy criminals, however, are likely to protect their privacy through means such as privacy coins, The Onion Router (TOR) internet browser, and virtual private networks (VPNs) to impede the tracing of their transactions and IP address. Indeed, the use of privacy-enhancing technologies in itself may be deemed high risk, and some crypto-asset businesses refuse to interact with customers making use of them. Despite the various risks and the FATF's statement that the crypto-asset industry in general may be deemed higher risk, it must be emphasised that the all-encompassing application of EDD measures to crypto-asset activity would be wholly inappropriate. Such an approach would run

78 cf JMLSG (n 8) para 5.1.4.
79 MLRs reg 37(1).
80 MLRs reg 33(1); cf JMLSG (n 8) para 5.1.8.
81 cf FATF (n 66) 19.
82 ibid., 26; cf JMLSG (n 60) para 22.62.

contrary to the RBA endorsed by the MLRs and the FATF, and onerous EDD requirements would risk stifling industry demand, competition, and innovation.[83]

FATF Travel Rule

Even if a crypto-asset business has strong internal AML controls, detection and tracing of illicit activity may be hindered when counterparty payees or payers provide little or no identification information. The FATF aimed to mitigate this money laundering risk by recommending that countries require VASPs to comply with recommendation 16, the 'travel rule'.[84] Under the travel rule, for all transfers of VAs over 1,000 euros or US dollars, VASPs and other obliged entities must collect and hold identification information on the transaction originator and beneficiary, screen the name of their counterparty originator or beneficiary for financial sanctions compliance and freeze or prohibit transactions where appropriate, and report suspicious transactions to the relevant FIU.[85] Ordering institutions must send the collected information to the beneficiary immediately and securely, and whereas the ordering must verify the accuracy of the originator information, the beneficiary must verify the accuracy of the beneficiary information.[86] For VA transfers below 1,000 euros or US dollars, the FATF suggests that countries could apply fewer requirements, but recommend that VASPs should be required to obtain the names of both the originator and the beneficiary and either their VA wallet addresses or a unique transaction reference number, verifying only their customer's information in the case of suspicious circumstances.[87] Where

83 EU Blockchain Observatory and Forum, 'Legal and Regulatory Framework of Blockchains and Smart Contracts' (*EU Blockchain Observatory and Forum*, 2019) 17 www.eublockchainforum.eu/sites/default/files/reports/report_legal_v1.0.pdf?width=1024&height=800&iframe=true. Accessed 31 October 2021.

84 cf FATF (n 66). For a detailed overview of the FATF's latest guidance on the travel rule, see: XReg Consulting, 'The Travel Rule: The Financial Action Task Force's updated guidance' (*XReg Consulting*, 2021) uploads-ssl.webflow.com/5df7642ffbd9264804671001/617a95a1bb2e99523784bdd7_Explainer%20travel%20rule%20changes%20-issue%201%20-FINAL.pdf. Accessed 31 October 2021.

85 cf FATF (n 67).

86 ibid.

87 ibid., 61.

a VA transfer only involves one VASP or other obliged entity, the FATF expects that entity to comply with the travel rule with regard to its customer, but not to send information to non-obliged entities such as individual users controlling private wallets.[88]

Identification of VASPs

Currently, challenges remain to be addressed before widespread compliance with the travel rule can be achieved. The two primary impediments to travel rule compliance are:

1. the process of identifying whether a counterparty is a VASP, verifying their identity and conducting counterparty VASP due diligence; and
2. ensuring secure, clear and accurate data transmission between VASPs.[89]

While traditional financial institutions have long complied with the travel rule through sophisticated communication channels such as SWIFT, VASPs often have no information on their counterparties beyond pseudonymous addresses, and no means of transmitting their own information to their counterparties.[90] One solution for identifying VASPs is to create a list of VASPs across the world,[91] with an additional list of all wallet addresses associated with each VASP.

Accurate and secure data collection and storage would be critical in making a VASP list a viable and reliable solution. Otherwise, illicit actors gaining access to lists of VASPs and wallet addresses could identify VASPs in control of specific high-value wallets and target them in cyberattacks to steal the crypto-assets. Further, inaccuracies in the lists may impede efforts to trace the audit trail beyond the counterparty, and could result in customer identification information being provided to the wrong entity. Equally, if illicit actors were able to compromise the lists and amend data or impersonate VASPs, they could ensure that inaccurate data was provided with respect to transactions they wish to conceal for the purposes of money laundering. Whether in

[88] ibid., 65.
[89] ibid., 62–64.
[90] Fedor Poskriakov et al., 'Cryptocurrency compliance and risks: A European KYC/AML perspective' in Josias Dewey (ed), *Blockchain & Cryptocurrency Regulation* (Global Legal Insights 2020) 119.
[91] cf FATF (n 67) 63.

conjunction with a VASP list or another solution, some form of VASP identity verification is necessary to mitigate the risk of impersonation. One solution to this issue proposed by the Travel Rule Information Sharing Architecture (TRISA) is to delegate this task to a designated certificate authority who verifies VASP identities and issues them digital certificates to use as proof of identity.[92] For this type of solution to support travel rule compliance in the global crypto-asset industry, it would have to be widely accepted by industry participants, and supplemented by alternative solutions if certain jurisdictions or VASPs do not accept this form of identity verification.

Data Transmission

To achieve compliance with both the travel rule and data protection legislation, VASPs must ensure the customer data being transmitted is accurate. The information required under the travel rule constitutes personal data within the scope of the EU General Data Protection Regulation[93] (GDPR), the UK GDPR, and the UK Data Protection Act (DPA).[94] As such, the processing of this data[95] must adhere to the DPA, which includes principles, requirements and rights of data protection and data accuracy. As a data controller,[96] a VASP must correct any inaccurate personal data they process upon request by the data subject,[97] and under the travel rule, they are obliged to verify the accuracy of the required information provided by their customer.

However, the travel rule does not require VASPs to verify the accuracy of information provided by their counterparties.[98] This may give rise to substantial money laundering risks as VASPs could provide inaccurate information which prevents the tracing of transactions, yet their counterparties would be unaware if they do not verify this

[92] TRISA, 'Travel Rule Information Sharing Architecture for Virtual Asset Service Providers' (*TRISA*, 2020) trisa.io/trisa-whitepaper. Accessed 31 October 2021.

[93] Council Directive 2016/679/EC of 27 April 2016 on the protection of natural persons with regard to the processing of personal data and on the free movement of such data [2016] OJ L 119/1.

[94] cf FATF (n 66) 29: Required information is listed in para 114. This information constitutes personal data as defined under both GDPR art 4(1) and DPA s 3(2).

[95] Data processing as defined under DPA s 3(4).

[96] Data controller as defined under DPA s 3(6).

[97] DPA s 46(1).

[98] ibid.

information. Similar risks arise when VASPs transact with counterparties which are not subject to the travel rule, such as private wallets, in which case counterparty information can be provided by the customer with no requirement for its accuracy to be verified by the VASP.[99] The VASP may then be exposed to money laundering risk as the customer could easily give false information which impedes AML investigations. In order to address these money laundering risks associated with inaccurate counterparty information, the travel rule could be amended to require at least a cursory appraisal of the accuracy of counterparty information. Alternatively, countries could implement this requirement in national legislation, though this approach could result in differences in national implementation of the FATF recommendations which enable regulatory arbitrage.

Regulatory Harmony

Although the introduction of various technical solutions has enabled significant progress towards widespread travel rule compliance, most jurisdictions have not yet imposed travel rule obligations on VASPs.[100] Prior to the 2021 UK government proposals to apply the travel rule to crypto-asset businesses,[101] the Treasury had decided to delay these until viable travel rule solutions were 'globally recognised', emphasising that 'it is imperative that there is international regulatory harmony to successfully counter the use of crypto-assets for illicit activity'.[102] Similar to the UK, the EU proposed to subject crypto-asset businesses to the travel rule[103] by revising the funds transfer regulation,[104] and the direct applicability of the regulation to all EU Member States prevents regulatory arbitrage across the bloc. Notwithstanding this, in light of the disparities between regulatory frameworks across the world, international regulatory harmony in travel rule compliance would require different solutions to have sufficient flexibility and inter-operability to be compatible with the requirements of

99 cf FATF (n 66) 30.

100 cf FATF (n 22) 17.

101 cf HM Treasury (n 70).

102 cf HMT (n 23) 9–10.

103 Commission, 'Proposal for a Regulation on information accompanying transfers of funds and certain crypto-assets (recast)' COM (2021) 422 final.

104 Council Regulation 2015/847/EC of 20 May 2015 on information accompanying transfers of funds [2015] OJ L 141/1.

each jurisdiction.[105] For example, differing requirements for AML, data protection and electronic identification across jurisdictions could require VASPs to provide different customer information depending on where their counterparty is situated.[106]

One major factor enhancing the inter-operability of travel rule solutions across borders is the adoption of international messaging standards. This can ensure that, regardless of the travel rule solution being used, VASPs are able to transmit and receive the information required under the travel rule as well as under relevant legislation. Also, having a standardised format enables the automation of information exchange, which minimises costs and risks.[107] One such set of standards has emerged and is widely accepted among industry participants: the interVASP Messaging Standards (IVMS101).[108] IVMS101 recognises and accounts for the differences in regulatory requirements and languages between jurisdictions, providing a flexible standard which enables the interoperability of travel rule solutions.[109]

8.4 Privacy Enhancement

Section 8.4 will explore three of the most prevalent means of enhancing privacy when dealing with crypto-assets, all of which are considered by the JMLSG to pose a high risk of money laundering.[110] Since privacy-enhancing technologies can 'obfuscate the identity of the sender, recipient, holder, or beneficial owner', they frustrate the primary technique of tackling crypto-asset ML risks: transaction tracing.[111] Nonetheless, private firms specialising in sophisticated blockchain analytics, such as Chainalysis, CipherTrace, and Elliptic, can in some cases trace transactions even where privacy-enhancing

105 cf FATF (n 22) 17.
106 ibid.
107 Joint Working Group on interVASP Messaging Standards, 'interVASP Messaging Standards' (*Joint Working Group on interVASP Messaging Standards*, 2020) 11. intervasp.org/wp-content/uploads/2020/05/IVMS101-interVASP-data-model-standard-issue-1-FINAL.pdf. Accessed 31 October 2021.
108 ibid.
109 ibid., 10.
110 cf JMLSG (n 60) para 22.34.
111 cf FATF (n 66) 28; Anton Moiseienko and Kayla Izenman, 'From Intention to Action: Next Steps in Preventing Criminal Abuse of Cryptocurrency' (*RUSI*, 2019) 20.

technologies have been used. Indeed, the JMLSG recommend that firms use blockchain analytics to manage and mitigate the money laundering risks associated with privacy-enhanced crypto-assets and technologies.[112] Where crypto-asset businesses are unable to manage the associated risks, however, the FATF recommends that countries prohibit them from dealing with these crypto-assets and activities.[113] Despite this, many forms of privacy-enhancement in the crypto-asset industry are not directly addressed under the UK's AML regime, allowing crypto-asset businesses to deal with them at their discretion subject to non-binding guidance from the JMLSG and FATF. For example, while the JMLSG and FATF identify them as higher-risk factors, there are no specific requirements under the MLRs relating to following three areas discussed further below:

1. privacy coins;
2. mixers and
3. decentralised finance (DeFi).[114]

Privacy Coins

Since the detection of crypto-asset money laundering requires the criminal source of funds to be identified, privacy coins present a major challenge to AML regulation by impeding the traceability of transactions (the ability to link a transaction's output to its input).[115] Privacy coins such as Monero, Zcash, and Dash leverage different techniques including advanced cryptography and mixed inputs in order to prevent the tracing of transactions and addresses by concealing the sender, recipient, and value of transactions. While privacy coins cannot secure absolute anonymity for users, they should be of concern to regulators who may see their supervisory and enforcement powers

[112] cf JMLSG (n 60) para 22.33.
[113] cf FATF (n 66) 28; updated 55.
[114] cf JMLSG (n 60) para 22.34; FATF, 'Virtual Assets Red Flag Indicators of Money Laundering and Terrorist Financing' (*FATF*, 2020) www.fatf-gafi.org/media/fatf/documents/recommendations/Virtual-Assets-Red-Flag-Indicators.pdf. Accessed 31 October 2021.
[115] Apolline Blandin et al., 'Global Cryptoasset Regulatory Landscape Study' (*Judge Business School*, 2020) 53; Malte Möser et al., 'An Empirical Analysis of Traceability in the Monero Blockchain' 2018 (3) Proceedings on Privacy Enhancing Technologies 1, 2.

limited by their inability to trace these transactions.[116] Currently, the investigative tools provided by even the most advanced blockchain analytics firms remain largely ineffective for tracing privacy coin transactions.[117] Though Chainalysis have recently announced their ability to trace most Zcash and Dash transactions, they can only reliably trace transactions which do not have privacy features enabled.[118] Monero, which does not offer the option of disabling its privacy features, continues to pose major difficulties in reliable transaction tracing, though some progress is being made by Chainalysis and CipherTrace.[119]

By default, Monero conceals information relating to the wallet and IP address of senders and recipients of transactions as well as the value of the transactions.[120] Monero demonstrates that advanced cryptography and tight requirements for anonymity embedded in its code can make privacy coins 'effectively untraceable'.[121] Indeed, some criminals have started requesting that payments be made in Monero in cases of ransomware attacks[122] and terrorist financing,[123] and started charging a premium for Bitcoin payments due to the relative difficulty of

[116] ibid.

[117] US Department of the Treasury, 'Pilot IRS Cryptocurrency Tracing' (*US Department of the Treasury*, 2020) 1. beta.sam.gov/opp/6c8e3cfe6059462c8cdd82cea4252966/view?keywords=cryptocurrency&sort=-modifiedDate&index=&is_active=true&page=1. Accessed 31 October 2021.

[118] Michael Kapilkov, 'Chainalysis Can Now Track Your "Privacy Coins" Zcash & Dash' (*Cointelegraph*, 2020) cointelegraph.com/news/chainalysis-can-now-track-your-privacy-coins-zcash-dash. Accessed 31 October 2021.

[119] Kollen Post, 'Chainalysis and Texas firm win million-dollar IRS contract to crack Monero' (*Cointelegraph*, 2020) cointelegraph.com/news/chainalysis-and-texas-firm-win-million-dollar-irs-contract-to-crack-monero. Accessed 31 October 2021; Rachel Wolfson, 'CipherTrace develops Monero tracing tool to aid US DHS investigations' (*Cointelegraph*, 2020) cointelegraph.com/news/ciphertrace-develops-monero-tracing-tool-to-aid-us-dhs-investigations. Accessed 31 October 2021.

[120] cf Moiseienko and Izenman (n 112) 20.

[121] cf Möser et al. (n 116) 1.

[122] Felipe Erazo, 'Major Argentine Telecom Falls Victim to $7.5M Monero Ransomware Attack' (*Cointelegraph*, 2020) cointelegraph.com/news/major-argentine-telecom-falls-victim-to-75m-monero-ransomware-attack. Accessed 31 October 2021.

[123] Andrey Shevchenko, 'ISIS-Affiliated News Website to Collect Donations with Monero' (*Cointelegraph*, 2020) cointelegraph.com/news/isis-affiliated-news-website-to-collect-donations-with-monero. Accessed 31 October 2021.

laundering Bitcoins.[124] Nonetheless, it must be emphasised that privacy coins may be *effectively* untraceable but not *absolutely* untraceable. Although it is practically impossible to decrypt the transaction information recorded on the blockchains of certain privacy coins such as Monero, future developments in blockchain analytics could enable the exposure of transaction information and the subsequent identification and prosecution of criminals. In light of the current limitations of blockchain analytics and investigations, however, regulation of privacy coins remains necessary to mitigate the associated risk of money laundering.

While the JMLSG guidance draws attention to the higher money laundering risk relating to privacy coins, there are no specific AML requirements under the MLRs beyond the standard requirements for crypto-asset businesses.[125] As such, the onus is on crypto-asset businesses to exercise discretion towards the use of privacy coins, and some have simply refused to deal with them due to money laundering risks.[126] Absolute rejection of privacy coins, however, is an unnecessarily extreme response to a form of technology which has various use cases which are legal. For example, businesses may want to keep transactions hidden from their competitors, and individuals may not want their political donations to be publicly known.[127] Since most Zcash and Dash transactions are actually traceable because the privacy features can be disabled, these coins should, when the privacy features are disabled, be accepted by crypto-asset businesses as readily as other traceable crypto-assets which pose similar money laundering risks.[128] Even more opaque privacy coins such as Monero could be accepted with the risks managed by stricter regulatory requirements. Though

[124] Adrian Zmudzinski, 'Sodinokibi Crypto Ransomware Switches from Bitcoin to Monero to Hide Money Trail' (*Cointelegraph*, 2020) cointelegraph .com/news/sodinokibi-crypto-ransomware-switches-from-bitcoin-to-monero-to-hide-money-trail. Accessed 31 October 2021.

[125] cf JMLSG (n 60) para 22.34.

[126] Cali Haan, 'Coinbase UK Delisting "Privacy Coin" ZCash' (*CrowdFundInsider*, 2019) www.crowdfundinsider.com/2019/08/150490-coinbase-uk-delisting-privacy-coin-zcash/. Accessed 31 October 2021.

[127] John Harvey and Ines Branco-Illodo, 'Why Cryptocurrencies Want Privacy: A Review Of Political Motivations And Branding Expressed In "Privacy Coin" Whitepapers' (2019) 19 Journal of Political Marketing 107, 124–125.

[128] cf Kapilkov (n 119).

some exchanges have delisted Monero and other privacy coins due to concerns around travel rule requirements, information can be shared separately from the crypto-asset transfer, for example, on a separate off-chain communications channel.[129] In any case, the use of off-chain communications may be advisable due to the risk of transfers of personal data on immutable blockchains breaching the data subject's right to erasure ('right to be forgotten') under the GDPR.[130] Where information is shared separately to the crypto-asset transfer via off-chain channels, travel rule compliance is attainable regardless of the crypto-asset's privacy and should not be used as an excuse to shun privacy coins.[131]

Due to their differing risks, the UK's AML regime should distinguish between the different types of privacy coins, and even between different types of transactions using the same coins. More detailed definitions of these types of crypto-assets should be included under the MLRs and within the JMLSG guidance, with bespoke AML requirements and guidance which accounts for the nuances and differing risks of different privacy coins and transactions. For example, specific and stringent AML requirements should apply to the use of opaque privacy coins such as Monero in order to mitigate the associated risks. Conversely, privacy coins such as Zcash and Dash should be subject to less stringent requirements under the MLRs when their privacy-enhancing features are disabled, and the JMLSG should specify in their guidance that such transactions are not to be treated as higher-risk factors by default. This would encourage crypto-asset businesses to adopt an RBA to privacy coin transactions without fears of criticism or punishment by regulators.

[129] FATF, 'Draft updated Guidance for a risk-based approach to virtual assets and VASPs' (*FATF*, 2021) 55 www.fatf-gafi.org/publications/fatfrecommendations/documents/public-consultation-guidance-vasp.html. Accessed 31 October 2021.

[130] Pierre Ostercamp, 'Central Bank Digital Currencies and the GDPR: Reconciling blockchains with the right to be forgotten' (2021) 3 UCL Centre for Blockchain Technologies Discussion Paper Series blockchain.cs.ucl.ac.uk/wp-content/uploads/2021/08/UCLCBT_DPS_Q22021.pdf. Accessed 31 October 2021.

[131] Travel rule solutions provided by firms such as Netki are compatible with privacy coins: Netki, 'TransactID – The Proven Travel Rule Solution' (*Netki*, 2020) netki.com/transactid. Accessed 31 October 2021.

Mixers

Mixers, also known as tumblers or washers, inhibit transaction tracing by mixing together various inputs before sending them to the output addresses.[132] Due to the multiplicity of transaction senders and recipients, it is difficult to identify which users are actually transacting with each other, even on otherwise transparent blockchains such as the Bitcoin blockchain.[133] While the use of mixers does not necessarily signify criminal activity,[134] they pose a higher risk of money laundering than traditional crypto-asset transactions where privacy-enhancement features are not used.[135] Though mixers are deemed high-risk by the JMLSG, there are no specific AML requirements or guidance relating to their use in the UK.[136] The application of the standard AML requirements and guidance of the MLRs and JMLSG depends on the nature of the mixer. Whereas centralised mixers (such as Chip Mixer) would constitute regulated crypto-asset businesses,[137] mixers based on open-source software including non-custodian wallets with integrated mixing functionalities (such as Wasabi Wallet) fall outside of the UK's AML regime.[138]

While various commentators propose that mixers should be required to comply with AML requirements,[139] those which are partly or fully decentralised may have no controlling entity which can be brought within the scope of the AML regime. If stringent requirements were applied to centralised mixing services, criminals would likely turn to unregulated mixers such as non-custodian mixers which

132 cf Moiseienko and Izenman (n 112) 11.

133 cf Fox (n 6) 139, 164; ECB and BoJ, 'Balancing confidentiality and auditability in a distributed ledger environment' (*ECB*, 2020) 13 www.ecb.europa.eu/paym/intro/publications/pdf/ecb.miptopical200212.en.pdf. Accessed 31 October 2021.

134 cf Moiseienko and Izenman (n 112) 24. Chainalysis recently found that of the mixers that they analysed, barely 10% of cryptoassets sent to them derived from criminal activity: Andrey Shevchenko, 'Remaining Anonymous: Which Crypto Privacy Solution Works Best?' (*Cointelegraph*, 2020) cointelegraph.com/news/remaining-anonymous-which-crypto-privacy-solution-works-best. Accessed 31 October 2021.

135 cf JMLSG (n 60) para 22.34.

136 ibid.

137 MLRs reg 14A(1)(b).

138 cf HM Treasury (n 23) 9; cf JMLSG (n 60) para 22.16.

139 cf Haffke et al. (n 21) 133; cf Moiseienko and Izenman (n 112) 11.

would not impose KYC requirements.[140] Since mixers may be unregulated and could facilitate money laundering, regulated crypto-asset businesses play a key role in mitigating the associated risks when receiving funds which have passed through mixers. Those providing on- and off-ramp services have a responsibility to take steps to prevent criminal funds from passing through them into the traditional financial system, and as such should be subject to specific and strict AML requirements under the MLRs for crypto-asset activity involving mixers, such as lower transaction thresholds for the application of due diligence measures.[141] Such requirements would constitute a proportionate response to the money laundering risk in light of the enhanced privacy associated with mixers, and the reliance on crypto-asset businesses as potentially the only regulated entity dealing with customers after mixing has occurred.

Decentralised Finance (DeFi)

DeFi comprises decentralised applications (DApps) providing financial services. DApps are software programs based on smart contracts ('self-executing agreements that are usually written in code in the blockchain'[142]), as such, DeFi protocols can be automated and operate without influence of centralised entities. Due to the lack of intermediaries and the absence or anonymity of individuals exerting control over protocols, it is difficult to apply regulation to DeFi. As such, DeFi remains mostly unregulated in the UK and across the world, except in some cases where a protocol in fact exhibits a degree of centralisation enabling the imposition of regulatory requirements on individuals which control or own the protocol. Since 'anyone in any country can access them with little or no KYC required', DeFi protocols have increasingly been exploited for the purpose of money laundering via crypto-assets, and are 'the next major threat vector for fraud

140 Chainalysis, 'The Chainalysis 2020 Crypto Crime Report' (*Chainalysis*, 2020) 81 blog.chainalysis.com/reports/cryptocurrency-crime-2020-report. Accessed 31 October 2021.

141 cf Moiseienko and Izenman (n 112) 24.

142 Florian Möslein, 'Conflicts of Laws and Codes: Defining the Boundaries of Digital Jurisdictions' in Philipp Hacker et al. (eds), *Regulating Blockchain: Techno-Social and Legal Challenges – An Introduction* (Oxford University Press 2019) 275.

and money laundering'.[143] Notably, Decentralised Exchanges (DEXes) can be exploited for money laundering purposes as they enable users to exchange crypto-assets without completing KYC or other regulatory requirements. DEXes are P2P exchanges based on smart contracts. P2P exchanges facilitate the matching of buyers and sellers of crypto-assets, and may act as an intermediary in trades.[144] Since the definition of crypto-asset business under the MLRs includes those 'arranging or making arrangements with a view to the exchange' of crypto-assets, P2P exchange platforms may be within the scope of the MLRs.[145] Whether or not P2P exchanges are regulated, or can be regulated, depends on their design and governance structure. In the UK, the scope of the MLRs does not include P2P exchange platforms which only allow participants to share bids and offers before trades are executed outside of the exchange, such as through private crypto-asset wallets.[146] Even where the MLRs are applicable, some P2P exchanges, including most DEXes, 'can be maintained by a dispersed community of users and therefore be highly resistant to attempts at regulating or closing it down'.[147]

Due to their decentralised nature, subjecting DEXes to AML requirements may be difficult or even impossible: it would require individuals who own or control the platform to be identified and regulated, and certain DEXes are under no such control.[148] DEXes may therefore fall outside of the scope of the MLRs,[149] and associated individuals such as software developers are more likely to fall outside of the MLRs if they do not profit or benefit from the DEX activity.[150] While DEXes may pose higher risks of money laundering, these risks could be mitigated by the AML requirements and supervision of

[143] CipherTrace, 'Cryptocurrency Crime and Anti-Money Laundering Report 2021' (*CipherTrace*, 2021) 6, 13 ciphertrace.com/wp-content/uploads/2021/01/CipherTrace-Cryptocurrency-Crime-and-Anti-Money-Laundering-Report-012821.pdf. Accessed 31 October 2021.

[144] cf FATF (n 66) 15.

[145] MLRs reg 14A(1).

[146] The JMLSG specified that the definition of 'cryptoasset business' under the MLRs did not intend to include P2P buyer and seller forums: cf JMLSG (n 60) para 22.11.

[147] cf Moiseienko and Izenman (n 112) 7.

[148] cf Blandin et al. (n 103) 52; cf Moiseienko and Izenman (n 112) 10.

[149] cf JMLSG (n 60) para 22.12.

[150] ibid.

regulated entities they interact with.[151] Regulated crypto-asset businesses should be aware of the higher risks associated with unregulated exchanges and take them into account when conducting risk assessments and due diligence. Further, specific and strict AML requirements should apply under the MLRs to crypto-asset businesses when conducting transactions involving unregulated exchanges, such as requirements to conduct due diligence at lower transaction thresholds. However, there are also risks that stringent AML requirements imposed on crypto-asset businesses would encourage both criminals and consumers to transact exclusively on unregulated exchanges to avoid KYC requirements, which would likely reduce regulatory visibility and impair the overall effectiveness of the AML regime.[152]

Some DeFi activities and associated crypto-assets may already fall within the FCA's regulatory perimeter, including activity involving regulated security tokens and e-money tokens.[153] While the UK government is considering the merits and feasibility of bringing specific DeFi activities within the regulatory perimeter, proposals are yet to be made.[154] In its recent updated guidance, the FATF clarified that its definitions of VA and VASP are intended to be expansive.[155] Similarly to the MLRs, however, their applicability to DeFi depends on the specific protocol, associated individuals, and the level of decentralisation.[156] According to the FATF's guidance, although DApps themselves would not qualify as VASPs, DApp creators, owners, operators, or others with 'control or sufficient influence in the DeFi arrangements' may be considered VASPs.[157] The FATF suggests considerations in identifying VASPs, such as which entities profit from or can make changes to the DeFi arrangement, yet discretion is left to countries to identify VASPs

[151] ECB Crypto-Assets Task Force, 'Crypto-Assets: Implications for financial stability, monetary policy, and payments and market infrastructures' (*ECB*, 2019) 29 www.ecb.europa.eu/pub/pdf/scpops/ecb.op223~3ce14e986c.en.pdf. Accessed 31 October 2021.

[152] cf FATF (n 22) 17.

[153] HM Treasury, 'UK regulatory approach to cryptoassets and stablecoins: consultation and call for evidence' (*HM Treasury*, 2021) 34 www.gov.uk/government/consultations/uk-regulatory-approach-to-cryptoassets-and-stablecoinsstablecoin-consultation-and-call-for-evidence. Accessed 31 October 2021.

[154] ibid.

[155] cf FATF (n 67) 5.

[156] ibid., 26–28.

[157] ibid.

in the DeFi sector on a case-by-case basis.[158] Similarly, FinCEN's 2019 guidance states that DApps and their owners or operators may be subject to US AML requirements, yet no detail is given on how these entities could be identified or subject to regulation.[159]

Due to the lack of detail and examples in the guidance to support identification of VASPs in the DeFi sector, and the considerable practical difficulties in regulating DeFi, application of the FATF recommendations to DeFi remains unclear. This lack of clarity leaves scope for regulatory arbitrage arising from inconsistent implementation of the recommendations across jurisdictions, and this risk should be addressed through further, more detailed guidance from the FATF around the application of its recommendations to DeFi. Equally, the application of the MLRs to DeFi is unclear, and clarification should be provided in guidance issued by the FCA or the JMLSG, notably on specific circumstances and examples in which DeFi arrangements and associated individuals may fall within the scope of the MLRs.

8.5 Conclusion

Overall, the UK's AML regime for crypto-assets is relatively comprehensive, aligning with of the FATF recommendations to cover a wide range of crypto-asset activities including crypto-to-crypto exchange. The regime is effective in tackling crypto-asset money laundering by requiring crypto-asset businesses to collect the information necessary to identify criminals from pseudonymous transactions, identify and manage risks, and report suspicions to the NCA. However, while these measures are effective in preventing money laundering in the areas within the scope of the regime, various gaps and inadequacies in the regime remain, and these allow money laundering risks to persist. Notably, these include the range of privacy-enhancing technologies which are specifically recognised by the JMLSG as higher-risk factors[160] yet are not subject to specific requirements under the MLRs and also lack specific guidance from the JMLSG. While the omission of specific requirements under the MLRs affords crypto-asset businesses more flexibility to adopt an RBA, some minimum requirements are

158 ibid.
159 cf FinCEN (n 32) 18.
160 cf JMLSG (n 60) para 22.34.

necessary with respect to higher-risk factors. For example, specific and strict requirements should be imposed on activity involving opaque privacy coins, mixers, and unregulated exchanges. Conversely, guidance on generally higher-risk factors should specify the situations in which these factors may actually be deemed low- or medium-risk, such as privacy coins when used without their privacy features. This would encourage crypto-asset businesses to adopt an RBA rather than shun various types of crypto-assets or activities due to them being labelled as higher risk. In addition, given the ambiguity under the MLRs and relevant guidance, the JMLSG or the FCA should issue updated guidance clarifying the application of the MLRs to DeFi, including details and examples of when DeFi arrangements and associated individuals would fall within the scope of the MLRs.

Another potentially higher-risk factor which should be specifically addressed in the MLRs and the JMLSG guidance is the use of private crypto-asset wallets. As it stands, crypto-asset businesses may transact with private wallets but should bear in mind the potential risks since private wallets are unregulated. Associated risks can be mitigated through a range of methods including those suggested by the FATF in its guidance. Crypto-asset businesses could also manage risks by requiring that customers provide information relating to their private wallet transactions, though the potential for customers to provide inaccurate information could conflict with the aims of the travel rule. Both the FATF and the JMLSG should provide more guidance on this matter, especially to support compliance once the UK imposes travel rule obligations on crypto-asset businesses. In addition, blockchain analytics can support risk assessments with respect to private wallet activities, helping crypto-asset businesses to adopt an appropriate RBA to this area.[161]

Looking to the future, even under a more robust regime with widespread travel rule compliance, the UK's AML regime may lack effectiveness in tackling crypto-asset money laundering in the event of the widespread adoption of crypto-assets in everyday use. Currently, the focus of crypto-asset regulation in the UK and worldwide

[161] Companies such as Coinfirm offer risk assessments for private wallets based on blockchain analytics: Coinfirm, 'Full Audit Trail' (*Coinfirm*, 2020) www.coinfirm.com/wp-content/uploads/2020/06/case002_03.pdf. Accessed 31 October 2021.

is on the regulation of on- and off-ramps and other intermediary service providers. However, widespread adoption of crypto-assets could enable their everyday use without the need for intermediary services, reducing the ability of regulatory authorities to detect and identify criminals via regulation of service providers. This would facilitate the use of cryptoassets for the purpose of money laundering and stimulate growth in P2P markets which may fall outside of the regulatory framework.[162] Though various solutions could address this issue, such as the imposition of restrictions on P2P exchanges and on service providers enabling transfers to and from private wallets, strict regulation would risk driving crypto-asset activity into unregulated or opaque areas such as DeFi and privacy coins.[163] In this case, the crypto-asset industry may take on the form of a two-tier system in which the top tier is regulated under the UK's AML regime, while the bottom 'underground' tier is unregulated and primarily or exclusively P2P. Tight controls would need to be imposed on the traffic between the two tiers to ensure that the potentially higher risks of unregulated crypto-assets and activities are identified and managed.

[162] cf JMLSG (n 60) para 22.34.
[163] cf FATF (n 22) 15.

9 *Triple-Entry Accounting, Blockchain, and Next of Kin*

Towards a Standardisation of Ledger Terminology

JUAN IGNACIO IBAÑEZ, CHRIS N. BAYER, PAOLO TASCA, AND JIAHUA XU

9.1 Introduction

Triple-entry accounting (TEA) is one of the most innovative concepts of the past decades. It introduces a shared transaction record that constitutes a single source of truth, which is secured through triple-signed receipts and is usually maintained by means of blockchain. This idea was first introduced through Ian Grigg's Ricardo Payment System beginning in 1995. In 1998, Todd Boyle independently started to develop shared transaction repositories (STRs), with some influence from William E. McCarthy's resource-event-agent (REA) accounting model. In 2004, Grigg and Boyle converged, and the latter's work was integrated onto the former's (Ibañez et al., 2023).

While TEA is extremely innovative, 'there is a dearth in academic research on the topic (TEA), which is extremely limited' (Cai, 2019). This includes attempts to specify the meaning of the terms at use. Meanwhile, practitioners appear not to be putting much effort into a comprehensive conceptualisation of TEA and related terms. In turn, they focus on the technical aspects of their product, while taking the vocabulary for granted. This is illustrated by the fact that most companies developing or commercialising TEA projects rarely specify the terms used in their whitepapers.

The concept of TEA is thus rarely defined. It appears, however, that it is often assumed to mean a shared ledger – and, if blockchain technology is used, it is advertised as a decentralised shared ledger. Nonetheless, were TEA equivalent to a shared ledger, there would be no need for the concept of TEA in the first place, which suggests instead that a TEA system is a sub-type of shared ledger.

Matters are complicated further by the question of whether Bitcoin is a TEA system. It is often described as one (Grigg, 2011; Tyra, 2014) but the reason therefore is unclear. Furthermore, were this to be the case, it would pose the question of whether all other cryptocurrencies are also TEA use cases. If they were all also TEA use cases, one would be left to wonder what distinguishes those products specifically advertised as TEA.

Consider furthermore that it is speculated that TEA was one of the influences behind Bitcoin itself (Ibañez et al., 2023), that is, behind the use case introducing blockchain technology as such. This raises the question of whether there is anything intrinsically TEA-like in blockchain technology, meaning that blockchains would constitute TEA by definition and that the term 'blockchain-based TEA systems' would be redundant, or the two concepts are not in perfect overlap.

This leads to the enquiry of what blockchain is, as well as what (if any) difference lies with the concept of distributed ledger technology or DLT. Nevertheless, these notions are also elusive: the prime characteristic of a DLT is not that it is distributed, as distributed systems need not be DLT. Many maintain that what distinguishes DLT from other shared ledger systems is not that DLT is distributed, but that it is decentralised (Fresno, 2018; TradeIX, 2018). However, a number of DLTs are not fully decentralised in every possible way. Bitcoin, for instance, displays centralisation in its mining pools (Kimani, 2018). Nevertheless, it would be hard to argue that this makes Bitcoin any less of a DLT.

A number of papers have attempted to build a taxonomy for blockchain/DLT systems (Ballandies et al., 2018; Beinke et al., 2018; Garay and Kiayias, 2020; Glaser and Bezzenberger, 2015; Ibañez et al., 2023; Ismail et al., 2019; Labazova et al., 2019; Mohsin et al., 2019; Sarkintudu et al., 2018; Tasca and Tessone, 2019; Walsh et al., 2016). Nevertheless, these works tend to focus on organising existing and possible systems into typologies, usually taking the higher-level categories for granted.[1]

For the reasons explained above, there is a deficit in this field of research. Existing categories are insufficient to give a proper account of TEA. This includes extant blockchain taxonomies.

[1] For an exception, see Rauchs et al. (2018).

This chapter sets out to fill in this gap. We build on existing research that describes the taxonomy and landscape of accounting and DLT. We find that an adequate terminology to give account of TEA requires the introduction of accounting vocabulary, not just for TEA, but also for DLT in general.

With this goal in mind, this chapter is structured in the following manner: first, we lay out the methods employed. Second, we present a background discussion of the distinction between distributed systems and decentralised systems, as well as the one between accounting and book-keeping, and journals and ledgers. Third, we define TEA and specify the architecture of a TEA system. Fourth, based on the previous steps, we attempt to standardise terminology, to clarify misunderstandings and set the stage for further analysis. Fifth, we conclude the chapter with summary observations and recommendations for further research.

9.2 Methodology

Approaching the topic from the perspective of accounting theory and practice, this chapter reviews usage in TEA use cases identified in Ibañez et al. (2021) by consulting their whitepapers. It further elaborates on the categories relevant to TEA and of the architectural requirements and possibilities of a TEA system. This is done, first, through a literature review. The literature consulted, quoted throughout the chapter, notably covers the disciplines of accounting and computing in general, and of TEA, cryptography, DLT, and blockchain in particular. Second, we conduct key informant interviews per phone or email correspondence with salient individuals in the world of TEA. The interviewees are listed in Section 9.5.

9.3 Results

Our research yielded the following findings the coherent usage of accounting vocabulary is necessary for a proper apprehension of TEA, DLT systems, and blockchain. It has been often stated that 'blockchain is fundamentally an accounting technology' (ICAEW, 2018), yet not only have the main usages of the blockchain so far, for example, cryptocurrencies – not been about accounting, but also accounting terminology has been used with excessive latitude until the present.

In this direction, we find that the specificity of DLT-based TEA systems can only be apprehended by applying the distinction, used in the accounting discipline, between book-keeping and accounting (Ibañez, 2022). Furthermore, we find that the distinction between journals and ledgers as the two possible types of books is also important to sustain this specificity. Moreover, we find that a correct conceptualisation of the term DLT requires preliminary awareness of series of contrasts.

This section contains a detailed presentation of our findings.

Conceptualisation of TEA in Whitepapers

As explained in the Introduction, TEA is a concept used in whitepapers, but seldom defined. This emerges from the consultation of the white papers of the TEA use cases identified in Ibañez et al. (2021). For instance, The Accounting Blockchain's whitepaper simply defines TEA as the act of recording a transaction in the sets of books of the two parties to the transactions simultaneously and does no further attempt at conceptualisation (AB, 2018).

Similarly, Provenance Blockchain does not mention the concept of TEA in its whitepaper (Figure Technologies), despite having been advertised as a TEA use paper by board member Pompliano (2019). The same is the case of another TEA use case: Auditchain (2018). In interviews conducted with Jason Meyers (founder of Auditchain) and Anthony Pompliano, both confirmed that the product put forward by their companies constituted TEA use cases.

Similarly, Open Transactions' whitepaper only states that 'we proposed the use of triple-signed receipts' (Odom, 2015), without further explanation. Request's whitepaper solely claims that 'it represents a switch from double-entry accounting to triple-entry accounting' (Request, 2018), also without further explanation. This is also the case for Ledgerium's whitepaper, which only mentions that 'we utilise a decentralised ledger through a triple entry accounting system' (Mehmood et al., 2019).

In a similar fashion, Corda's sole public explanation of the term is that the design was 'inspired by previous work, including that (...) on triple entry accounting' (Brown, 2018: 17). Similarly, PayPie (2018: 5) only explains that 'Adding blockchain record in the world of debit and credit effectively creates a triple entry accounting system'. Only

Pacio (2020) whitepaper contains some conceptual effort, with a detailed Standardised Semantic Information Model describing how its TEA system would work, as well as prerequisites for a functional TEA system.

Preliminary Concepts: Decentralisation, Distribution, Accounting, and DLT

In this section, we point out the distinction between distributed and decentralised systems, together with the divide between (triple-entry) accounting and (triple-entry) book-keeping, and between distributed book technology (DBT), distributed journal technology (DJT), and DLT.

The Distinction Between the Centralised, the Decentralised, and the Distributed

In 1964, Baran (1964) claimed that there were two types of networks: 'centralised (or star) and distributed (or grid or mesh)'. Baran also argued that 'in practice, a mixture of star and mesh is used to form communication networks (…) a "decentralised" network'. Baran's typology is shown in Figure 9.1.

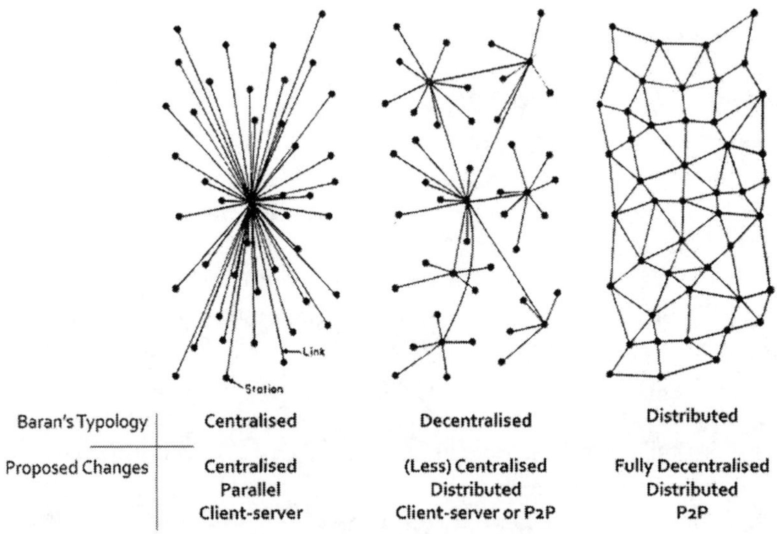

Figure 9.1 Centralised, decentralised and distributed networks according to Baran (1964) and revised categories

This distinction has found wide adoption within the blockchain community, but results are anachronistic. Fundamentally, it does not match current use in computing, and thus creates a series of false impressions (see also Buterin 2017). In fact, the names applicable to the second and third diagrams should arguably be reversed (Grange, 2016).

Despite not capturing the distinction between systems that are centralised by design and systems that moved to a degree of centralisation from an originally decentralised design, Baran's illustration of a centralised network is not controversial. However, the depiction of a decentralised network could be challenged, on the grounds that there is a centre to the network. Moreover, Baran appears to depict decentralisation as equivalent to deconcentration of functions. Although the fact that some nodes are shown as more connected than others is not problematic in itself, the depiction of decentralisation as a central node delegating connections to intermediate centres may lead to confusion.

Currently, a better understanding for the term 'decentralised' is, as the name suggests, a system lacking a (decision-making and single point of failure)[2] centre. The Internet is an example of a decentralised system. While there is still no ultimate centre, the Internet is also not fully decentralised, as there are a number of decision-making centres or 'hubs' within its structure. Cash transactions, by definition, are almost completely decentralised. Therefore, there is a gradient between the centralised and the fully decentralised, in the middle of which the partly decentralised exists.

Whether a system is distributed, in turn, is an entirely different affair. In a distributed computing system, each independent computer or node (with a local memory) communicates with the others through message-passing. This comes in opposition to the alternative of having one shared memory, that is, of being a 'parallel system', such that the collection of independent nodes appears to the users as a single computer (van Steen and Tanenbaum, 2016). For instance, if the customer of a bank notices no difference between doing a transaction in

[2] According to Ethereum co-founder Vitalik Buterin, to the two aforementioned dimensions of decentralisation (political and architectural, respectively) one should add a third one: logical decentralisation, namely whether the system's interface looks monolithic or not. 'One simple heuristic is: if you cut the system in half, including both providers and users, will both halves continue to fully operate as independent units?' (Buterin, 2017).

one office of a bank and another one on the other side of the country (despite there being numerous computers in the system, plus a master computer per office and a central computer at the headquarters), it is a distributed system (van Steen and Tanenbaum, 2016).

What Baran's third diagram shows is not what is currently known as a distributed network, but a purely peer-to-peer (P2P) network. A distributed system may be centralised or decentralised. A P2P system is a particular type of distributed system in which the clients also act as servers: they share their hardware resources for other users to access without the need for intermediaries, that is, they are 'servents' (clients + servers) – in contrast to the client/server model. As a result, it is usually decentralised.

A P2P system may have a central entity, but if this is the case, it is known as hybrid P2P system. Pure P2P systems are decentralised: the nodes are equipotent and, thus, there are no hubs (Schollmeier, 2001). File-sharing mechanisms such as Napster and BitTorrent constitute examples of P2P systems. Bitcoin is an example of a P2P system that has ended up forming hubs (mining pools) and thus does not exhibit full decentralisation.

In conclusion, as shown in Figure 9.2, whether a system is decentralised (or centralised), distributed (or parallel), and/or P2P (or client/server) depends on the answer to different questions. The anachronism given by the application of Baran's typology misconstrues this as if 'centralised', 'decentralised' and 'distributed' were three possible answers to one common question, which is not the case.

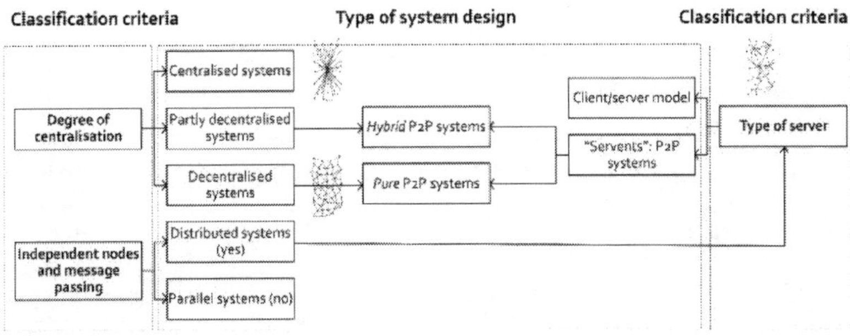

Figure 9.2 Whether a computing system is centralised, decentralised, distributed, or peer-to-peer (P2P) constitutes in each case an answer to a different question. The categories should thus not be construed as a continuum

The Difference Between Book-keeping and Accounting
This chapter distinguishes types of triple-entry systems based on whether they merely keep a shared record of transactions, or whether they undertake a more complex processing task on the basis of that information. For this purpose, the distinction between book-keeping and accounting is used (Ibañez et al., 2023; Ibañez, 2022). However, we should note that the meanings assigned to recordkeeping, book-keeping, and accounting in the literature are not completely homogeneous.

This dispute is difficult to settle because the peer-reviewed literature has not directly dealt with this question. At best, published papers spend no more than one sentence on each term, whereas handbooks and manuals provide definitions outright without justifying them.

While some believe that there is no difference between book-keeping and accounting (Ibañez et al., 2023), most do. Edwards (1960), for example, claims that recordkeeping would be to preserve the documentary evidence of a particular transaction. Book-keeping, in turn, would be a historical stage that came after recordkeeping and consists of 'analysing, classifying, and recording transactions'. Finally, the ulterior stage of accounting is 'bookkeeping with additional refinements of financial summarisation and a control function added'.

However, the majority position seems to be that book-keeping and ('mere') recordkeeping are synonyms, whereas accounting 'builds on top of bookkeeping to make that information flow to the decision-making areas of the firm, by means of systematising, compiling, collating, synthesising, processing, analysing and/or auditing' (Ibañez et al., 2023; Ibañez, 2022). This position is found in the peer-reviewed literature (Rukhiran and Netinant, 2018; Vollmer, 2003) and in many instruction manuals and handbooks (Jnr, 1977; Ge, 2005; Mutero et al., 2017; Peters-Richardson, 2011; Wild et al., 2011). This is the distinction that we follow.[3]

We find that the suggestion by Grigg (2017b, 2019) – see also Ibañez et al. (2023); Ibañez (2022) – of importing this distinction to the classification of triple-entry systems allows to apprehend their differences

[3] In practice, this differentiation still leaves some room for debate. One may argue over where the line between accounting and book-keeping lies, since, for example, when recording a transaction, some classification may be involved, but only through the mechanical application of rules discovered or invented in the accounting profession.

better. It is thus recommendable to differentiate between triple-entry book-keeping (TEB) and TEA. TEB systems simply record transactions in a triple-entry fashion (e.g., Bitcoin, see Grigg (2011); Ibañez et al. (2023)) and TEA systems involve an accounting software built on a layer of TEB (Ibañez, 2022).

An Accounting Typology for Blockchain-inspired Technology

With the aforementioned categories clarified, we can proceed to establish a typology that functions as a proper 'toolbox' to give an account of the TEA phenomenon. Before explaining triple-entry recordkeeping, we need to understand recordkeeping itself.

Recordkeeping is also known as book-keeping because the instrument where a firm's transactions with other companies are recorded is called a 'book'. The book where transaction raw data is first recorded – sequentially – is called a journal. Accounting records are different from book-keeping records in that transactions are recorded analytically, rather than just sequentially: transactions are classified so that the resulting record shows information that is meaningful for business life (for instance, it facilitates decision-making or financial reporting). Thus, the accounting process takes the information from the journal and posts it in a second book, where information is organised analytically. This book is known as ledger. In consequence, *accounting happens in ledgers, whereas book-keeping is limited to journals.*

If the two companies engaging in a transaction use the same book, it is known as a shared book. It is hard to conceive a shared book on paper. Rather, shared books are generally held in computer systems common to (or connected to) both firms. Computer systems may be parallel or distributed. If the book is held on a distributed system, it is a *distributed book*. If, as a consequence of being unable to trust each other (i.e., being *adversarial*), the computers (nodes) in the system resort to verification techniques to maintain a consensus[4] about the transaction history, the technology for this distributed book receives a particular industry name: DBT.[5]

[4] Trust and consensus solve are ways to implement the 'what you see is what I see' principle, known by the WYSIWIS acronym.

[5] For examples of usage of the term DBT, see Liu and Yu (2018).

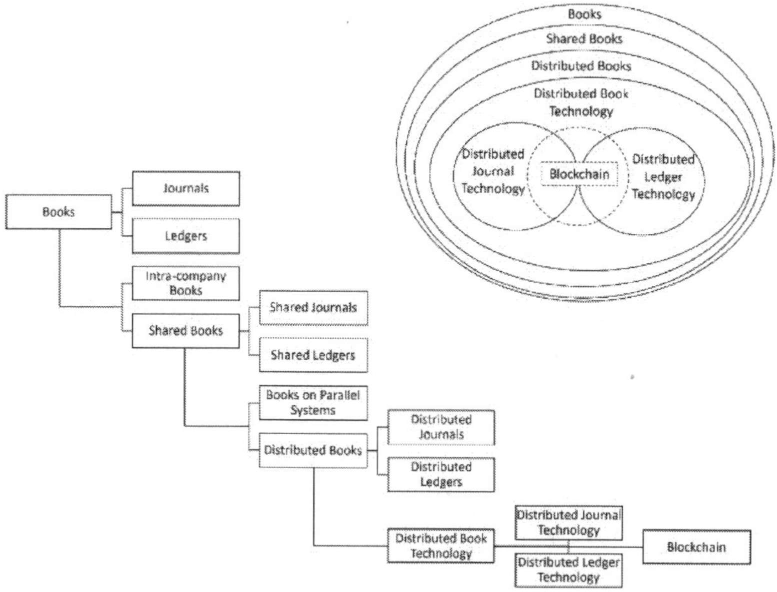

Figure 9.3 A representation, from an accounting perspective, of the 'family tree' of categories of DLT, the technology to which TEA systems usually resort to (though in principle it is not required)

If the DBT record is a journal, the system may be called DJT. If it is ledger, DLT.[6] Hence, under a proper usage of accounting terminology, and because *not all books are ledgers*, DLT is thus a subtype of DBT, despite the former usually being mistaken for the latter.

A particular subtype of DBT is known as 'blockchain'. Blockchain's main characteristic is that transaction data is stored in data packages called 'blocks' which include cryptographic references to previous blocks, thus forming a chain of blocks. All blockchains are DBT, but not all DBT is blockchained. However, DBT is based on/inspired by blockchain. Therefore, blockchains and DBT are in the same industry category.[7]

Figure 9.3 describes these categories in a more systematic manner.

[6] For works advocating a proper usage of the terms DLT and DJT, see Rauchs et al. (2018), University of Derby (2019) and Shea (2015).

[7] This definition is not shared by all. Odom (personal communication, 27 February 2020), for instance, claims that blockchains and DLT are the same, and that they are necessarily PoW-based decentralised systems: 'There is no such actual thing as a "DLT" unless it includes proof-of-work. Any such

The Concept of Triple-entry Accounting

The purpose of this section is threefold. First, to describe TEA as a three-dimensional (3D) accounting device which comes to address certain problems in traditional, redundant, double-entry accounting (as it was originally described by Todd Boyle). Second, we define what TEA is. Third, we enumerate the essential and nonessential features of a TEA system.

Three-dimensional Accounting

Although there are at least two parties to a transaction, the transaction is just one economic event. However, the parties keep historically independent and mirroring records of this event. In other words, there are two records for each transaction. A sale, for instance, is 'recorded into receivables by a seller, (...) [and] as a purchase, into accounts payable by a buyer' (Boyle, 2000b). Furthermore, each party records the transaction in a double-entry manner. 'That's quadruple entry. Since every transaction in the developed world also causes quadruple entries when it clears [through] a bank, that's octuple entry' (Boyle (2000b); italics are ours). We can call this 'redundant book-keeping'.

Any triple-entry system is an interparty book-keeping system which eliminates this redundancy: there is a shared transaction repository keeping a single record of the transaction. Boyle (2003a, c), see also Ibañez et al. (2023), explains that, in this context, book-keeping becomes at least 3D, because there is a need to represent transactions from the viewpoint of its two parties (even if stored in a viewpoint-independent manner): the sending side and the receiving side. Attempts at representing three dimensions in two dimensions will necessarily result in redundancy, that is, recording the same transaction over and over (e.g., different, mirroring books for each party to the transaction).

Historically, 3D accounting records were not available. At present, however, computer-based shared ledgers can maintain a shared record in a 3D manner. Ibañez et al. (2023) provide a representation of 3D[8] accounting as explained in Figure 9.4.

project without proof-of-work is actually under centralised control, though it may contain "distributed" elements in its design'.

[8] More dimensions can be added, resulting in a hypercube (Boyle, 2003a).

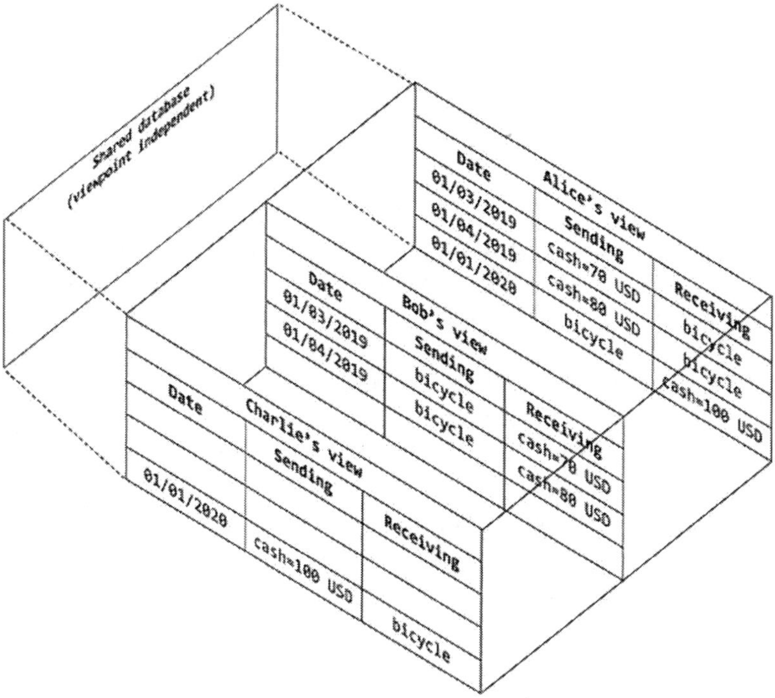

Figure 9.4 Three-dimensional accounting, in which N sheets equal the N parties to the system (Ibañez et al. (2023); based on Boyle (2003a, c)).

Triple-entry Accounting: A Concept

TEB is a particular proposal for a shared transaction record (and thus, for 3D accounting). It relies on signed receipts to reach an agreement on the content of the shared record. As explained by Ibañez et al. (2023):

In order to update the shared record with a new transaction record, two parties need to be involved: one initiates a transaction entry – called "request", "offer" or "transaction draft" – and the other accepts it. This can be seen as a signature-gathering process: one party adds their signature to the transaction entry draft and the counterparty accepts by countersigning, before the entry gets processed by the STR which can be a middleware server or a distributed ledger; the STR checks the validity of the signatures and then, if everything is in order, signs off on the entry (…). This generates a hashed triple-signed receipt, such that all the parties hold the same data that cannot be manipulated or lost: a single, shared entry serving as the single source of truth.

The two fathers of TEB, Ian Grigg and Todd Boyle, conceived this sort of three-pronged consensus mechanism. However, it is worth noting that only Grigg named the system 'triple-entry' because of the tripartite consensus involving three signed messages (Grigg, 2005; Ibañez et al., 2023). Boyle (2001a, b) called it in this manner because he had envisioned two (optional) private transaction stubs on top of the shared entry for the parties to insert nonessential data[9]. (Ibañez, 2022).

As anticipated, based on the prior distinction between book-keeping and accounting, we can conceive something beyond a 'mere' shared record of transactions: a triple-entry system with an accounting solution. This constitutes TEA. TEB requires a shared journal, whereas TEA requires either a shared ledger or a shared journal enabling individual ledgers. Given that accounting presupposes book-keeping (see Ibañez et al. 2023), but the reverse is not true, all TEA systems are TEB systems, but not all TEB systems have an accounting layer.

Note that a TEA system is not bound to any particular technology, but most current TEA systems resort to DLT. Bitcoin is a well-known triple-entry system using DBT (Ibañez, 2022) but, since it does not have an accounting layer, it is not TEA and does not involve a distributed ledger. Strictly speaking, Bitcoin is a TEB system with DJT technology.

Note too that the three entries in TEA are not three mirroring records of a transaction, but three signature entries or signed messages. This means that TEA records may be compatible with both a single-entry and a double-entry representation of transactions.[10]

Criteria for TEA With the categories discussed in the previous subsection in mind, we can establish that a TEA system has intrinsic requisites and two near-essential features, numbered below. Furthermore, we have identified 14 important characteristics that a TEA system may have, despite them not being definitionally essential.

9 For a discussion of the many possible meanings of the word 'entry' and whether TEA should be called 'single-entry' instead of 'triple-entry', see Ibañez et al. (2023).

10 For a more detailed discussion of the polysemy of the term 'entry', see Ibañez et al. (2023).

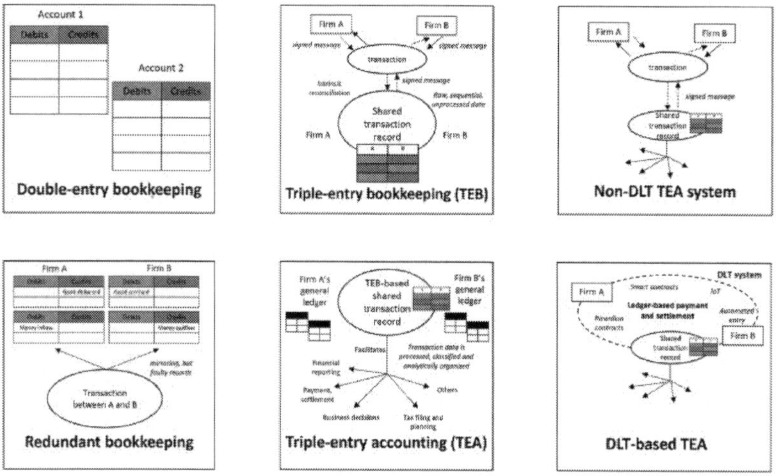

Figure 9.5 DLT-based TEA systems in comparison with other categories. Note that TEA systems may not only record, but also enable the transaction, that the record is shared between the parties (intrinsic reconciliation, unlike traditional, redundant book-keeping), and that transaction data is processed and organised to facilitate business life.

TEA – Operational Criteria

(a) Shared transaction record (single truth): a TEA system keeps a record of the transactions between two or more unrelated parties in a shared journal or ledger. This condition is informed by the *What You See Is What I See (WYSIWIS)* principle.[11]

(b) Three-pronged consensus: either in a digital cheque model through three signed messages resulting in a triple-signed receipt (sequential offer-acceptance-validation structure) or in a digital cash model with asynchronous acceptance.

(c) Ledger/accounting layer: transactions should not just be recorded in an unprocessed manner. Raw transaction data should be fed to each party's general ledger or it should be processed in such a way that it facilitates corporate life (decision-making, financial analysis and forecasting, invoicing, tax planning, financial reporting, etc.).

[11] The WYSIWIS principle does not preclude the possibility of restricted viewing permissions, as long as the information that both parties have still emerged from a central, shared record.

Near-essential Features

(a) Immutability of transactions: while a shared record solves the problem of redundant/duplicate records, it creates a security challenge (on top of the pre-existing possibility of tampering). This is the need to trust that the other party will not alter the dominating record in their favour. Immutability of transactions fixes this problem.

In principle, a TEA system without this security feature is conceivable. However, Grigg's three-way consensus through digitally signed receipts ensures immutability by design. Furthermore, the low degree of trust characterising businesses since before the first double-entry systems, makes the immutability of the shared record of transactions such a practical imperative that it can be regarded as an essential requisite. This has historically been the case.[12]

Note that since no system can be regarded to be absolutely immutable, the word 'immutability' should be applied within reasonable bounds to systems that are significantly harder to modify than their competitors. Furthermore, as noted in Ibañez et al. (2021), immutability should not be absolute as it is also necessary to acknowledge that business process is often tentative and unfinished.

(b) Digital character: it is hard to maintain an analogical shared transaction record unless one of the parties is willing to entrust the other with the maintenance of the record. Because TEA is itself a concept designed for this kind of trust not to be needed, a digital system results in a practical imperative.

(c) Digital identity verification: although Grigg claimed that digital cash systems do not depend on identity (Saia et al., 2021), the TEA whitepaper proposed binding identity in a Ricardian contract. Boyle (2003g) argued that a TEA system requires at least an alias, which means it cannot be a completely anonymous system.[13]

[12] Grigg (2005) called for a secure, 'reliable', 'bullet proof accounting system', to 'keep a record safe' from unconsented changes, fraud and theft. 'Computer science introduces concepts such as transactions, which are defined as units of work that are atomic, consistent, isolated, and durable' (Grigg (2005) italics are ours). Boyle (2000d) also stated that the economics of a public transaction record depend 'on achieving security, which is why he proposed a "true, unforgeable record"'. See also Pacio (2020).

[13] Boyle (2003f) went beyond to state that there is also a practical requisite to comply with anti-terrorism and anti-money laundering legislation.

In practice, most TEA systems will need to consider identity for practical reasons.

Architectural Add-ons

(a) Network-based settlement/payment: in theory, a TEA system can function as a mere archive, recording transactions common to two or more parties that conduct their dealings elsewhere. However, if the network both enables and records payment, an enhancement in efficiency may be achieved (Boyle, 1999, 2001b, 2003b).

(b) Smart contracts-enabling network: network-based settlement/payment does not presuppose smart contracts, but the latter might increase the value of the former feature by making the network more versatile. Furthermore, smart contracts may play a role in automating accounting practices (Ibañez et al., 2023).

(c) Ricardian contract-enabling network: neither network-based settlement/payment nor smart contracts imply Ricardian contracts, but the latter might enhance the appeal of the former by improving the legal standing of network-based transactions.

(d) Distributed ledger (more than one node): the shared ledger is set up on a system of distributed computing, that is, with independent nodes communicating through message passing.
  - DLT: the distributed ledger is a decentralised, blockchained, or blockchain-inspired system for nodes lacking mutual trust.
    - Blockchain (permissioned or otherwise): a blockchain is not necessary to enable, notify, store, and timestamp transactions. However, it might prove to be the most efficient method to do all of the above.

(e) 'Stub – shared entry – stub' structure: to enable the recording of information that is non-essential from the shared perspective, but that could be very important for each party's internal accounting.

(f) General ledger for transactions: a TEA system need not involve a master record of a firm's transactions. Nevertheless, if it did so, the system would be in a position to compete with other general ledger software accounting solutions (see Ibañez et al. 2021).

(g) General ledger for reporting: to facilitate financial reporting, tax reporting, sales reporting, etc., is not an essential feature of a TEA system, but its presence may improve the system's appeal.

(h) Viewing permissions: a TEA repository with recorded transactions may be public (e.g., gossip protocols) or private. A private TEA could, for example, be encrypted, only allowing people with access rights to view the transactions (Boyle, 2000c, 2001a, 2003b, d). However, making this optional for each transaction, 'according to entity preference', would constitute a valuable feature (Pacio, 2020).

Other Features

(a) Scalability and high throughput: to be viable to meet business needs in the modern world (Barett et al., 2019; Pacio, 2020).
(b) Compliance with financial regulations: to improve the appeal of the system (Pacio, 2020).
(c) Affordability: so that even small businesses can use the system (Auditchain, 2018; Pacio, 2020).
(d) User-friendliness: so that even small businesses can use the system (Boyle, 2000a; Hildebrand, 2018; Pacio, 2020).

Glossary Table

Having defined TEA and explicated the concepts necessary to apprehend the specificity of the notion and its implementation, we can proceed to summarise some of the most fundamental terms to explain TEA.

Book	A record of transactions. It may be either a journal or a ledger.
Journal	The book of first entry where raw (unprocessed) transaction data is recorded sequentially.
Ledger	The book of second/final entry to which the transactions recorded in a journal are processed and imported ('posted'), but in an analytical order.
General ledger	A master collection of books containing all of a company's transactions (usually in a summarised form, as subsidiary ledgers – subledgers – contain the details). It is the central transaction repository. In software applications, this repository is often split in two modules (Boyle, 2003e): • The General Ledger for Transactions (GLT), where objectively verifiable transaction data is posted; and • The General Ledger for Reporting (GLR), where the architecture of the ledger is reorganised through subjective adjustments to serve downstream integration and reporting requirements.

Shared book	A shared journal or shared ledger.
Shared journal	A journal maintaining transaction records for two or more unrelated parties.
Shared ledger	A ledger maintaining transaction records for two or more unrelated parties.
Shared transaction repository (STR)[14]	A particular concept of a shared book by Boyle (2003g), allowing any party to any inter-company transaction to: 1. post a copy of (the time, content, and parties to) the transaction; 2. notify the other party; 3. enable the counterparty to post an unforgeably timestamped, non-repudiable acceptance of the transaction; and 4. provide persistent storage of the (single history of) transactions to achieve intrinsic, robust reconciliation. While originally conceived as a middleware server with an operator (Boyle, 2001b) and in consecutive steps, it may well be set up in a decentralised system, and the steps may well collapse into one. The STR does not need to allow for payment and settlement within the network, but it probably only makes economic sense if that is the case (Boyle, 2001b) because otherwise it will not be able to replace the banking system (Boyle, 1999, 2003b).
Distributed book	A journal (transactions are unprocessed and sequentially organised) or ledger (transactions are processed, consolidated, and analytically organised) set up on a network of computers conforming to a distributed system (instead of a parallel system). For both distributed journals and distributed ledgers, the distributed database may be, in order of decentralisation[15]:

[14] Originally named 'public transaction repository' or PTR (Boyle, 2000d).
[15] See also Grigg (2016): 'Todd Boyle's concept could not work without a server, a quorum or a blockchain'.

	1. a traditional database in which a computer stores a master database which is then duplicated through the network (in discrete intervals), requiring trust on all the nodes, that is, in the network operator; 2. a traditional database in which specialised software tracks changes over all the databases and replicates them across the network (on an ongoing basis), requiring trust on all the nodes, that is, in the network operator; and 3. a DBT system.
Distributed book technology (DBT)	An industry term for a particular kind of distributed book – usually either blockchain or blockchain-inspired technology: a record of transactions stored in a database set up over a network of computers/nodes which cannot trust each other (Brown, 2016),[16] and thus resort to verification/validation (and time-stamping with unique cryptographic signatures) to maintain a consensus about (the single set of) shared facts. In other words, the network operator does not maintain the records by itself (it is not 'central').
Distributed journal technology (DJT)	A DBT system storing raw transaction data, sequentially and in a journal.
Distributed ledger technology (DLT)	A DBT system going beyond first entry to processing, consolidating, and organising transactions, that is, a DBT system with a ledger instead of a journal. The term DLT is often incorrectly applied to DJTs, despite there being no shared ledger, but only a shared journal.

[16] One could further distinguish between fully trustless DBT systems and walled garden DBT systems with a gatekeeper (Grigg, 2017a).

Blockchain	A particular kind of DBT[17] (DJT or DLT), managed by a P2P network, storing data in packages called 'blocks',[18] each with a unique 'hash' (cryptographic signature) logically dependent on the hash of the previous block to which it is connected, thus forming a linear chain of blocks. A new block can only be added after cryptographic verification by the network, which ensures that there is only one chain of blocks, and thus, a single set of shared facts. A blockchain may be (Carlyle, 2020; Tholen et al., 2019): Open: anyone can read the information in the blocks. Permissionless: anyone can also write on the blocks and take part in the verification process. Permissioned: permission is required for writing and verifying. Closed: only authorised parties can read. Consortium: (only) authorised parties can write and verify. Private permissioned or 'enterprise': only the network operator can write and verify.
Triple-entry bookkeeping (TEB)	Shared book built through signed messages resulting in cite receipts. Recordkeeping is sequential and journalised. Todd Boyle's STR, Ian Grigg's Ricardo Payment System, and Satoshi Nakamoto's Bitcoin are examples of TEB.

[17] Using the terms 'blockchain' and 'DLT' interchangeably is a common practice. Many choose to do this despite being aware of the distinction, in order to conform to popular usage (Aste et al., 2017; Tholen et al., 2019). We do not do this. Instead, we always stick to the specific meaning of each term (except in literal quotes).

[18] In proof-of-work systems such as Bitcoin, a block includes a concatenation of transactions (the set is determined by the wish of the miner seeking to verify that set of transactions), the answer to a cryptographic puzzle called 'nonce', and the hash.

Triple-entry accounting (TEA)	A TEB system with an accounting layer, that is, at least one of the following two characteristics: • The STR is not limited to just sequentially storing transactions, but also to classifying and interpreting them, and facilitating decision-making, financial analysis and forecasting, tax planning, and financial reporting.[19] • As in Boyle (2003g) original formulation, the STR serves as a subledger for each of both parties to a transaction's general ledger: both general ledgers retrieve the transaction data from the STR. It involves a shared ledger underpinned by triple-signed receipts formed through offer, acceptance, and validation.
Bitcoin	A (currently hybrid) P2P payment system constituting both a permissionless public blockchain and an 'asynchronous' TEB system (Ibañez et al., 2023) without an accounting layer.
Resources, events, agents (REA)	An ontology[20] for an accounting system which replaces the classical double-entry system with an information system integrated to all functional areas of an enterprise, not just limited to the accounting department. For this purpose, it proposes a single, shared record of transactions. When applied to inter-company transactions,[21] it is compatible with TEA and may even serve to supplement TEA, to which it is genealogically related (Ibañez et al. 2023).

[19] While 'book-keeping' consists in recording transactions, 'accounting' consists in all of the above.
[20] 'A number of abstractions that generalise business events' (Boyle, 2000b).
[21] REA was mainly conceived for intra-business organisation, but is applicable to intercompany transactions. A number of works have developed this possibility, applying it to supply chain management (Haugen and McCarthy, 2000).

Open-edi distributed business transaction repository (OeDBTR)	A term within the REA ontology for a single-entry system which tracks the immutable history of changes triggering changes of state in multiple business entities, relying on the independent view of the transaction as a single source of truth and the open-edi electronic data interchange standard (McCarthy and Holman, 2019). An OeDBTR does not require DLT, but DLT 'exhibits all of the principles of the distributed repository in which to store business transactions' (Holman, 2019).
Momentum accounting	An accounting system which, aside from wealth and income (the rate of change in wealth), records the rate of change in income. Its inventor, Ijiri (1982), named it 'triple-entry book-keeping' but it is really accounting[22] (Grigg, 2017b, 2019). Despite other works of Ijiri that had a minor indirect impact on the TEA concept discussed in this chapter, momentum accounting is almost unrelated to it (Ibañez et al., 2023).
Russian triple-entry	Also known as 'triple-book system', it is an accounting system which proposes a continuous update of inventory and the usage of only three books: capital book, systematic accounts book, and balance book (Faccia et al., 2020; Platonova, 2016). It is also unrelated to TEA.
Signature	Any token that attests an agreement at a particular point in time.

Other Double-entry Accounting Iterations

A number of other digital means seek to enhance conventional double-entry accounting and are worth mentioning:

[22] At present, both Ijiri's and Grigg's notions of triple-entry are used, but Grigg's definition has found wider adoption (Gröblacher and Mizdraković, 2019), particularly in cryptographic circles.

Immutable Double-entry Accounting (IDEA)

The company Pacio (2020) has proposed a concept of blockchain-based double-entry accounting adding a layer of immutability to "classic" double entry accounting (CDEA). It would constitute a better fit than TEA for 'single-entry counterparty (inter-entity) transactions', which 'do not cover the internal transactions such as depreciation, payroll, etc.' (ibid: 5). IDEA is different from other DLT-based accounting services in that the system should be 'readily upgradeable to TEA', so as to serve as an interim step to it. This requires the ability to scale.

Plain Text Accounting (PTA)

PTA is a type of accounting software aimed at making accounting less convoluted, more accessible, more easily understood, and less subject to intellectual property constraints. It gets its name from the fact that it relies on plain .txt files – rather than, for example, SQL files. In order to achieve this, accounting data is stored in a simplified and human-readable way (Michael, 2019).

PTA has a number of relations to TEA. First, some of its advocates maintain that PTA is a necessary (or preferable) prior step to TEA and DLT. To 'move accounting to the blockchain at this point when everyone is still using CSV files and the proprietary software of large (...) corporations (e.g., Quickbooks and Intuit) is premature. We need a common open standard first and to then build tools around that. (...) Before blockchains can/should be used for accounting in the triple-entry form, we should have a common standard for double entry book-keeping that is in plain text' (Buchman, personal communication, 7 January 2020).

Furthermore, just like TEA and REA advocates, PTA advocates point out that CDEA is viewpoint-dependent: it only includes the partial view of a transaction of the party owning the ledger. This means that in order to 'model the finances of several entities simultaneously', redundant entries are needed. The PTA tool 'Transity', for example, allows the automatic change of viewpoints for each of the parties modelled, which constitutes a partial workaround (Sieber, 2018).

9.4 Conclusion

TEA is one of the most innovative concepts at the forefront of blockchain research. Its historical influence is remarkable (Ibañez et al., 2023) and potential efficiency effects are copious. At present, numerous companies compete to win the race towards the development of a widely-adopted, blockchain-based TEA system. However, the taxonomical deficit characterising this field of research impedes apprehension of what TEA even is.

Due to insufficient usage of accounting vocabulary in blockchain research, it is often unclear what 'three entries' means in this context, whether Bitcoin is a TEA system, what the difference is between Bitcoin and a TEA software, whether blockchains are necessarily TEA or vice versa, and why, if TEA is a proposal for a shared ledger system, TEA records are different from other shared ledgers. This further reveals that the terms 'shared ledger', 'distributed ledger', 'decentralised ledger' and 'distributed technology' are often used imprecisely, creating difficulties for the understanding of the underlying technologies.

With the aim of filling this gap, in this chapter, we set out to achieve a number of goals. First, we provide a proposal for a terminological standardisation that allows us to give a proper account of the TEA phenomenon. Notably, we lay out the basic characteristics of a TEA system. We also distinguish 'bare' triple-entry systems or TEB systems (such as Bitcoin), from TEA systems. While the TEA systems reviewed are DLT-based, we further distinguish DLT technology from basic DJT technology (again, the Bitcoin example). As a prior step, we also argue against the widely used distinction of centralised, decentralised, and distributed authored by Baran.

Our work constitutes an early-stage approximation, shedding light on the conceptual and linguistical complexities surrounding the emergent technology of TEA. Although aware of the preliminary character of our terminology, we hope that it will constitute a useful contribution to the ongoing efforts in the field of TEA and blockchain technology.

9.5 Acknowledgements

We thank the following individuals for answering our questions per email correspondence or per interview:

Individual	Position
Chris Odom	Founder of Open-Transactions
David Hartley	CEO of Pacio
G. Ken Holman	CTO at Crane Softwrights Ltd and former editor of ISO/IEC 15944-21
Ian Grigg	Co-founder at Solidus/Chamapesa
Jason Meyers	Founder at Auditchain
Robert Haugen	Developer at Mikorizal Software
Todd Boyle	Founder at International Accounting Services

Bibliography

AB (2018). Accounting blockchain whitepaper.

Aste, T., Tasca, P., and Di Matteo, T. (2017). Blockchain technologies: The foreseeable impact on society and industry.

Auditchain (2018). Auditchain: Decentralized continuous audit & reporting protocol ecosystem.

Ballandies, M. C., Dapp, M. M., and Pournaras, E. (2018). Decrypting distributed ledger design-taxonomy. *Classification and Blockchain Community Evaluation.*

Baran, P. (1964). On distributed communications networks. *IEEE transactions on Communications Systems*, 12(1):1–9.

Barett, J., Sheth, S., and Vile, A. (2019). From PoC to production: Implementing an enterprise blockchain solution. *Thought Works*.

Beinke, J. H., Nguyen, D., and Teuteberg, F. (2018). Towards a business model taxonomy of startups in the finance sector using blockchain.

Boyle, T. (1999). Differentiating between web-based GLs.

Boyle, T. (2000a). CDEA general ledger schema.

Boyle, T. (2000b). Draft schema for general ledger.

Boyle, T. (2000c). FAQ.

Boyle, T. (2000d). The public transaction repository (PTR) project.

Boyle, T. (2001a). Re: Initial draft of CPP-CPA specification.

Boyle, T. (2001b). The shared transaction repository (STR) ver. 0.60 spec.

Boyle, T. (2003a). Accounting hypercubes on the internet.

Boyle, T. (2003b). The AR/AP cloud.

Boyle, T. (2003c). The argument to abolish double-entry accounting and abolish the assets=liabilities + owner's equity equation.

Boyle, T. (2003d). File-based commerce (FBC) architecture ver. 0.31 spec. business requirements viewpoint.

Boyle, T. (2003e). GLT and GLR: Component architecture for general ledgers.

Boyle, T. (2003f). Ledger ontology.

Boyle, T. (2003g). Shared transaction repository (STR) ... a high level software specification.

Brown, R. (2016). On distributed databases and distributed ledgers. *Richard Gendal Brown: Thoughts on the Future of Finance*, pages 18–23.

Buterin, V. (2017). The meaning of decentralization. *Medium*.

Cai, C. W. (2019). Triple-entry accounting with blockchain: How far have we come? *Accounting & Finance*, 61(1):71–93.

Carlyle, J. (2020). How "public-permissioned" blockchains are not an oxymoron.

Edwards, J. D. (1960). Early bookkeeping and its development into accounting. *Business History Review*, 34(4):446–458.

Faccia, A., Moşteanu, N. R., and Leonardo, L. P. (2020). Blockchain hash, the missing axis of the accounts to settle the triple entry bookkeeping system. In *Proceedings of the 2020 12th International Conference on Information Management and Engineering*, pages 18–23.

Fresno, B. d. (2018). ¿ Cuál es la diferencia entre una DLT y'blockchain'.

Garay, J. and Kiayias, A. (2020). Sok: A consensus taxonomy in the blockchain era. In *Cryptographers' track at the RSA conference*, pages 284–318. Springer.

Ge (2005). Accounting english. *Ge*.

Glaser, F. and Bezzenberger, L. (2015). Beyond cryptocurrencies-a taxonomy of decentralized consensus systems. In *23rd European conference on information systems (ECIS), Münster, Germany*.

Grange, E. (2016). Mesh world P2P simulation hypothesis. *DelphiTools. Available at www.delphitools.info/DWSH/(25/01/2020)*.

Grigg, I. (2005). Triple entry accounting. *Systemics Inc*, pages 1–10.

Grigg, I. (2011). Is Bitcoin a triple entry system? *Financial Cryptography*.

Grigg, I. (2016). Yup – Todd Boyle's concept could not work without a server, a quorum or a blockchain. That's why it's called triple entry.

Grigg, I. (2017a). Eos-an introduction. *White paper*. whitepaper database.com/eos-whitepaper

Grigg, I. (2017b). Oddly, Yuji called it 3E bookkeeping, we called it 3E accounting, and arguably we should have reversed.

Grigg, I. (2019). It's tricky – term was coined 20 years ago by Todd Boyle. My paper was 2004 or so. Oddly – paper is "3E accounting" but techniques are really bookkeeping. Yuri Ijiri's work was originally labelled "triple entry bookkeeping" but is really accounting... Confusion abounds...

Gröblacher, M. and Mizdraković, V. (2019). Triple-entry bookkeeping: History and benefits of the concept. *Digitization and Smart Financial Reporting*, page 58.

Haugen, R. and McCarthy, W. E. (2000). Rea, a semantic model for internet supply chain collaboration. In *OOPSLA Workshop on Business Object Components: Enterprise Application Integration, OOPSLA.*

Hildebrand, G. (2018). The strikingly simple new way to get paid in cryptocurrency. *Medium.* Available at medium.com/gilded/the-strikingly-simple-new-way-to-get-paid-incryptocurrency-609ecbd8a80a (30/01/2020)

Holman, K. (2019). Blockchain and eBusiness.

Ibañez, J. I. (2022). Triple-entry accounting with blockchain. In *Blockchain Technology: Advances in Research and Applications.* Nova, New York.

Ibañez, J. I., Bayer, C. N., Tasca, P., & Xu, J. (2023). REA, Triple-Entry Accounting and Blockchain: Converging Paths to Shared Ledger Systems. *Journal of Risk and Financial Management,* 16(9), 382. https://doi.org/10.3390/jrfm16090382

Ibañez, J. I., Bayer, C. N., Tasca, P., and Xu, J. (2021). The efficiency of single truth: Triple-entry accounting. *Available at SSRN 3770034.*

ICAEW (2018). Blockchain and the future of accountancy.

Ijiri, Y. (1982). *Triple-entry bookkeeping and income momentum.* American Accounting Association.

Ismail, L., Hameed, H., AlShamsi, M., AlHammadi, M., and AlDhanhani, N. (2019). Towards a blockchain deployment at uae university: Performance evaluation and blockchain taxonomy. In *Proceedings of the 2019 International Conference on Blockchain Technology*, pages 30–38.

Jnr, C. A. (1977). The visible hand: Managerial revolution in american business.

Kimani, M. (2018). Blockchain, Identity, Chamas and Africa: A Q & A with Ian Grigg.

Labazova, O., Dehling, T., and Sunyaev, A. (2019). From hype to reality: A taxonomy of blockchain applications. In *Proceedings of the 52nd Hawaii International Conference on System Sciences (HICSS 2019).*

Liu, X. and Yu, T. (2018). An automatic pattern recognition value system with listed banks based on blockchain. In *2018 IEEE 3rd Advanced Information Technology, Electronic and Automation Control Conference (IAEAC).*

McCarthy, W. and Holman, G. (2019). Blockchain and eBusiness. The open-edi distributed business transaction repository. ISO/IEC 15944-21 OeDBTR. *E-Invoicing Exchange Summit Singapore 2019.*

Mehmood, F., Cheah, I., Golash, R., and Ma, L. (2019). Ledgerium whitepaper, version 2.2.

Michael, S. (2019). Plain text accounting.

Mohsin, A. H., Zaidan, A., Zaidan, B., Albahri, O. S., Albahri, A. S., Alsalem, M., and Mohammed, K. (2019). Blockchain authentication of network applications: Taxonomy, classification, capabilities, open challenges, motivations, recommendations and future directions. *Computer Standards & Interfaces*, 64:41–60.

Mutero, J. et al. (2017). Introduction to bookkeeping: A flexible learning course.

Odom, C. (2015). Open-transactions: Secure contracts between untrusted parties.

Pacio (2020). Pacio white paper.

Peters-Richardson, J. (2011). Introduction to accounting.

Platonova, N. V. (2016). FV Ezersky and the development of accounting thought and practices in Russia. *Vestnik NSUEM*, (4):160–170.

Pompliano, A. (2019). Funding the future of finance. Off The Chain. pomp.substack.com/p/funding-the-future-of-finance

Rauchs, M., Glidden, A., Gordon, B., Pieters, G. C., Recanatini, M., Rostand, F., Vagneur, K., and Zhang, B. Z. (2018). Distributed ledger technology systems: A conceptual framework. *Available at SSRN 3230013*.

Request (2018). The future of commerce: A decentralized network for payment requests.

Rukhiran, M. and Netinant, P. (2018). The house bookkeeping conceptual framework for supporting adaptability using three dimensions layering. *Advanced Science Letters*, 24(7):5234–5238.

Saia, A. R., Buckleya, J., Fitzgeralda, B., and LeGearb, A. (2021). Taxonomy of centralization in public blockchain systems: A systematic literature review. *Information Processing & Management*, 58(4).

Sarkintudu, S. M., Ibrahim, H. H., and Abdwahab, A. B. (2018). Taxonomy development of blockchain platforms: Information systems perspectives. In *AIP Conference Proceedings*, volume 2016, page 020130. AIP Publishing LLC.

Schollmeier, R. (2001). A definition of peer-to-peer networking for the classification of peer-to-peer architectures and applications. In *Proceedings First International Conference on Peer-to-Peer Computing*, pages 101–102. IEEE.

Shea, R. (2015). The blockchain is a journal.

Sieber, A. (2018). Transity – the future of plain text accounting.

Tasca, P. and Tessone, C. J. (2019). A taxonomy of blockchain technologies: Principles of identification and classification. Ledger 4 (2019). *arXiv preprint ArXiv:1708.04872*.

Tholen, J., de Vries, D., Daluz, A., Antonovici, C.-C., Van Brug, W., Abelson, R., and Lovell, D. (2019). Is there a role for blockchain in responsible supply chains. In *Joint document by the OECD and KPMG. OECD Global Blockchain Policy Forum.*

TradeIX (2018). The difference between blockchain and distributed ledger technology.

Tyra, J. (2014). Triple entry bookkeeping with bitcoin. *Bitcoin Magazine*, 2014.

University of Derby (2019). Distributed ledger technologies.

van Steen, M. and Tanenbaum, A. S. (2016). A brief introduction to distributed systems. *Computing*, 98(10):967–1009.

Vollmer, H. (2003). Bookkeeping, accounting, calculative practice: The sociological suspense of calculation. *Critical Perspectives on Accounting*, 14(3):353–381.

Walsh, C., OReilly, P., Gleasure, R., Feller, J., Li, S., and Cristoforo, J. (2016). New kid on the block: A strategic archetypes approach to understanding the blockchain.

Wild, J. J., Shaw, K. W., and Chiappetta, B. (2011). Fundamental accounting principles.

PART IV

Cryptocurrency Economics and Monetary Policies

10 Monetary Policy in a World with Cryptocurrencies, Stablecoins, and Central Banks Digital Currency (CBDC)

DANIEL HELLER*

10.1 Monetary Policy Implementation

Most modern central banks have a dual mandate. They are typically tasked to achieve price stability[1] (the 'inflation target') and low unemployment or high economic growth (the 'output target').[2] Central banks then set a target for a short-term interest rate that they viewed to be appropriate for fulfilling their mandate. This can be a band for short-term interbank rates, as in the case of the Federal Reserve (the 'federal funds rate'), or an interest rate for refinancing operations between the central bank and eligible financial market participants, as in the case of The European Central Bank (ECB) and The Bank of England (BoE).

While every central bank has its own, unique monetary policy framework, they deploy three common tools to manage the target interest rates.

First, the central bank sets an interest rate for overnight borrowing at very short notice (referred to as marginal lending rate or discount rate). Such (collateralised) loans can be tapped by market participants if they face an unforeseen liquidity shortfall at the end of a settlement day. The interest rate for such loans is higher than the target rate, indicating a penalty markup. As supply through the lending facility is elastic (i.e., the central bank satisfies any demand by eligible participants), interbank overnight rates generally don't move above the marginal lending rate.

* I would like to thank Katrin Assenmacher, Petra Gerlach, Carlos Lenz, Dirk Niepelt, Olaf Ransome and anonymous referee for excellent comments on an earlier draft

[1] Price stability is usually defined as an inflation rate of 2%.

[2] The European Central Bank has a hierarchical mandate, with price stability being the primary objective.

Second, the central bank sets an interest rate on overnight deposits that eligible financial market participants (banks and central counterpartys (CCPs)) hold with the central bank ('deposit rate'). The deposit rate is lower than the target rate. Again, this implies that the deposit rate provides a floor to interbank overnight rates.

Third, central banks influence the supply of reserves through credit operation (repo) and purchases of securities. Since the Global Financial Crisis (2007–2012) targeted securities purchases have become a standard instrument of many central banks. By being large amounts of government bonds, for instance, a central bank aims at impacting longer-term interest rates and the refinancing costs for sovereign debt.

The combination of these three tools ensures that the central bank is always in a position to keep the targeted interest rates where it wants them to be. More than two decades ago, Woodford (2000) showed that in well-functioning markets for liquidity, the central bank can manage short-term interest rates even if demand for central bank money is zero. Even if new currencies and new forms of money are introduced, the central bank won't lose the ability to control short-term interest rates and therefore implement monetary policy. This outcome hinges on the domestic currency still being the unit of account. If there is dollarisation through a foreign currency, possibly in the form of a stablecoin, the domestic interest rate ceases to matter, and monetary policy loses its influence.

Figure 10.1 illustrates how the Federal Reserve influences the federal funds rate (a market rate for unsecured overnight lending between financial market participants). In 2022, the Federal Reserve increased the target band for the federal funds rate (50 basis points) seven times. In order to ensure that the actual federal funds rates stay within the target band, the Federal Reserve pays interest on the reserves depository institutions hold at the central bank. The interest rate on reserves is set in a way that it is always slightly below the upper limit of the target band. If the federal funds rate were to rise too much above the interest rates of safe reserves, supply in the interbank market would increase, leading to a decrease in the federal funds rate.

Figure 10.1 shows that the effective federal funds rate (an average of observed individual contracts between market participants) has always stayed within the target band in 2022 despite several interest rate hikes. Thus, the interest rate on reserves has been a very effective monetary policy tool. It should be noted, however, it is not always

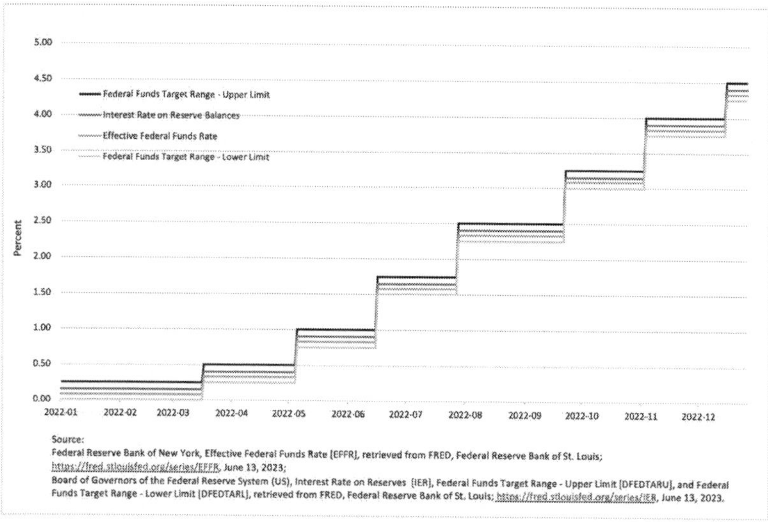

Figure 10.1 Target Rates of the Federal Reserve

easy to keep monetary policy market rates on target. For the period of very low interest rates after the Great Financial Crisis of 2008–10, Williamson (2016) observed out 'interest rate control is more complicated than you thought' and that 'theory and reality sometimes do not agree'.

10.2 New Forms of Money

This section illustrates the effects of recent innovations in money on the balance sheets of the various stakeholders. Similar approaches have been used by Bindseil (2020) for central bank digital currency (CBDC) for the public and Malloy and Lowe (2021) for stablecoins.

It is helpful to start by looking at the balance sheet effects of a standard monetary policy operation through a repo. The effects are shown in Table 10.1. If the central bank engages in a repo of 110 with a commercial bank, this is equivalent to a transfer of securities/bonds to the central bank in exchange for cash. At the end of the repo contract, for example, after 2 weeks, the flows are reversed, that is, the central bank returns the securities and the bank the cash. At the beginning of the contract, the assets of the central bank increased by 110, booked as 'repos'. Since the central bank transfers cash to the counterparty, its

Table 10.1 *Monetary policy operation through repos*

	Assets		Liabilities	
Central bank	repos	+100	Banknotes	
	Bonds		Deposits of banks	+100
Commercial bank	Central bank deposits	+100	Sight deposits	
	Loans		Bonds issued	
	Bonds		repos with central bank	+100
Households and firms	Sight deposits		Debt	
	Real assets			
	Bonds			
	Banknotes			

liabilities also increase by 110 (booked as 'Deposits of banks'). In the balance sheet of the commercial bank, the transaction is reflected by an increase of 110 in 'Central bank deposits' (assets) and 'repos with central bank' (liabilities). It should be noted that due to accounting rules, a repo transaction does not alter the number of securities shown in the balance sheets of the counterparties. However, the commercial bank has fewer 'unencumbered assets' during the duration of the repo, which is relevant from a liquidity regulation point of view. Finally, households and firms are not directly affected by the repo transaction of the central bank.

10.3 Stablecoins

Next, we look into the effects of a stablecoin arrangement. We assume the most straightforward arrangement in which the stablecoin issuer promises to peg the value of the stablecoin to a single sovereign currency like the US dollar or the euro. For such a peg to be credible, the stablecoin issuer holds all its assets as deposits in the banking system, that is, it doesn't have access to an account at the central bank and doesn't hold bonds. Clients purchase such a stablecoin by transferring the amount due through the banking system.

Table 10.2 ***Stablecoin issuer holding only bank deposits***

	Assets		Liabilities	
Central bank	repos Bonds		Banknotes Deposits of banks	
Commercial bank	Central bank deposits Loans Bonds		Sight deposits Bonds issued repos with central bank	−50+50=0
Stablecoin issuer	Sight deposits	+50	Stablecoins issued	+50
Households and firms	Sight deposits Real assets Stablecoins Bonds Banknotes	−50 +50	Debt	

The balance sheet effects are shown in Table 10.2. We assume that a household buys stablecoins for 50. Thus, the household has fewer deposits (−50) and more stable coins (+50) leaving the sum of its assets unchanged. Similarly, commercial banks debit the deposits of the household by 50 and credit the account of the stablecoin issuer, leaving the total amount of deposits unchanged. Finally, the stablecoin issuer now has assets of 50 (booked as 'sight deposits') and liabilities of 50 (the stablecoins it has issued). The balance sheet of the central bank doesn't change.

A probably more realistic setup would be for the stablecoin issuer also to hold bonds in addition to bank deposits.[3]

By adjusting its assets, the stablecoin issuer has to buy bonds that were previously held by someone (a commercial bank or a household). In Table 10.3, it is assumed that the issuer buys bonds for 11 from households and for 11 from commercial banks. Thus, it will have

[3] Another extension would be to allow the stablecoin issuer to hold central bank deposits. Since central banks have been reluctant to provide accounts to such schemes, this option is not discussed here.

Table 10.3 *Stablecoin issuer holding deposits and bonds*

	Assets		Liabilities	
Central bank	repos		Banknotes	
	Bonds		Deposits of banks	
Commercial bank	Central bank deposits		Sight deposits	−10−10+10=−10
	Loans		Bonds issued	
	Bonds	−10	repos with central bank	
Stablecoin issuer	Sight deposits	+50−20=30	Stablecoins issued	+50
	Bonds	+20		
Households and firms	Sight deposits	−50+10	Debt	
	Real assets			
	Stablecoins	+50		
	Bonds	−10		
	Banknotes			

sight deposits with banks of 30 (50-11-11) and bonds of 20. Households will receive sight deposits with banks for 11 leading to a net reduction of 40 instead of 50, and they will have fewer bonds (−11). Commercial banks will have fewer assets (sale of bonds for 11 to stablecoin issuers) and fewer liabilities (sight deposits of stablecoin issuer are reduced as a result of the bond purchase). Again, the balance sheet of the central bank isn't affected by any of these transactions.

Since the introduction of the stablecoin arrangements doesn't change the balance sheet of the central bank, the monetary policy won't be affected. But there could be an impact on financial stability. Households substitute bank deposits for stablecoins and depends. If the stablecoin arrangement is less sound than the bank (i.e., if the probability of default is higher), the risks to financial stability increase. More precisely, the risk of a run on the stablecoin arrangement is higher than the risk of a run on a bank. From a public policy perspective, it is thus essential that stablecoin arrangements are safe and have to meet high prudential standards. Like banks, the stablecoin issuer will have to have enough capital and highly liquid assets to be able to cope with an extreme, but the plausible withdrawal of liabilities (the stablecoins). The recent proposal by CPMI and IOSCO (International Organization of Securities Commissions) – the standard – setting bodies for Financial Market Infrastructures – to have systemically important stablecoin arrangements comply with the Principles for Financial Market Infrastructure (Committee on Payments and Market Infrastructures and International Organization of Securities Commissions, 2021).

10.4 Retail CBDC

Central banks around the world have recently launched projects to investigate the possible introduction of digital banknotes or retail CBDC. These projects are attracting widespread attention from various communities. Quarles (2021), for instance, observes that 'public interest' in a 'digital dollar has reached fever pitch'. Bank of Canada, European Central Bank, Bank of Japan, Sveriges Riksbank, Swiss National Bank, Bank of England, Board of Governors of the Federal Reserve, and Bank for International Settlements (2020) outline the key design features of potential CBDC.

Table 10.4 *Balance sheets with retail CBDC*

	Assets		Liabilities	
Central bank	repos Bonds		Banknotes Deposits of banks CBDC	−10 −40 +10+40=50
Commercial bank	Central bank deposit Loans Bonds	−40	Sight deposits Bonds issued repos with central bank	−40
Households and firms	Sight deposits Real assets Bonds Banknotes CBDC	−40 −10 +10+40=50	Debt	

Like banknotes and deposits by banks, retail CBDC would be a liability of the central bank and an asset of households and firms. They can acquire CBDC either with banknotes or sight deposits. Table 10.4 illustrates the balance sheet mechanics in more detail.

Let us assume that households want to hold CBDC of 50. To this aim, they exchange banknotes of 11 and sight deposits of 40. The exchange of the banknotes will not affect the commercial banks, even if the transactions are operationally performed through commercial banks. The structure of the liabilities of the central bank will change (banknotes −11; CBDC +11). The assets of the households also change (banknotes −11; CBDC +11).

The purchase of CBDC through sight deposits is more complex, as the commercial bank has to buy CBDC on behalf of its client from the central bank. The commercial bank will have an outflow of sight deposits of 40, and it has to pay to the CBDC with its deposits at the central bank.[4] The commercial bank will have an outflow of sight

[4] This would be essentially the same process as today when a bank client withdraws banknotes from an ATM.

deposits of 40, and it has to pay for the CBDC with its deposits at the central bank. The effect is that its balance sheet shrinks. In turn, the composition of the central bank liabilities changes. The deposits of banks go down by 40, but CBDC issued increases by 40, leaving the size of its balance sheet unchanged.

A large demand for retail CBDC could lead to such a large decrease in central bank deposits that banks could find it difficult to meet the minimum reserve requirement (a fraction of the deposits of a bank). An extreme outcome could be that aggregate central bank deposits by the banking sector could fall below the minimum reserve requirement. The central bank would not remain passive at the sideline and let this happen. Baeriswyl et al. (2021) point out that if retail CBDC reduces the central bank deposits to close to the minimum requirement, short-term interest rates would increase. But as shown above, they wouldn't move out the upper limit of the interest rate channel (i.e., the marginal lending rate or discount rate) of the central bank. Also, recent monetary policies (also referred to as 'quantitative easing') and the associated increase in central bank balance sheets have made minimum reserve requirements a meaningless constraint. Another concern related to retail CBDC is that the reduction of the deposit base of banks could reduce the provision of credit by banks to the economy. Ultimately, this could hurt growth and output (Carstens, 2019).

But as pointed out by Brunnermeier and Niepelt (2019), the central bank could, if it wanted to, offset the reduction of deposits in the banking sector. It would just have to offer additional repos to the banking sector. These repos would have to be renewed upon expiration to compensate for the permanent loss of deposits of banks. Table 10.5 shows the impact on the balance sheets. The loss of deposits of 40 in the banking sector would have to be compensated by central bank repos of 40. This would keep the balance sheet of the banking sector at its original size, and leave the balance sheet of the households unaffected. But it would increase the balance sheet of the central bank by 40. Thus, if central banks want to avoid a negative impact on private sector credit provision from the introduction of CBDC ('do not harm') they would need to accept an expansion of their balance sheets.

Finally, retail CBDC would have a negative impact on financial stability if doubts about the solvency of banks and stablecoin issuers would lead to a run into CBDC (large scale substitution of bank

Table 10.5 *Balance sheets with retail CBDC and offsetting operation by central bank*

	Assets		Liabilities	
Central bank	repos	+40	Banknotes	−10
	Bonds		Deposits of banks	−40+40
			CBDC	+10+40=50
Commercial bank	Central bank deposits	−40+40	Sight deposits	−40
	Loans		Bonds issued	
	Bonds		repos with central bank	+40
Households and firms	Sight deposits	−40	Debt	
	Real assets			
	Bonds			
	Banknotes	−10		
	CBDC	+10+40=50		

deposits and stablecoin holdings for retail CBDC). Such risk isn't new. Today, households can already convert bank deposits into banknotes (central bank non-digital currency) or move deposits to another bank (e.g., once with state guarantee). There are several ways to minimise this run risk; one being a cap on retail CBDC holdings, another being credible deposit insurance schemes and adequate regulation and oversight of stablecoin issuers.

10.5 Crypto Currencies

The last use case to be discussed here is new blockchain-based currencies like Bitcoin and Ether ('cryptocurrencies') cryptocurrencies. They are defined by not having an 'issuer' as such, but by being created by a software protocol. The creation of new coins is typically rules-based and written in software code. Newly issued coins

Table 10.6 *Balance sheets with crypto currency*

	Assets		Liabilities	
Central bank	repos		Banknotes	
	Bonds		Deposits of banks	−10+10
Commercial bank	Central bank deposits		Sight deposits	+10−10
	Loans		Bonds issued	
	Bonds		repos with central bank	
Households and firms	Sight deposits	+10−10	Debt	
	Real assets			
	Bonds			
	Banknotes			
	Cryptocurrency	+20(−10+10)		

('primary market') cannot be bought from someone, they are distributed by the protocol as a reward to those who validated transactions in the network (so-called 'miners'). Cryptocurrency coins or tokens can be bought in exchange for sovereign currency or another cryptocurrency, but only after they have been brought into circulation by the software protocol through the miners ('secondary market').

Even though cryptocurrencies are created 'out of nothing' meaning that they are just given to miners as a reward for validation services, they are still reflected in households' balances sheets. In Table 10.6, it is assumed that a cryptocurrency mining household receives cryptocurrencies valued at 20 in a sovereign currency. As mentioned, cryptocurrencies can be traded against other currencies, which means that their balance sheet value is fluctuating with their exchange rates. It should be noted that any foreign exchange transaction of cryptocurrency against the sovereign currency will leave the aggregate balance sheet of households and firms as well as commercial banks unaffected. If, for instance, cryptocurrencies valued at 11 are sold, the sight deposit of the seller increases by 11 and of the buyer decreases by then.

10.6 Conclusion

The impact of new forms of money such as stablecoin arrangements and retail CBDC, as well as cryptocurrencies on the effectiveness of monetary policy appears to be modest. In essence, stablecoins are very similar to bank deposits; and most importantly, they only lead to a re-allocation of bank deposits and bonds between stablecoin issuers, households, and commercial banks. But to avoid runs on stablecoin issuers, sound regulation of oversight similar to existing banks and financial market infrastructures is indispensable. Similarly, secondary markets for cryptocurrencies just trigger an exchange of bank deposits between the buyers of the cryptocurrencies and the sellers, leaving aggregate balance sheets unaffected.

A possible introduction of retail CBDC as a new risk-free form of money would lead to re-allocation of assets by households. They would hold fewer banknotes and bank deposits. The reduction in bank deposits would shrink the balance sheet of banks and impair their ability to provide credit. However, a central bank could offset this effect by increasing its credit provision to the banking sector. It may also be necessary for central banks to increase their supply of deposits to banks should minimum reserve requirements become (more) binding as demand for retail CBDC increases.

Bibliography

Baeriswyl, R., Reynard, S., and Swoboda, A. (2021). Retail CBDC purposes and risk transfers to the central bank.

Bank of Canada, European Central Bank, Bank of Japan, Sveriges Riksbank, Swiss National Bank, Bank of England, Board of Governors of the Federal Reserve and Bank for International Settlements (2020). Central bank digital currencies: Foundational principles and core features. Technical report.

Bindseil, U. (2020). Tiered CBDC and the financial system. Frankfurt: European Central Bank.

Brunnermeier, M. K. and Niepelt, D. (2019). On the equivalence of private and public money. *Journal of Monetary Economics*, 106:29–41.

Carstens, A. (2019). The future of money and payments.

Committee on Payments and Market Infrastructures (2019). Wholesale digital tokens. Technical report, Bank for International Settlements.

Committee on Payments and Market Infrastructures and International Organization of Securities Commissions (2021). Application of the principles for financial market infrastructures to stablecoin arrangements. Technical report, Bank for International Settlements.

Financial Stability Board (2020). Regulation, supervision and oversight of "global stablecoin" arrangements. Technical report, Financial Stability Board.

Malloy, M. and Lowe, D. (2021). Global stablecoins: Monetary policy implementation considerations from a U.S. perspective. *Finance and Economics Discussion*.

Quarles, R. K. (2021). Parachute pants and central bank money. Technical report, Board of Governors of the Federal Reserve System.

Williamson, S. D. (2016). Interest rate control is more complicated than you thought.

Woodford, M. (2000). Monetary policy in a world without money.

11 *Yields*
The Galapagos Syndrome of Cryptofinance

BERNHARD K. MEISTER AND HENRY C. W. PRICE

11.1 Introduction: Decentralised Finance Needs Yield

The combined market capitalisation of cryptocurrencies has grown exponentially and stands as of June 2021 at around $1.5 trillion after breaching briefly $2 trillion in May. This remarkable expansion in value from zero in 2009 has not gone unnoticed by the general public and has been observed with astonishment by practitioners of legacy finance, but it still represents less than 1% of global wealth (Credit Suisse, 2020).

Many attempts exist within the technical constrains of the trust- and permission-less framework governing cryptofinance to translate existing and to construct novel financial products and structures. This area is called decentralised finance (DeFi). It covers exchanging, lending, and tokenising[1] of assets and has recently in a variety of metrics, for example, total value locked (TVL), transacted volume, products available, and number of participants, increased dramatically. In the past year, there has been a jump by a factor of 60 according to DeFi Pulse of the 'collateral for loans, trades and other transactions in DeFi applications' (Kruppa, 2021), and according to the data aggregator DeFi Llama[2] the TVL, one of the key measures used to estimate market size, in DeFi first breached $150 billion in May 2021. The constantly changing amounts and rankings for popular DeFi products and platforms can be found on the public dashboards of DeFi Llama.

Crypto-optimists regard DeFi as a way to improve efficiency, transparency, interoperability, accessibility, and inclusivity beyond what has been achieved in traditional finance, even if unlimited transparency

[1] In the rest of the chapter, the term 'token' will be used loosely. We will not be restricted to the UK's Financial Conduct Authority (FCA) definition: www.fca.org.uk/firms/cryptoassets

[2] DefiLlama – DeFi dashboard, www.defillama.com

and unimpeded access do not necessarily entail social and economic benefits – see for example an article by Dennett and Roy (2015).

For the purpose of this chapter, yield-based investments are defined as the combination of a positive return accumulating in a regular almost clock-like fashion with a short position in an out-of-the-money option corresponding to tail risk. An example from legacy finance would be a credit-risky bond which combines interest accrual with the downside risk of the issuer declaring bankruptcy and defaulting on the obligation to pay interest and principal. Due to the heightened volatility of cryptocurrencies, yield-based strategies might seem like trying 'to pick up pennies in front of a steam roller', but with rigorous portfolio diversification, the idiosyncratic risk associated with tail events often becomes manageable.

In the derivatives ranking by notional of legacy finance fixed income dominates, see the statistical release for 2020 of the Bank of International Settlement (2021), but this does not extend to gross or net exposure, since volatilities of interest rates are often smaller by an order of magnitude than volatilities of other asset classes. This already suggests a challenge for DeFi fixed income products, since crypto collateral is normally linked to the notional amount and not exposure, whereas margin payments between counterparties via exchanges, clearing houses, or credit support annex (CSA) in legacy finance are mostly based on the more dynamic and complex to determine net exposure.[3]

Positions on a blockchain updated by proof-of-work (PoW), most prominently Bitcoin, earn zero return similar to holdings in cash.[4] This implies a vanishing short rate, which clashes with 'conventional' interest rate models, which take a non-zero short rate to be a 'primitive', that is, a necessary building block for term structure, discount rates, and a requirement to flexibly model pay-off structures. In a paper by Brody et al. (2020), it was shown how to overcome this difficulty.

For blockchains with proof-of-stake (PoS) updating, for example, Ethereum is in the process of switching from PoW to PoS, staked

[3] Attempts in DeFi to develop zero knowledge dynamic credit risk monitoring and margining systems, for example, X-Margin, have persuaded some venture capital (VC) investors, but have gained up to now limited traction.

[4] In conventional interest rate modelling cash is usually ignored, since a central bank backed riskless short rate exists, but for cryptocurrencies, ignoring positions directly held on the blockchain is not feasible.

tokens have a non-zero yield, which relates a largely deterministic return to the amount committed. In addition, validators are able to exploit maximal/miner extractable value (MEV) linked to the ability to select and order transactions from the Mempool for blockchain inclusion, but also incur in the process obligations. Non-staked tokens can participate in DeFi or gain convenience yield from immediate accessibility, which can for example pay for imminent blockchain fees. The risk-adjusted benefits for the marginal investor in these three forms of token usage have to match to avoid runaway effects. The relevant return data for staked Ethereum is presented in Section 11.2.

Besides conventional fixed income products, there are other areas of DeFi where yield-like returns exist. DEXs provide such an opportunity to liquidity providers (LPs), who lock up token pairs in pools to allow liquidity takers (LTs) to switch between them for a fee. The LTs garner the fees but are short of an option associated with exchange rate fluctuations. This will be discussed in Section 11.3.

DEXs are alternative liquidity sources with universal access. A natural extension of the crypto-anarchist ideals set forth in the cypherpunk movement of the 1990s and crystallised in Bitcoin by Satoshi Nakamoto. By removing the middleman, as well as any form of control, DEXs are furthermore a response to failures of legacy finance. On CEXs, users are required to transfer custody of their assets to a third party, which entails risk. The temporary freezing of assets as well as the collapse of exchanges, for example, Mt Gox of Japan in 2014, has shown that this risk is non-negligible. DEXs are increasingly coming under official scrutiny, as they circumvent money laundering rules, and mix assets without regard for regulations.

Another area of interest is modelling. For the cryptocurrency interest-rate derivatives market to bloom, pricing, replication, and hedging need to function smoothly. Models are required that are convincing and common to market participants. This is a necessary but not a sufficient condition for the establishment of a capital efficient crypto fixed income market. A way to evaluate a simplified version of these loans without the detailed examination of the liquidation mechanisms, which differ from platform to platform, is given in Section 11.4.

A proposal for a crypto product linking collateral not to notional but exposure is presented in Section 11.5. A natural candidate is a modified version of a cross currency swap traditionally used by banks to exchange collateral and interest payments in different currencies without taking directional foreign exchange risk. Section 11.6 covers yields of short-dated loans on CEXs.

Perpetuals swaps traded on CEXs enable speculators to leverage their capital close to a stratospheric hundred times. Speculators are willing to pay a premium over spot to access leverage motivated by the chance to invest in possibly highly lucrative momentum strategies, whereas LPs get a return associated with the size of the premium but have to take on unpopular positions with drift and jump risk. The basis of perpetual and finite duration futures is the topic of Section 11.7.

The interest rate implied by crypto-options is the topic of Section 11.8. A conclusion rounds off the Section 11.9.

11.2 Protocol Defined Return and Ethereum 2.0

In this section, information about the evolving Ethereum 2.0 protocol and the associated Beacon Chain is presented. The Ethereum 1.0 blockchain is currently separated from the Beacon Chain to reduce risk in the transition. The new protocol is not finalised and evolves with the EIPs (Ethereum Improvement Proposals[5]). The novelty of the protocol and the complexity of the switch to PoS involving multiple stages have led to a lack of data for staking returns in the academic literature. Before we present the data, which covers the period from December 2020 (Launch of the Beacon Chain) to September 2021, a rough introduction to some relevant parts of staking is provided, as it exists in June 2021. To participate in staking, at least 32 ETH has to be pledged for the whole trial period. The volume weighted staking return as used by Attestant[6], R_{stake} between time $t-1$ and t for an eligible validator is given by

$$R_{stake} = 365 \times \left(\frac{V_t}{V_{t-1}} - 1 \right)$$

where V_{t-1} is the validator balance at time $t-1$ and V_t is the validator balance at time t. The validator balance is taken always at 00:00 UTC. An eligible validator is a validator that is in the 'Active' state

[5] eips.ethereum.org
[6] www.attestant.io/metrics/aor/

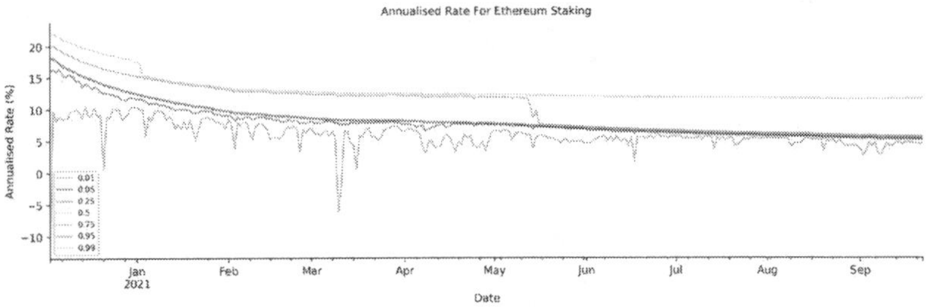

Figure 11.1 Staking rewards for all validators active in each 24 hour period; shown are returns in percent of the 1st, 5th, 25th, 50th, 75th, 95th and 99th percentile. Source: www.attestant.io

at time $t-1$ and remains continuously in the 'Active' state until, and including, time t. The validator must also maintain a minimal balance of 32 ETH during the entire period. Balance changes in Figure 11.1 are obtained from all validators active within the previous 24 hours.[7] The Ethereum 2.0 upgrade has incorporated a further range of interesting features. For the more technical aspects, we refer readers to the voluminous Ethereum 2.0 documentation. This includes the work a validator has to perform and how, as a result, the balance V_{t-1} is converted into V_t.

Some pertinent features necessary for understanding Figure 11.1 are that stakers can neither at this stage withdraw funds back to Ethereum 1 nor can they switch funds to a different validator to increase their yield. As a result, the ability to optimise allocations between validators is restricted. In addition, there is a ceiling on individual validator balances that are eligible to receive returns, and initially high returns are whittled down as the surplus unable to generate returns increases. However, it must be noted that when Ethereum 2 is fully operational, validators will receive fees from transactions as well as block rewards increasing returns for staked assets.

Features of the chart are:

First, returns started high, are slowly declining and converging, that is, the spread between different percentiles is decreasing.

Second, the erratic returns of the 1st percentile, which on occasion have been negative, are due to a failure to adequately fulfil the required tasks. Negative returns can be caused by 'Slashing', when incorrect

[7] Data provided by www.attestant.io

information is validated, or to a lesser extent from inaction. Punishment is increased with the amount of network disruption. For example, all validators, who failed to validate, are slashed jointly using the following equation: $Slash\ Cost = 3 \times N_{\%}$. As a consequence, a pool controlling 1/3 of the network could have a 100% loss.

Third, there are also those validators that perform exceptionally well, that is, they perform a special validator function. This allows them to choose a block for which they are rewarded in ETH, which is reminiscent of Bitcoin mining. However, unlike in Bitcoin, these special rewards are based solely on luck and not influenced by the computational capacity of the validators. Except for this random element, returns are more predictable and they directly follow from the number of active validators, which is a known quantity.

Fourth, the 'step functions' observable in the return of the highest two percentiles could either be due to protocol changes or discrete effects linked to the number of validators winning top-tier rewards, usually given to block proposers in the ETH committee system.

As the overall number of participants grows, the chance of obtaining these slots diminishes. To determine if protocol changes or marginal validator returns are responsible for jumps, one only needs to consider a more fine-grained percentile graph.

Dedicated standalone entities provide both bespoke and non-pooled services, where funds are segregated, not mixed in validators, and security is ensured. Exchanges also offer for a fee staking services to enhance yield on positions under custody.

Although Ethereum 2.0 is perhaps the highest profile staking protocol, it is not the first to adopt PoS. The main other staking cryptocurrencies are Tezos, which calls staking 'baking', Algorand, and Cardano. The protocols differ, but all rely on dedicated 'collateral' to perform the network verification function.

11.3 Automated Market Maker and Yield

DeFi has expanded into a number of different directions. In Section 11.3, Automated Market Makers (AMMs), a core component of DeFi, are introduced, and in Section 11.3, the financial mechanics of AMMs are discussed. In Figure 11.3, some challenges facing AMMs and the yield of an exemplary AMM are presented.

Introduction to AMMs

Arguably the biggest growth has been in AMMs facilitating token exchanges, which are in competition with CEX. Big participants, or maybe they should already be called incumbents despite the novelty of the field, are for example Uniswap, Balancer, Curve, Pancakeswap, and Sushiswap. On these DEXs LPs, which earn yield in the form of a stream of commissions but are exposed to jump risk in the token exchange rate, are matched to LTs wanting to exchange one token for another.

AMMs are substantial. Uniswap, which is in its third major incarnation, alone has executed as of 30 June 2021 trades worth almost $300 billion, supports 40,000+ token pairs of different sizes, and has combined liquidity of over $3 billion according to the Uniswap website. These numbers are impressive for any exchange, but especially for an originally one-person project[8] started in 2017 on a shoestring. It then moved through various stages and was deployed on the Ethereum Mainnet in November 2018. It is based on an open-source code, which can and has been forked and adapted by competitors such as Sushiswap.

Uniswap and other AMMs are not directly comparable to traditional exchange, since their legal status is both contentious and recognisably different. A simplistic way to highlight the difference is by pointing out the distinction between the verb 'to exchange' and the noun 'the exchange'. The Uniswap AMM should be viewed as a software protocol deployed on the Ethereum blockchain built and supported by an entity called Uniswap with a peculiar institutional structure controlled by the UNI governance token held with variable lock-ups by users, team, investors, and advisers with a market capitalisation of just under $10 billion as of June 2021.

The Financial Mechanics of AMMs

This section serves as a limited introduction to the financial mechanics of AMMs as employed by Uniswap and similar protocols; details of these mechanics are subject to change. For full details of the evolv-

[8] "A short history of Uniswap" can be found at uniswap.org/blog/uniswap-history

ing smart contract implementations, see the websites of the providers, which also explain how specific tokens, for example, UNI of Uniswap, are created to differentiate protocols from competitors, to attract liquidity, and to deal with governance issues including the determination of contract specifications. One major challenge faced when translating the functionality associated with limit-order-based exchanges, which offer a plethora of order types and differentiate between market participants, to the distributed Ethereum Virtual Machine was to reduce memory and computational requirements. Many AMMs including Uniswap use a simplified market maker model associated with the acronym CPMM ('Constant Product Market Maker').

In this type of market, each token pair is called a pool and divided into two types of participants. These are LPs and LTs. The smart contract employs a simple deterministic formula to incorporate the two types of actions each market participant is able to perform after a pool is created. The key formula is $xy = k$. x and y are respectively the two tokens which form a particular pool. The ratio x/y can be viewed as the exchange rate associated with the pool. Details can be found in a paper by Zhang et al. (2018) and in the whitepapers and other materials of the various AMM platforms. The pool is stocked by LPs, who can add and subtract liquidity. This means LPs provide or withdraw supplies of tokens at predefined ratios. Subtleties involving the submission of a combination of tokens which do not exactly match the pool ratio are ignored. The LTs also have two ways to interact with the protocol. LTs can either send an amount of the first token in the pool to receive an amount of the second token, or they can do the reverse. The amounts received are predetermined by the pool composition and incorporate a fee proportional to the trade size to incentive LPs to commit liquidity. As these four interactions with the smart contract governing the pool occur, the composition of the pool is dynamically adjusted.

Arbitrageurs observe a host of DEXs and CEXs and ideally keep prices aligned within the limits set by transaction and other frictional costs. As a pool gets larger, that is, LPs add liquidity, the market impact of an LT order of fixed size is reduced, whereas a reduction of tokens in the pool increases market impact. The reverse is true for LTs. If an LT wants to switch a large amount, then the execution price moves further. This is a form of price impact or slippage.

The fee charged in a pool can be adjusted as part of the governance procedure involving UNI tokens. The current fee on Uniswap V3 is tiered, 0.05%, 0.3%, or 1%, and depends on the token pair chosen. Pools with higher volatility are riskier and normally require a higher fee. Various costs due to interaction with the blockchain, for example, gas in the case of Ethereum, are the responsibility of LPs and LTs and can lead to inertia. DEXs are dynamic and constantly tinker with their business model. In Uniswap V3, the newest version of Uniswap launched in May 2021, LPs can concentrate liquidity in particular exchange rate ranges, which is of particular benefit for stablecoin token pairs with smaller volatilities and also lower fees.

LPs lock up their assets when they enter a pool. On exit, LPs get a proportion of the accumulated fee commensurate with their relative stake in the pool plus an appropriate proportion of the liquidity pool itself. The fee creates an incentive and is similar to a yield, but it is tempered by the risk associated with being short volatility in the exchange rate of the underlying token pair. This risk is slightly incongruously called 'impermanent loss'. It is the relative loss due to the change in the pool composition from the LP's entry and exit points. In other words, if the investor had retained the initial position ignoring the accumulated fee, then this would have been more valuable than getting the final mix of tokens, which reflects the change in the pool exchange rate. Examples are provided in Zhang et al. (2018). Besides relative losses, one can also consider numeraire dependent absolute value changes of the pool portfolio. This comparison can show both gains and losses and is depicted in Figure 11.2, which shows for USD as the numeraire the cumulative absolute impermanent gain or loss for the ETH-USDT pool. Absolute value changes are of importance for the overwhelming majority of investors, who have either reporting or financial obligations in a specific currency.

In Figure 11.3, the price dynamic of an Uniswap token pool controlled by an AMM is captured beautifully. In this case, it is the token pair of wrapped ETH (WETH, but subsequently written as ETH) and the stablecoin Tether (USDT). What would normally correspond to the bid-offer spread on CEXs is dependent on the 0.3% fee and the pool size. The bid-offer spread on DEXs increases with the size of the fee and decreases with the size of the pool. As the price drops in a conventional exchange 'bids are hit', but on an AMM, tokens are exchanged (orange circles: ETH is exchanged for USDT) such

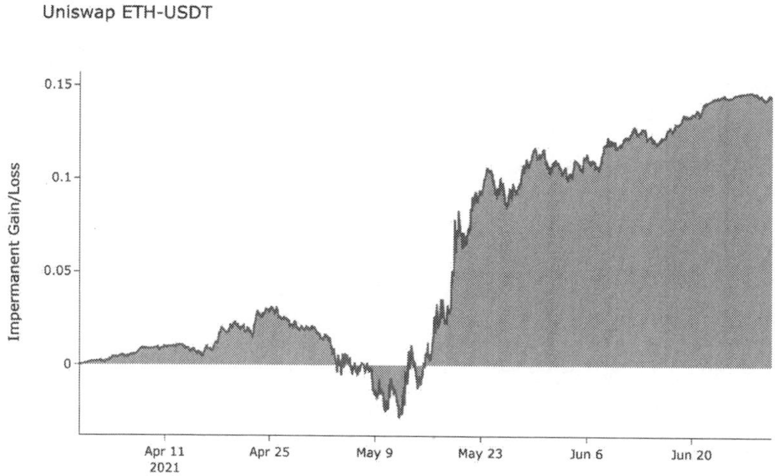

Figure 11.2 Cumulative Impermanent Gain/Loss for the Uniswap ETH-USDT token pool as fraction of initial notional with USD as the numeraire, Data Source: www.intotheblock.com

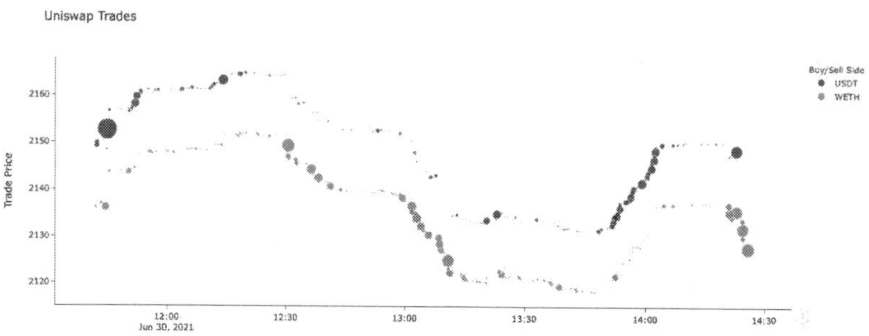

Figure 11.3 Two hours in the life of the Uniswap WETH-USDT Token Pool, Source: pools.fyi

that the price drops. Trade size is depicted by the circle area, which seems to expand when prices move. There is asymmetry in up- and down-trending markets, that is, sell-side trades are more prominent in a downward move and buy-side trades, more prominent in an upward move. These concentrated larger trades with the commensurately larger slippage can be profitable when markets trend and are likely to have originated with arbitrageurs exploiting prior price moves on CEXs. From this graph alone, one cannot tell with certainty if the Uniswap DEX leads or lags other DEXs or CEXs. The hypothesis would nevertheless be that the liquidity pattern observed is suggestive of this DEX being a follower. This is bolstered by the fact that CEXs can react faster to market news than DEXs dependent on sluggish blockchain updating times.

Challenges of AMMs

In Figure 11.3, challenges facing AMMs and yield data are presented. The competition between pools exists in multiple dimensions and is a fascinating example of game theory in action. Yield-enhancement subsidies to increase the competitiveness of particular protocols using platform specific tokens lead to possible distortions. Benefits for LPs can be detrimental for LTs and vice versa. Balancing short-term and long-term greed can be particularly difficult and might not have stable solutions in such a transient and transparent environment.

Let us briefly describe the case of a LP participating in an idealised pool for the duration T. If for example the exchange rate follows approximately a random walk with volatility σ per unit of time, then the 'impermanent risk' is expected to be proportional to $\sigma\sqrt{T}$, whereas the average fee of α per unit of time should accumulate linearly at the rate αT, and should eventually dominate. The amount gained on average per unit of time in the large T limit is $\lim_{T\to\infty}(\alpha T - \sigma\sqrt{T})/T = \alpha$.

A way to compare various pools is to look at the associated Sharpe ratios, which are $(\mu_i - r)/\sigma_i$, where r is the riskless rate, μ_i is the return and σ_i the volatility of the ith-pool. The riskless rate in many major fiat/numeraire currencies is currently approximately zero, and from the time series of returns the Sharpe ratios can be computed. Ignoring correlation and instead assuming the time series of the pools are approximately independent, which is an extreme idealisation, one could rank the pools in a simple way. Portfolio optimisation using the Kelly criterion can be applied (Kelly, 1956; Lv and Meister, 2009, 2010) to optimise investments in pools taking the covariance of returns into account.

AMMs are accessed through the blockchain, and preferential access leads to profits (Zhou et al., 2020). Miners can select and reorder Mempool submissions, for example, front- and back-running orders, to create MEVs – see Daian et al. (2019) for an early discussion. This has created a hyper-profitable cottage industry together with service providers such as flashbots.net, who consider what is arguably a vice, that is, a (possibly unavoidable) friction cost for investors, as a profit-generating virtue.

11.4 Over-Collateralised Cryptoloans

This section on cryptoloans divides into three subsections. In this section cryptoloans are introduced and market data is presented, in Figure 11.4, a toy model is analysed, and in Equation 12.4, liquidation mechanisms are described.

What are Cryptoloans?

Cryptoloans are a form of over-collateralised lending managed by a smart contract. Potential lenders send tokens, often in the form of stablecoins, to a lending pool, whereas the borrowers deposit collateral often in the form of Ether and in return gain access to a fixed amount of stablecoins. Due to the trustless nature of the exchanges, the value of the collateral is around 150% of the borrowed amount. There are also off-blockchain providers where interest rates are tiered with the level of initial collateral. If the value of the collateral falls below a certain threshold compared to the borrowed amount, a liquidation procedure ensues to protect the lenders. Liquidation normally involves a penalty and can be in the form of a fixed time unwind auction or based on an oracle-specified price. For an extensive analysis, see a recent paper by Qin et al. (2021) and co-authors mainly from Imperial College. Significant deleveraging occurs when token prices jump dramatically, as has happened on 19 May 2021.

The attempt to automatically re-margin or faithfully unwind the initially over-collateralised loan through smart contract appeals, but it is technically cumbersome and as a consequence involves operational risk, and more importantly is costly in on-chain computation and data.

The interest rate borrowers pay depends on the volatility of the token pair and the amount of collateral required, but also on the utilisation of the lending pool. The interest rate model used differs from platform to platform. On Aave, it has the form of a hockey stick. For a lending pool utilisation of up to 80%, the interest rate increases

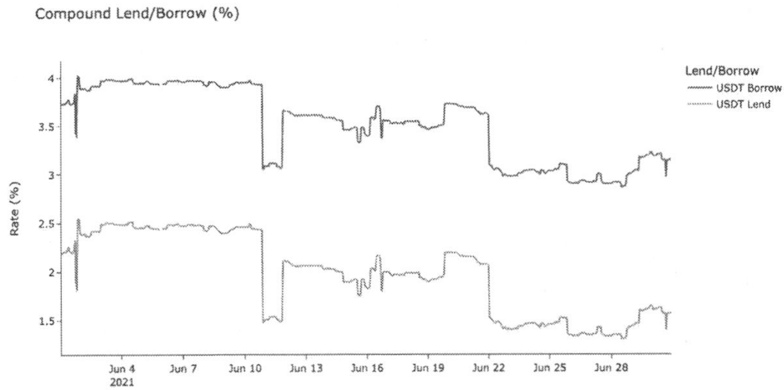

Figure 11.4 Annualised Interest Rate for borrowing and lending of USDT on Compound with ETH as collateral. Source: compound

slowly, but above this utilisation rate, it increases at a steeper slope. This is to ensure that lenders of tokens in demand benefit from scarcity. Other platforms, for example, MakerDAO, Compound, and Curve, provide variations of the theme. More details of the ever-changing protocols can be found on the respective websites. The constantly shifting rankings for loan platforms as well as other DeFi products can be found on the website www.DeFiLlama.com. Figure 11.4 shows the volatile borrowing and lending rates in June 2021 for USDT on Compound with ETH as collateral. The rates are a multiple of what is available for USD in legacy finance and an indication of market segmentation.

Pricing and Modelling of Cryptoloans

Cryptoloans need to be modelled and priced. We next present a simplified evaluation based on an option introduced by Margrabe (1978) and consistent with Black-Scholes-Merton option theory, where one party has the right to choose between two risky assets at maturity. The model has its limitations, since the underlying price process is assumed to be a geometric Brownian Motion, but it can provide a starting point for further investigations. Collateralised options can be priced for more general price processes – including jumps or stochastic volatility. The main weakness of the model is the neglect of the liquidation process. This will be partly rectified in the next subsection.

One can view a collateralised loan in the static hedge case as an option on the minimum of two assets, since the token amount used to over-collateralise the loan can fall below the value of the loan notional plus interest at maturity. The value of the option in the Black-Scholes-Merton model is dependent only on the interest of the two tokens, their correlation, and their respective implied volatilities.

The payout for the borrower is $Max[A, B]$, where A is the collateral in the form of token α and B the amount of token β to be paid at maturity time T. The payout for the lender is $\mathrm{Min}[A, B]$ and the sum of the pay-outs is the $A + B$. The value of such an option at time $t = 0$ is:

$$\begin{aligned} Max[A, B] &= B + Max[0, A - B] \\ &= B + e^{-r_\alpha T} AN(d_1) + e^{-r_\beta T} BN(d_2), \end{aligned}$$

where $N(\cdot)$ is the standard normal cumulative distribution function, and

$$\begin{aligned} d_1 &= \frac{\log(A/B) + r_\beta - r_\alpha + \frac{1}{2}\sigma^2 T}{\sigma\sqrt{T}}, \\ d_2 &= d_1 - \sigma\sqrt{T}, \\ \sigma^2 &= \sigma_\alpha^2 - 2\sigma_\alpha\sigma_\beta\rho_{\alpha,\beta} + \sigma_\beta^2, \end{aligned}$$

with σ_α and σ_β the volatilities of tokens α and β, respectively, and $\rho_{\alpha,\beta}$ the correlation between the two tokens. The interest rates r_α and r_β are the interest rates of the two tokens. All the prices, volatilities, and interest rates are given with respect to the numeraire, for example, the US dollar. If one of the two assets is the numeraire itself (or an asset with zero volatility and drift with respect to the numeraire like an eternally tethered stablecoin), then the formula simplifies. For example for A, as the notional amount denominated in the numeraire, it becomes

$$B + Max[0, A - B] = B + AN(d) + e^{-r_\beta T} BN(d - \sigma_\beta\sqrt{T}),$$

with

$$d = \frac{\log(A/B) + r_\beta + \frac{1}{2}\sigma_\beta^2 T}{\sigma_\beta\sqrt{T}}.$$

The European and American versions of this option have equal values, since early exercise is under the artificial conditions considered, that is, no dividends and the underlying process is a geometric Brownian motion, never advantageous. The existence of multiple collateral tokens, as exist in some protocols (Balancer has up to 8 for some markets), complicates the calculation of maximum and minimum values. A solution for prices limited to geometric Brownian motions was discussed in 'Options on the maximum or the minimum of several assets' by Johnson (1987).

Liquidation of Cryptoloans

By ignoring the liquidation procedure, a simple but insufficient formula was derived. As a next step, one can incorporate a pared down version of a liquidation penalty function, which awards a fixed amount, that is, a fraction of the notional, to the lender, if some collaterlisation limit is reached. This could be modelled as a one-touch option.[9] The liquidation penalty on the lending platform Compound is 8%, while on Aave, it is 5–15%. The value of a loan is in the simplest penalty case, where margins cannot be replenished, the combination of two options, which can still be priced directly. Various subtleties inherent in the actual liquidation process involving for example time delays %, an auction mechanism, or the existence of a centralised recovery fund inhibit accurate option replication and add non-negligible noise (Qin et al., 2021).

The ability to disentangle loans in terms of a combination of options provides a useful way to build a bridge to the nascent crypto options market. It offers a way to price and hedge crypto options and allows the liquidity of the loan market to leach into the less liquid options market.

A way to enhance the utilisation of collateral would be to allow the lending contract to re-lend part of the collateral, that is, a form of recycling, in a separate loan. The advantage would be a more efficient use of capital, whereas the disadvantage would be the increased risk of losses. As collateral chains get longer, the risk, if the various exchange rates are independent, would be approximately additive, but if it involves triangles of currencies, that is, from A to B to C and back to A, then the risk would stay in a tighter range.

[9] For the value of one-touch options in the Black-Scholes-Merton framework and beyond, see Chapter 11 of the comprehensive book by Lipton (2001).

11.5 Efficient Use of Collateral to Enable Leverage and Enhance Yield

One of the issues that has plagued crypto-finance is the difficulty to generate leverage. In this section, we propose a structured product as a prototype solution. It is based on a cross currency swap and separates credit from foreign exchange risk. These swaps are widely used by, for example, Japanese Maruyama and Washimi (2021), who fund themselves in their home currency at a stable low rate, but lend internationally in dollars.

Cross-currency swaps are a tailor-made solution, because they allow Japanese banks to fund positions in a foreign currency without the associated foreign exchange risk. Credit risk Japanese banks can manage through the construction of a diversified portfolio of loans, whereas foreign exchange risk is concentrated and would otherwise necessitate a hedge.

The contract starts with a notional exchange denominated in two currencies at an agreed exchange rate normally close to the current spot rate and it ends at the termination date with a reversal of the notional exchange at the same initial exchange rate. At regular intervals during the lifetime of the swap, cash flows linked to either fixed or floating rates in the two currencies plus a potential spread are exchanged.

Next we describe how this can be translated into the trustless cryptocurrency framework,[10] and why it is beneficial. The first and last step would be identical, that is, the initial and final exchange of notional via an intermediary smart contract, allowing both sides to reuse the notional. To avoid losses due to currency movements, each side is required to deposit an initial margin into the smart contract. An oracle monitors the exchange rate and observes if the margin of either side falls below some critical threshold. If this occurs and the margin is not replenished, the contract is prematurely terminated. Each side keeps the exchanged notional amount and the party, whose margin limit has not been breached, acquires enough of the margin of the other party to be made whole. A version of this contract without an oracle, but with either side able to prematurely terminate the contract for a fixed fee, is also possible.

[10] MK2 Finance in collaboration with others is developing such a contract.

Details about buffers and various other payments, which take into account supply and demand, as well as penalties for early liquidation require careful consideration. One should note that an unexpected jump in the exchange rate can exhaust the margin buffer. Therefore, buffers should take into account the volatility of the exchange rate. Asymmetry of possible movements could as well as supply and demand lead to the initial and final exchange rates or the margins to differ by a market-determined factor. The importance for both sides to have access to the notional minus a margin enhances symmetry, currently not available in crypto-loan deals, and will fuel reuse of the notional.

The buffer corresponds to a hair-cut and might reasonably increase with the square root of the duration of the arrangement. If the buffer corresponds to $x\%$, then the total leverage gained by each side, assuming maximal recycling of the notional, would be slightly under $1/(x\%)$. This turbo-charges crypto-finance but entails risk, since the underlying historical volatilities guiding the choice of $x\%$ might change spontaneously across the board leading to wild deleveraging. Even with the current over-collateralised contracts, DeFi TLV dropped by a third in the recent period of volatility in May 2021, see the dashboards of DeFi Llama.

11.6 Short-dated Cryptoloans on Decentralised Finances

In the subsequent short sections, we switch from DeFi to centralised finance (CeFi). We start with the presentation of data of different short-dated loans from the crypto-exchange Bitfinex.

The three graphs of Figure 11.5 show the lending rate per day for BTC, ETH, and USD loans of 2 days, which is the most liquid duration. A limit order book is used to match borrowers and lenders. The market has existed comparatively long and provided an early opportunity to establish leveraged positions in cryptocurrencies.

11.7 The Basis of Perpetual and Finite Duration Futures

In this section, we study the different types of CEX futures. Accessibility of leverage differs in the futures and spot markets. In this section, there is a discussion of the history of perpetuals and some related market data and in the subsequent subsection, the same is done for finite duration futures.

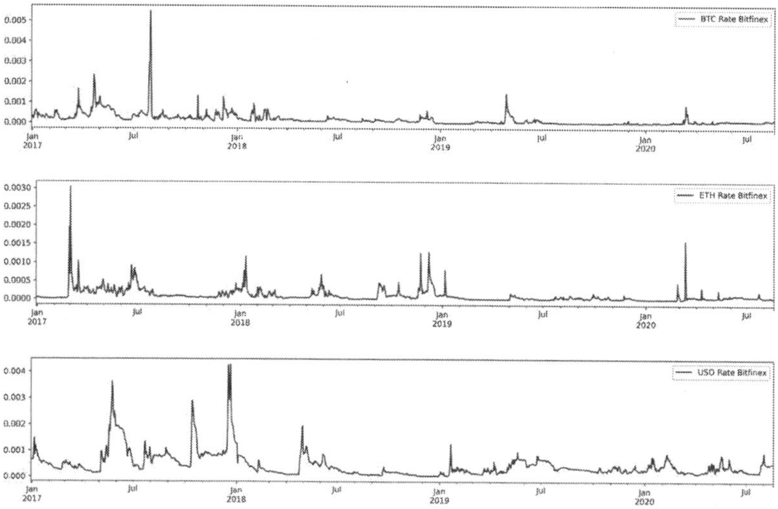

Figure 11.5 Weekly rolling average of the interest rate in % per 365 days on Bitfinex for short dated BTC, ETH, and USD loans (for details: www.docs.bitfinex/v1/reference#rest-public-fundingbook)

The Basis of Perpetual Futures

In the early 1990s, Shiller (1993) introduced a novel way for pricing perpetual claims on indices. Together with Case, he introduced a real estate-based index, which after multiple re-incarnations turned into the 'S&P CoreLogic Case-Shiller U.S. National Home Price Index'. Futures and options written on this index are listed on the Chicago Mercantile Exchange (CME). Undated gold futures traded already in Hong Kong in the 1980s and can be viewed as precursors of perpetual futures (Jr and K, 1988).

Starting from 2016, crypto exchanges have been offering perpetual and inverse perpetual contracts[11] on Bitcoin and other tokens. Before we discuss the modifications introduced in the crypto-market, it is important to provide a brief overview of Shiller's original concept, which involves extending the daily settlement mechanism beyond changes in future prices by incorporating an additional term. This term serves to link the traded perpetuals to a potentially non-traded index. Conventional futures with the daily settlement price F_t and a

[11] If the base/numeraire currency of the future is switched, for example, from $ to BTC, then one uses the moniker 'inverse'.

finite duration have a physical or cash settlement at the expiry date, whereas day-to-day price changes of the form $F_t - F_{t-1}$ link directly to matching cash flows between the counterparties. Since there is no expiry date for perpetuals, a method needs to be found to link the futures price to the index value. This is achieved by adding an extra term of the form $d_t - r_t F_{t-1}$. The dividend payments d_t, for example, lumpy rental payments, are balanced with the riskless return r_t, for example, a short-term risk-free rate associated with government debt, times the notional of the index. This additional daily exchange can be understood as representing the payout associated with owning the index minus the funding cost for such a position.

A similar methodology for linking flows between longs and shorts applies to perpetual crypto-currency futures. The conventional daily settlement interval is reduced to 8 hours on BitMex and other periods on other exchanges. In addition, there is the challenge of defining a meaningful anchor to link the futures price to an index. The first question is the choice of appropriate index. This is solved by choosing the Bitcoin spot rate either of the exchange where the perpetual is listed or some other related rate. Next, one has to associate a dividend d_t with the index as well as define the respective interest rate r_t. Crypto-currencies do not pay dividends. BitMex overcame this difficulty by choosing a different kind of anchor, which in first approximation, when futures and spot price significantly deviate,[12] is proportional to the percentage difference between spot and a suitably adjusted futures price. Deribit launched perpetuals in 2018 with a simpler formula for the anchor.[13] As in the original perpetuals, the main payment for each period is due to the price change of the futures themselves. The added

[12] This is the case, when the percentage difference between futures and spot reflected in *Premium Index*(P) is significantly larger in absolute terms than 0.05%, that is, when the 'clamp' function in:

$$\begin{aligned} \textit{Funding Rate}(F) = \textit{Premium Index}(P) + \textit{clamp}(\textit{InterestRate}(I) \\ - \textit{PremiumIndex}(P), 0.05\%, -0.05\%) \end{aligned}$$

applies and $F \approx P$. The future price used is itself adjusted in a 'unique' way to avoid price anomalies and avoid 'unnecessary liquidation' according to the BitMex website. One should keep in mind that with maximal leverage of the kind offered, liquidation is unlikely to be an uncommon occurrence.

The authors are not convinced, if in this context 'unique' warrants an unqualified recommendation.

[13] For contract specifications, see the Deribit website, www.deribit.com.

anchor payment per futures contract is defined as the product of funding rate and time fraction, where the time fraction is again divided into 8-hour slices, and the funding rate is given by

$$Maximum(0.05\%, Premium\ Rate) + Minimum(-0.05\%, Premium\ Rate)$$

and the premium rate is given by

$$Premium\ Rate = ((Mark\ Price - Deribit\ Index)/Deribit\ Index) \times 100\%$$

where the Deribit index is the spot rate at the relevant time and the 'Mark Price' corresponds to the relevant futures price adjusted to take into account bid-offer spreads and protect against potential market distortions. The other two markets, Binance and Bybit, have their own formulas for aligning perpetuals with spot, that is, with details to be found on the exchange websites.

The benefits to speculators of trading in futures over spot are the additional leverage. The initial margin for perpetuals on BitMex is only 1% complemented by a maintenance margin of 0.35%. This converts into high double digit leverage, which seems ridiculously high, since double digit percentage daily moves are not uncommon. This hyper-charges profits as well as losses and is particularly attractive for high-conviction momentum traders and as importantly the exchange itself. Consequently, when simple momentum trading signals based on moving averages are strong, the perpetual outperforms the spot since speculators are willing to pay to access leverage. Figure 11.6 shows the often lengthy periods of premiums and discounts between perpetual futures and spot. This enabled hardy investors to accumulate return while being exposed to adverse moves in the underlying.

The Basis of Finite Duration Futures

A short section about interest rates implied from cryptocurrency futures of different maturities.

In Figure 11.7, the difference on BitMex, an innovator in the area of crypto-futures, between the perpetual and the shortest active future contract, is plotted. During the run up of the Bitcoin price in 2020 and early 2021, the implied interest rate was consistently positive across many crypto-exchanges. The futures basis on the CME exhibited the same behaviour. Various explanations have been proffered. It is likely

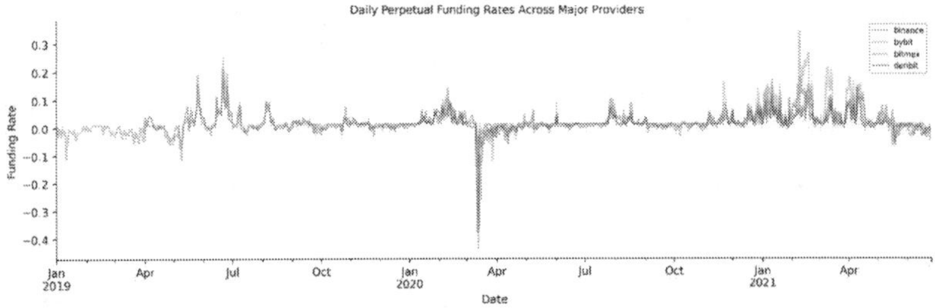

Figure 11.6 Funding Rates of Perpetuals in Percent on Multiple Exchanges. The Sign and Size of the Funding Rates are aligned across the Exchanges. Data Source: cryptoquant.com

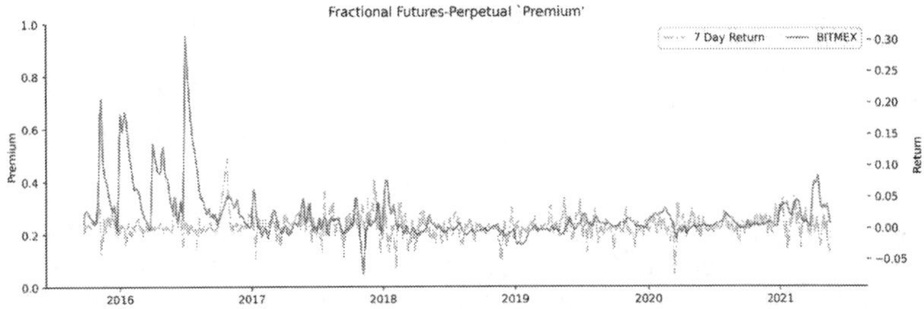

Figure 11.7 Weekly rolling average of the Premium between the perpetual and the closest futures contract to expiry: $\frac{F(t)-Perp(t)}{Perp(t)}$

that restrictions on the availability of leverage played a role in the creation of a positive basis. Futures positions are more efficient than positions in spot, since many of the more popular exchanges (Binance, Deribit, and Huobi, for example) only require an initial margin of between 20 and 50% for futures, while spot positions require full funding.

As a result, a spread developed between spot and futures of different maturities. Short-dated futures are cheaper to align with the spot price than long dated futures, which require a longer commitment of capital with its associated cost. This in itself leads to an upward sloping futures curve, but is maybe not an exhaustive explanation. Another possible reason is the difficulty for longer dated borrowing in cryptocurrencies due to the lack of general leverage and the limited connectivity between cryptofinance and the wider capital market.

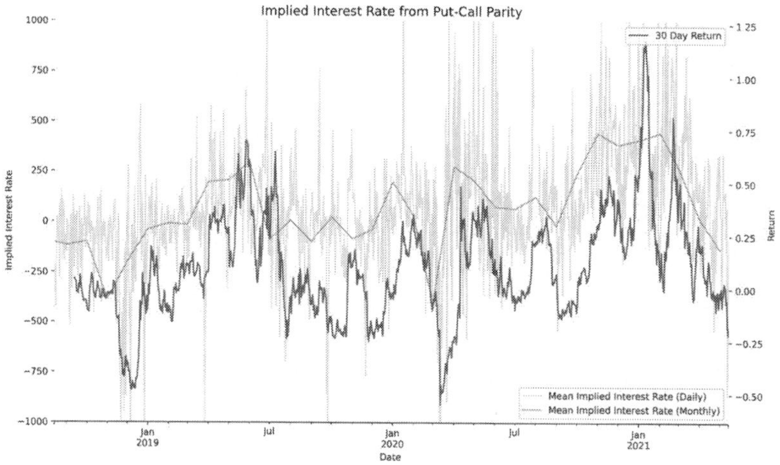

Figure 11.8 Put-Call parity implied interest rate, in annualised percent, from Options compared to the 30-day return of the underlying perpetual. Source: Deribit

11.8 Crypto-Options Market and Yield

This is another short section on CEX-traded products. Implied interest is derived from the Deribit options market, the largest crypto-option market, using put-call parity.[14] All expiries and strikes are used, since the liquidity of individual options is patchy, and both the weekly and calendar month average is plotted. The option implied interest rate, especially recently, plotted in Figure 11.8 follows a similar dynamic as the interest rate associated with the futures in Section 11.8. Implied yield, including convenience yield, has been discussed in Geman and Price (2020, 2021) for Deribit options and CME futures.

In Alexander and Imeraj (2021), much is made out of the fact that not just futures but also options on the Deribit exchange are of the 'inverse' variety. We cannot fully share this excitement. Inverse options, that is, options where the numeraire currency is in Bitcoin

14 The put-call parity is $B_t = -\frac{C_t - P_t - S_t}{K}$, where C_t is the call price, P_t the put price, and S_t the price of the perpetual contract, which acts as an underlying. The implied interest rate is $r = -\frac{\ln B_t}{T-t}$. It is calculated expiry by expiry and strike by strike for a given day and then re-sampled, and the mean is taken across all instruments. $T - t$ is the time to expiry.

but the notional amount is in USD, can be related by put-call symmetry to conventional options in the Black-Scholes valuation.

11.9 Conclusion: Challenges of DeFi are Tied to Yield

Although the abstract stated that positions on the blockchain have no intrinsic yield, that is, do not pay interest, this section described several interest-bearing crypto products. How can this apparent contradiction be resolved? Unencumbered by obligations and constraints, blockchain positions are instantly available, bypassing block size and updating constraints, and are accompanied by a convenience yield comparable to cash in fiat currencies[15] as compensation for forgone interest payments.

Yields in traditional finance and cryptofinance can vary significantly (Szalay, 2021). This is partly because of market segmentation imposed by technological, regulatory, and institutional barriers and partly because yields are commensurate with risk. For instance, stablecoins pegged to the USD offer significantly higher yields on DEXs and CEXs than deposits in traditional finance. This is because of varying risk profiles. While bank deposits are frequently insured, stablecoins – particularly the dominant Tether – are viewed with suspicion for the possibility of breaking their pegs.[16]

[15] As a caveat, in mathematical finance, incorporating cash is a challenge, and similarly pure blockchain positions, if one ignores the somewhat artificial catch-all of convenience yield, pose a modelling difficulty.

[16] In an episode aired on 16 June 2021, the stablecoin Iron of Iron. Finance mostly but not completely backed by USDC and reliant for stability on minting the associated token Titan broke its peg. When the price of Titan fell after an earlier rapid appreciation, a gap opened up between the price on Sushiswap, a decentralised exchange (DEX), and the lagging TWAP ('time weighted average price'), which functioned as the oracle for the stability mechanism. As a consequence, the incentive system designed to support Iron when the coin was below $1 by allowing arbitrageurs to buy Iron in the market and then redeem it at the full value as a mix of USDC and Titan failed, since the market discount in Iron was insufficient to compensate for the difference between the TWAP and the rapidly vanishing market value of Titan. Without the buying support of arbitrageurs Iron failed to recover and Titan fell further, as faith was lost in the mechanism. This lead to a vicious spiral with ever increasing price reductions in Titan driving the value from over $60 to close to zero. The TLV tumbled within a day by 99 + % from a peak of over $2 billion. For a fuller analysis, one has to also consider minting, that is, the creation of Iron, and more importantly, the motivation of Titan sellers. A

The introduction of staking, which enables the pledging of on-chain positions using token-specific mechanisms, has ideally created something strikingly similar to the short-term rates provided by central banks for fiat currencies. This affects the dynamics of DeFi, and the ramifications will only become clear over time.

This chapter's centrepiece are various yield-generating products and strategies that are currently popular for cryptocurrencies. The majority of these are less than 5 years old, and several have only recently gained prominence, with their TLVs reaching billions within months. Due to their complexity and the market's byzantine structure, each of them provides ample opportunity for additional research. We presented novel data from DEXs, CEXs, and the Ethereum 2.0 staking protocol. This chapter illustrates that cryptofinance is still grappling with leverage and yield enhancement.

Iterative development is used to create DeFi applications. Evolutionary improvement occurs through successive generations. Flawed approaches are forked away and vanish in an ideal world before any 'damage' is done. The term 'damage' is relative, and billions of dollars worth of tokens have already been lost due to various failures.[17] There could be a 'winner-takes-all' outcome, with the vast majority of attempts failing quickly and spectacularly, or there could be cycling through various phases with no stable tokens or DEXs.[18] The function of tokens as 'means of exchange' may preclude the existence of an equilibrium solution. Rather than 'failure being an impossibility', failure should be considered the default outcome.

Cryptofinance is embedded in economic history. Finance is littered with ostensibly limitless wealth schemes. The Mississippi and South Sea bubbles, which peaked in the early 1720s and were associated with France and Britain, are particularly well-known. In France, John Law,

good analysis, including market data for the critical day, can be found on the blog of I. (Kuznetsov, 2021).

[17] A recent episode involved the Uranium (a fission bomb) project, which reached a critical mass of $50 Million and blew up, because a security flaw in the smart code went unnoticed.

[18] Tokens and DEXs could also be confronted with an unending series of forks in their technology development path. Any potentially hard-to-reverse sub-optimal choice throws them out of the race since a multitude of competitors can spring up, copy all their correct historical decisions and overtake incumbents. Reputation or legitimacy mentioned as a way to protect a leadership position might not suffice, since as traders know, 'one is only as good as the last trade'.

an enterprising Scotsman, on the rise and possibly on the take, convinced the court to grant the Mississippi company a broad monopoly in exchange for the country's debt being assigned to a company-linked bank. This captured the public imagination, and the company's market value briefly exceeded France's GDP[19] before collapsing. This inauspicious affair fostered a (un)healthy scepticism of financial innovation. Whereas the South Sea bubble did not have the same effect on financial markets in Britain. Finance in its various forms, from double-entry book-keeping to access to the London capital market, underpinned the East India Company's success. This company, which at one point controlled a significant portion of the Indian subcontinent, accounted for half of global trade, was involved in large-scale famines, including the devastating one in 1770, and maintained a standing army comprising over 250,000 soldiers. The moral of the story: getting finance right is critical. For the same reason, a sound framework and finely tuned parameters[20] will be critical for DeFi to enable leverage and sustainable yields.

Cryptofinance's Galapagos syndrome with rich innovation isolated from traditional finance may be coming to an end, as high-profile institutions invest in the more vanilla end of the crypto spectrum, mostly Bitcoin.[21] Corporations such as MicroStrategy and Tesla and a host of banks are notable examples. Terms such as Hybrid Finance (HyFi) are gaining prominence as traditional players and regulators circle the new asset class and stake claims in cyberspace as they see fit.

Institutional involvement is not necessarily at odds with the original premise of crypto. Namely that legacy finance provides insufficient yield and is inherently unstable. This is already enshrined in the Bitcoin's genesis block as,[22] 'The Times 03/Jan/2009 Chancellor on brink of second bailout for banks'. How long can institutions resist the siren call of alternative yields in cryptofinance?

We gratefully acknowledge conversations with DC Brody and Sreejith Das.

[19] The joint crypto market capitalisation is only about 2% of world GDP, and by this measure could still have some room to grow.

[20] This is not easy, and even the designers of the board game Monopoly needed more than a decade to come up with amenable rules.

[21] bitcointreasuries.net

[22] en.bitcoin.it/wiki/Genesis_block

Bibliography

Alexander, C. and Imeraj, A. (2021). Inverse options in a black-scholes world. arXiv:2107.12041.

BIS (2021). Statistical release: Otc derivatives statistics at end-december 2020. *www.bis.org*.

Brody, D. C., Hughston, L. P., and Meister, B. K. (2020). Theory of cryptocurrency interest rates. *SIAM Journal on Financial Mathematics*, 11(1):148–168.

Credit Suisse (2020). The global wealth report 2020. *Credit Suisse Research Institute*.

Daian, P., Goldfeder, S., Kell, T., Li, Y., Zhao, X., Bentov, I., Breidenbach, L., and Juels, A. (2019). Flash boys 2.0: Frontrunning, transaction reordering, and consensus instability in decentralized exchanges. arXiv:1904.05234.

Dennett, D. and Roy, D. (2015). Our transparent future. *Scientific American*, 312:64–69.

Geman, H. and Price, H. (2020). In the vaults: Bitcoin futures and storage insurance. *The Actuary*.

Geman, H. and Price, H. (2021). Bitcoin spot and derivatives markets: Searching for completeness. *Risk and Decision Analysis*, 8(3–4):113–125.

Johnson, H. (1987). Options on the maximum or the minimum of several assets. *The Journal of Financial and Quantitative Analysis*, 22:277.

Jr, G. and K, A. (1988). Undated futures markets. *Journal of Futures Markets*, 8(1):89–97.

Kelly, J. L. (1956). A new interpretation of information rate. *Bell System Technical Journal*, 35:917–926.

Kruppa, M. (2021). Silicon Valley bets on crypto projects to disrupt finance. *Appeared on FT.com on 3/6/2021*.

Kuznetsov, I. (2021). Analysis of the TITAN fall – going the distance. *Jeiwan.net*.

Lipton, A. (2001). *Mathematical methods for foreign exchange: A financial engineer's approach*. World Scientific.

Lv, Y. and Meister, B. K. (2009). Application of the Kelly criterion to Ornstein-Uhlenbeck processes. In *International Conference on Complex Sciences*, pages 1051–1062. Springer.

Lv, Y. and Meister, B. K. (2010). Implication of the Kelly criterion for multidimensional processes. *International Journal of Theoretical and Applied Finance*, 13(01):93–112.

Margrabe, W. (1978). The value of an option to exchange one asset for another. *The Journal of Finance*, 33(1):177–186.

Maruyama, R. and Washimi, K. (2021). Cross-currency swap market through the lens of OTC derivative transaction data: Impact of

COVID-19 and subsequent recovery. *Bank of Japan Review*, 2021-J-4, 2021-E-1.

Qin, K., Zhou, L., Gamito, P., Jovanovic, P., and Gervais, A. (2021). An empirical study of DeFi liquidations: Incentives, risks, and instabilities. *arXiv:2106.06389*.

Shiller, R. J. (1993). Measuring asset values for cash settlement in derivative markets: Hedonic repeated measures indices and perpetual futures. *The Journal of Finance*, 48:911–931.

Szalay, E. (2021). The Tether equation for investors: Risk vs yield. *Appeared on FT.com on 29/10/2021*.

Zhang, Y., Chen, X., and Park, D. (2018). Formal specification of constant product (xy= k) market maker model and implementation. *White paper*.

Zhou, L., Qin, K., Torres, C. F., Le, D. V., and Gervais, A. (2020). High-frequency trading on decentralized on-chain exchanges. arXiv:2009.14021.

12 *The 'Klair Effect'*
A New Monetary Framework on Controlling Inflation Using CBDC

SARBJIT KLAIR

12.1 Introduction

There have been many discussions concerning central bank digital currency (CBDC) and its disruptive properties, which show their usefulness compared to fiat currencies. However, the discussions have not extended to more meaningful applications to the world of CBDCs. This chapter aims to extend our understanding and the use cases for CBDCs in line with domestic and international economic policies.

Bitcoin has illustrated its functions using a 'proof-of-work' system to verify transactions on the blockchain. What further magnifies Bitcoin's interest is that there will only be 21 million Bitcoin available. Once all this amount has been mined via its 'proof-of-work' system, there will be no more mined. With this fixed supply brings forth fluctuated demand, where Bitcoin's price is determined directly by these variables. This has conceptualised the notion that Bitcoin is 'deflationary' by substance. But how can we utilise this deflationary model in the real world? When we think of centralisation, we associate it with control, organisation, and management, and this association can be extended to CBDCs.

This deflationary proposition for CBDCs is called the 'Klair Effect'. During the pandemic and every financial crisis, quantitative easing has been at the full front of a country's monetary policy, but what does the government do with the money it intends to inject into the economy but no longer wishes to proceed with quantitative easing. This chapter will look at the central banks' ability to 'delete' unused cash on their balance sheet.

The Klair Effect can be contrasted with quantitative easing to control the inflation rate through CBDCs, given the controllability and managing properties of CBDCs.

CBDCs will become essential tools for central banks to continue payments in a safe means, but it is worth noting the following:

1. A central bank should not compromise monetary or financial stability by issuing a CBDC;
2. CBDCs will co-exist with current forms of money; and,
3. CBDCs should promote innovation and efficiencies in payment transactions.[1]

This idea has been a product of my solitude for 2 years, and I am proud to share this with the UCL Centre for Blockchain Technologies. I trust that you will enjoy reading it, as much as I have writing it.

12.2 What are CBDCs

CBDCs are known as a 'central bank digital currency'. These currencies are unique due to their blockchain capabilities and transmit value for low fees, and quick payment settlements between individuals and organisations have placed CBDCs in the spotlight. Blockchain technology allows individuals to copy and view transactions on a public ledger, where this information is distributed and not controlled by a centralised authority.

A CBDC is similar to a crypto-asset, but happens to be government-issued and will not use the decentralised properties of blockchain technology for anyone to copy or view the transaction history. Instead, a CBDC uses distributive ledger technology (DLT), which allows the central bank to control the currency's total supply and manage the digital currency.

12.3 Monetary Challenges and the Need for CBDCs

Confidence in Central Banks

In countries, where access to physical cash is somewhat scarce or going down, there is a concern that households will no longer have access to risk-free central bank money. If people do not have confidence in the cash system, they may withdraw their funds and revert to other assets that hold 'inherent value'. The use of a CBDC reinforces a type of digital presence for households and businesses, which provides confidence

[1] Bank for International Settlements, 'Central bank digital currencies: foundational principles and core features', Page 1, Report No.1 (2020). Available at: www.bis.org/publ/othp33.pdf

and allows central banks to govern and monitor the economy's cash system as a country becomes more reliant on digital payment systems.

Efficiency in Transmitting Value

During the COVID-19 pandemic, we have seen developing countries struggling to distribute food and monetary supplies to those in need. However, suppose the monetary supplies have ceased to operate in normal conditions. In that case, the use of a CBDC could be seen as a viable substitute, where the CBDC payment system could be an alternative way of transmitting value from one party to another and distributing money to accounts more efficiently and pragmatically. It also means an offline infrastructure is created for this value to be transmitted along with the independencies of mobile devices and electricity.

The immediate downturn is using online systems to facilitate the CBDC framework because it may be prone to cyber-attacks. If an attack is successful, it would affect many participants in the supply chain and threaten the confidence and integrity of the CBDC.

Effective Cross-Border Payments System[2]

Cross-border payments are financial transactions where the payer and the recipient are based in different countries. These types of payments include wholesale and retail payments, including remittances.

- **Wholesale cross-border payments:** these are between financial institutions to support customers' activities, or their own cross-border activities such as borrowing and lending, foreign exchange and the trading of equity and debt, derivatives, and other financial instruments.
- **Retail cross-border payments:** these payments are made between businesses and individuals. This includes remittance, where individuals may send funds from one country to another.

A domestic CBDC can be used to send payments to and from another jurisdiction receptive to CBDCs. It also minimises barriers and allows for seamless transactions between participants because the ability to

[2] Bank of England, 'Cross-Border Payments', Date: 15 June 2021. Available at: www.bankofengland.co.uk/payment-and-settlement/cross-border-payments

settle payments in a matter of seconds would facilitate efficiencies in transferring value.

12.4 How Do Central Banks Issue Money

Central banks issue three types of money: physical cash, electronic cash reserves, and private money. Physical cash is accessible amongst people and businesses, whereas cash reserves are electronic, which is available to financial institutions. The third type is private money which is widely accessible through electronic commercial bank deposits. Central banks support commercial bank money in different ways:

1. Allows commercial banks to settle inter-bank payments using central bank money;
2. Enabling convertibility between commercial and central bank money through banknote provisions; and,
3. Offering contingent liquidity through the lender of last resort function.[3]

It should be noted that physical cash and cash reserves are a liability to a central bank, commercial bank deposits are not. Thus, CBDC would be a new type of central bank money for a country to consider, but the CBDC would be provided and distributed similarly to physical cash.

A central bank's balance sheet is divided into assets and liabilities. A central bank's ability to supply money is to achieve specific objectives for a given economy, such as; low inflation, economic growth, or an increase in employment. Money is created and destroyed electronically as a form of information. The creation of this money is recorded on the balance sheet, and equally if it is removed, this is also noted on the balance sheet.

It may be difficult to understand a bank's balance sheet, but we are focused on the assets and liabilities that are necessary to understand the money supply process.

The central bank's assets include:

- **Loans** – these are made to commercial banks;
- **Securities** – mainly in the form of Treasuries; and,

[3] Bank for International Settlements, "Central bank digital currencies: foundational principles and core features", Page 1, Report No.1 (2020). Available at: www.bis.org/publ/othp33.pdf

Table 12.1 *Central Bank Balance Sheet*

	Assets	Liabilities
Banker's bank	Loans	Bank accounts
Government's bank	Securities	Currency
	Foreign exchange reserves	Government's account

- **Foreign exchange reserves** – these are made in the form of foreign bonds issued by foreign governments.

Central bank's liabilities include:

- **Commercial bank accounts** – this is known as reserves, where commercial banks keep their deposits with the Federal Reserve central bank;
- **Currency** – this is held by the public; and,
- **Federal government bank account** – this is the federal bank, where it will deposit its revenues and pay its bills electronically.

Central banks provide regular updates on their balance sheets to maintain transparency and minimise information asymmetries. In addition, it allows market participants to keep an eye on the behaviours of the central bank and whether the economy is headed in the right direction or not.

When the Federal Reserve purchases \$1 million Treasuries from a primary dealer, a bank will note this amount in the bank's reserve account by \$1 million. This is how money is created, rather than money being transferred between bank accounts. While this money is made out of nothing, it will be recorded on the Federal Reserve's balance sheet. In Table 12.1, we can see that a commercial bank's account is a liability for the Federal Reserve, it will increase its liability equally, which is offset by the Treasury, which is an asset. When the Federal Reserve looks to decrease the money supply, it sells these Treasuries to these primary dealers, debiting the dealer's account, transferring the Treasury amount to the dealer, and reducing the Federal Reserve's liability and its assets by the same amount.

Table 12.2 ***Central Bank Balance Sheet After Treasury Purchase***

Central bank balance Sheet		Banking systems' balance sheet	
Assets	Liabilities	Assets	Liabilities
Securities+£200 billion	Reserves+£200 billion	Securities+£200 billion Reserves+£200 billion	

12.5 Central Bank Transactions: Controlling and Managing Money Supply

There are three ways in which Central banks change the money supply in a given economy, these include;

- **Open-market operations** – where the central bank buys and sells securities, this takes the shape of Government Treasuries;
- **Foreign exchange intervention** – where a central bank exchanges domestic currency for a foreign currency; and
- **Discount loans** – this is a loan made by the central bank to a commercial bank.

Open-Market Operations

When the Federal Reserve buys and sells securities on the open market, it will take the shape of Government Treasuries, this will be done to its primary dealers as an open-market operation. In the United States, the financial market is predominantly held in the United States, which means the New York Federal Reserve will buy and sell these securities.

In times of a crisis, the Federal Reserve will look to stimulate an economy, it will increase the money supply by purchasing by (X) amount. This transaction expands the Federal Reserve's balance sheet because it increases the liabilities by (X) amount and its assets by the same amount.

The primary dealers' reserves held at a central bank are a liability, and this is seen in Table 12.2. When the Federal Reserve purchases the Treasuries, it increases the demand for the Treasuries; this causes the Treasury price to increase, which is subject to the interest rate. The lower interest rate makes money more readily available in the hope of stimulating the economy. Ultimately, this causes the money supply to increase because non-spendable Treasuries will be exchanged for reserve balance (See Central Bank Balance Sheet).

Foreign Exchange Transactions

A foreign exchange market intervention influences the foreign exchange rate, but it is not very practical to use this method. Instead, the central bank will hold onto foreign exchange currencies on its balance sheet to hedge against domestic currency risks. The central bank will hold foreign reserves to provide liquidity to serve its economy's needs and keep currencies with a higher value than its domestic currency. For example, the central bank will hold foreign bonds than the currency itself, if it wishes to purchase the US dollar, it will buy US Dollars with Pound Sterling, then buy the bonds, and this is transmitted into book value.

Discount Loans

A discount loan is a loan made by the central bank to a commercial bank. Commercial banks will borrow from the central bank to cover any shortfalls in their reserves. When this money is borrowed from the central bank, it is collateralised with Treasuries. This increases the money supply (intentionally or unintentionally) because the reserves are spendable and Treasuries are not. However, when the commercial bank pays the central bank, it will receive its collateral back, and its reserve account is reduced by the original loan, which reduces the money supply again. Typically, discount loans are overnight but can be extended in times of financial downfall.

In 'normal' market conditions, commercial banks will borrow from one another in the inter-bank market using a benchmark rate such as 'SONIA' or 'EURIBOR' to calculate interest rates on the requested loan amount. These loans are provided without collateral.

12.6 'Klair Effect': A New Paradigm for Quantitative Tightening

Basics of Quantitative Easing and Quantitative Tightening

Quantitative tightening is a monetary policy applied to decrease the amount of liquidity within the economy. This policy is the opposite of 'quantitative easing', which increases money supply to stimulate an economy.

Central banks applied quantitative easing worldwide to counter recessions, which were seen in the 2007–2008 subprime mortgage crisis. More recently, this has applied to the 2020 COVID-19 recession, which has created a recession globally. To combat the 2020 COVID-19 recession, the Federal Reserve provided support packages for the US, including:

- Near-zero interest rates – this includes lowering the cost of borrowing on mortgages, car loans, and other loans, which will ultimately reduce the interest income paid to savers.
- Encouraging banks to lend – the Federal Reserve has lowered the rate that it charges for loans from its 'discount window'[4] by 2%, from 2.25% to 0.25%. These are short-term loans that are taken out at the end of one day and repaid the following morning, but the Federal Reserve has extended this period to 90 days.
- Supporting corporations and businesses – the Federal Reserve provided new bond issuances with corporate credit facilities, which allowed companies to access credit to maintain business operations and capacity during periods of downturn in relation to the COVID pandemic. In the United Kingdom, the government has provided support packages for businesses and households with interest-free loans and grants to sustain the impact of the pandemic and the reduction of services.

While there are support packages from the Federal Reserve and government packages to sustain market shocks worldwide, the use of quantitative easing must be considered in a dire light, and one of the main consequences is the increase in inflation rates.

In Annex 1, I have illustrated how traditional Quantitative Easing works. Once the newly printed money has entered the real economy, there is no way of acquiring it back or simply 'deleting' the new printed money supply.[5] The CBDC database keeps a record of

[4] By providing accessible funding, the 'discount window' helps deposit institutions such as banks to manage their liquidity risks and avoid negative consequences for their customers, such as bank runs in times of financial downturns

[5] See Annex 1 for more information.

the amount of money held by every entity, such as people or businesses. This can be reviewed periodically to see how funds have been exchanged between participants to understand consumption and saving behaviours.

Goal of Quantitative Tightening

The ultimate goal of quantitative tightening is to normalise interest rates to avoid an increasing inflation rate by raising the cost of access to money and reducing demand for goods and services in the economy. Most people have not heard of the term 'quantitative tightening', nor understand its existence, and it is with good standing. In 2018, quantitative tightening was agreed in the United States, Bank of Japan, and European Central Bank to relieve some debt on its balance sheet, but in 2019, this ended due to negative market conditions and a slowdown in the world economy due to the US–China Trade War saga.[6]

The truth is that quantitative tightening has not been taken to a mainstream level, and our attachment to quantitative easing heightens this position. However, it should be understood that the limitation of quantitative tightening is subject to the current functionality and utility of a country's financial system. Sure, a central bank cannot control how its citizens consume, invest, or save their money. But, the central bank can supervise and monitor consumer and investor behaviour using various factors and indicators. There are still limitations on the country's money and its application, and CBDCs will advance central banks in their ability to extend their monetary policy.

The digitisation of CBDCs allows the central bank to understand how much money is being consumed, invested, and saved on a granular level rather than speculate on the finer details. Although the money supply is vastly increased using quantitative easing in times of crisis, it becomes difficult to reverse this notion when there is excess liquidity in the economy. Either this extra liquidity is held on the balance sheet (liability), or the central bank speculates the primary dealer will request these funds to provide loans to corporations and households later.

[6] Bloomberg, 'Federal Reserve Move Ends the Short Era of Global Quantitative Tightening'. Date: 1 August 2019. Available at: www.bloomberg.com/news/articles/2019-08-01/fed-move-ends-the-short-era-of-global-quantitative-tightening

Effects of Inflation

When inflation rises, the amount of goods and services that can be purchased decreases. The value of assets rises, so those who own physical assets such as property and stocks benefit from the price/value distribution of their holdings going up. Despite this, those who seek to acquire them will need to pay more for them.

Policymakers and economists favour a low and steady inflation rate with a target of on or around 2%. The desire to maintain a low, stable inflation rate and price stability for goods and services ensures the usefulness of money as a means of exchange, unit of account, and a store of value. If inflation is not stable, it causes participants to look for alternative means to transact value between themselves. Prices no longer reflect the supply and demand. It drives economic inefficiencies, and businesses become uncertain of their ability to maintain and create infrastructure because lenders require a higher rate of return on their principal loans due to the fear of uncertainty.

COVID-19 has dramatically altered the spending patterns of UK consumers, as people avoid their means of social leisure such as bars, gyms, and the cinema. In 2019 and 2020, it was not a normal year for spending because it was led by behavioural changes and lockdown measures concerning social distancing. The cost of clothing and footwear prices increased in May 2021[7] and contributed to the 12-month consumer price indices (CPIs) inflation rate (see Figure 12.1). In addition, transport and recreation and culture costs have increased between April and May 2021. Consumers will have felt the rate of inflation, principally for the cost of fuel with an increase of 17.9%, which has been the highest rate since February 2017.[8] As of June 2021, the UK inflation rate stands at 2.1%.[9]

The CPI measures changes in the prices of goods and services by households. During 2019 and 2020, we were confronted with governmental policies to combat the coronavirus, which led the demand for goods and services to go down, and their supplies remain stagnate.

[7] Office for National Statistics, 'Consumer Price Inflation, UK: May 2021'. Available at: www.ons.gov.uk/economy/inflationandpriceindices/bulletins/consumerpriceinflation/may2021

[8] ibid.

[9] Office for National Statistics, 'CPIH Annual Rate 00: All Items 2015=100', 16 June 2021. Available at: www.ons.gov.uk/economy/inflationandpriceindices/timeseries/l55o/mm23

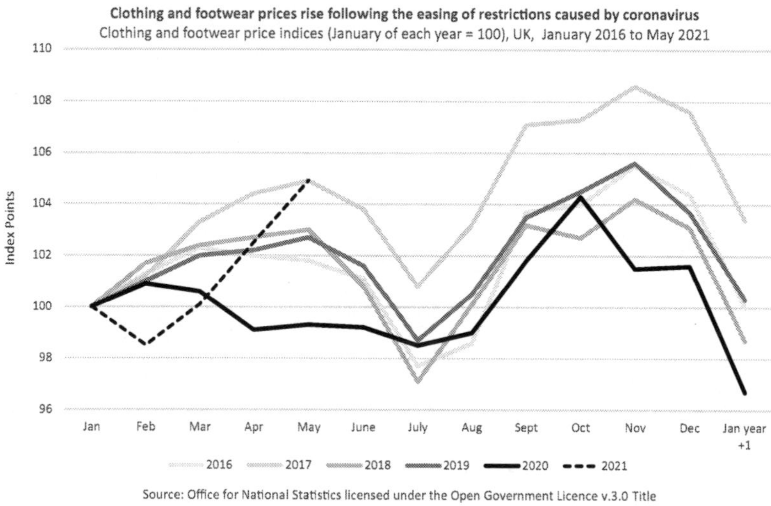

Figure 12.1 Clothing and Footwear Indices: January 2016 to May 2021[10]

While the government provides loans and grants to support households and corporations throughout the COVID-19 pandemic, this type of quantitative easing has contributed to today's current inflation spikes.

We now turn to more recent times, namely Figure 12.2, which shows the extent to which the different categories of consumptive goods have contributed to the CPI, including the Owner Occupiers' Housing Cost (CPIH).

From April 2021, transport has shown an uptrend in comparison to other categories, which has been caused by the increase of fuel prices. In August 2020, the CPIH for transport was −0.10, a year later, it is now 0.87. This is the biggest increase on this graph, but at the same time, this is understandable. Like transport, many other activities such as leisure took a major hit due to lockdown restrictions, but as soon as these measures began to lift, we see drastic increases, especially when we compare the yearly figures. In light of this, we see a large spike in leisure activities such as restaurants and hotels between July 2021 and August 2021. We can also see the housing and housing services remain steady from April 2021 that contributed heavily to the 3% inflation rate.

[10] Supra, at page 9.

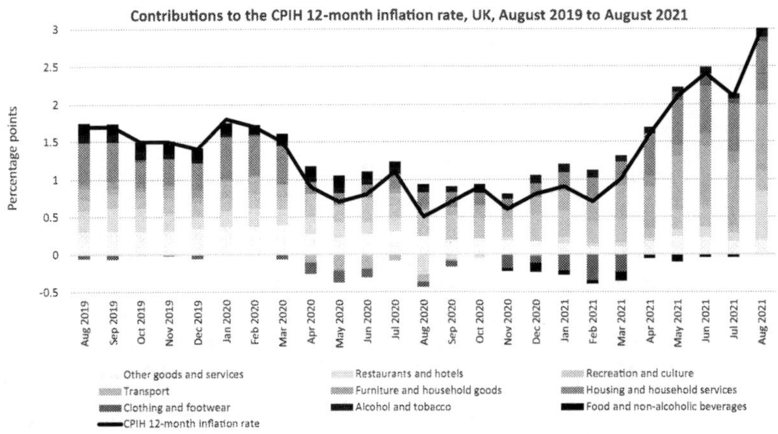

Figure 12.2 Contributions to the CPIH 12-month Inflation Rate: August 2019 to August 2021

Countries such as Venezuela have seen a surge in inflation rates, which has rendered their currency worthless, and the pandemic has accelerated this currency position.[11] In the United Kingdom and the United States, a popular monetary tool to reduce the rate of inflation is increasing interest rates to encourage saving, so people will save their money instead of spending it. In the short term, it reduces spending and can slow down economic growth and inflation rate down the line. Nevertheless, it takes time to see how effective the policy is, which cannot be ideally seen in the short term.

12.7 Klair Effect: How Is It Used

The 'Klair Effect' is a form of quantitative tightening, but it does not use the apparatus of interest rates to control the inflation rate; instead, a 'delete button' to control the money supply on a central banks' balance sheet.

There is an obvious concern, if an increase in interest rates cannot control the money supply, while quantitative easing causes inflation without an intended economic growth target, this leads to stagflation

[11] Trading Economics, 'Venezuela Inflation Rate', Date: 2021. Available at: tradingeconomics.com/venezuela/inflation-cpi

in the economy, thus the Klair Effect to 'delete' a CBDC amount can prevent destabilisation in economies.

There are three ways for the deletion process to occur;

- After the creation of the CBDC, if the CBDC is no longer needed, it can be deleted;
- Purchasing CBDCs in the economy (households and corporations) and deleting this money; and,
- If the central bank converts and transfers its 'fiat currency' liabilities into CBDCs, and no longer needs it, it can 'delete' the CBDC value total to the initial transferred amount.

After the creation of the CBDC, if the CBDC is no longer needed, it can be deleted.

I am not proposing that the money is just 'deleted', but the purpose of the 'deletion' is to moderate the monetary supply. If the central bank creates £500 million worth of CBDCs and injects £200 million worth into the economy, it now has £300 million remaining in its liabilities. If the central bank proposes £25 million worth of CBDCs to be injected for the next 12 months to support the economy, but the central bank decides against this notion, it can remove this liability from its balance sheet. The CBDC is created similarly to that of a fiat currency, but its digitisation allows it to be deleted.[12]

There are different ways in which quantitative easing can be used to stimulate an economy, where it may provide grants and loans to households and corporations as a means to support consumptive behaviour or reduce interest rates and incentivise corporations to take loans to increase employment rates. But the design flaw is that central banks do not have control over their own monetary supply, once the money goes into the economy, it cannot get it back. In the case of CBDCs, it completely changes the dynamic of this perceptive because the central bank can create money and delete it.

When a central bank decides to provide quantitative easing, it can provide grants, loans, and other forms of stimulus to encourage spending. This money will be directly injected into the economy, and if the central bank decides to change its plan, there is no actual means of 'retrieving' the sum. This money is circulating into the economy for

[12] This is seen in Tables 12.5 and 12.7 in more detail below.

whatever means the individual, household, or corporation wishes to use it. At first glance, it may seem trivial, and there is nothing to worry about, but this can unintentionally increase inflation due to the increased money supply.

If this capital injection was made using CBDCs, this money supply could be controlled, managed, and organised by the central bank. This also means that if the central bank finds itself holding excess money on its balance sheet, it has the option to remove it and enable the implementation of other monetary policies to control the inflation rate, such as raising interest rates or prioritizing its balance of payments.

The ability to manage stimulus or quantitative easing policies on a micro-level allows for more control and supervision of a domestic currency, especially where inflation becomes heightened in poor economic conditions. Suppose policymakers have the idea of 'pumping money into the economy to keep it stabilised in the short-term'. In that case, there is no possibility of controlling the amount of inflation in the future. Giving central banks the ability to 'create' money and 'delete' unused money will maximise the possibility of furthering economic policy.

Assume the central bank will stimulate the economy using CBDCs on the condition that GDP is below 1%. This stimulus package will consist of £50 million in CBDCs being injected into the economy. However, if the GDP figure is above 1%, this means the central bank will not stimulate the economy with the proposed sum. However, this unused money remains on the central bank's balance sheet, using the 'Klair Effect', it can be deleted to reduce its liabilities. If it does not choose to delete the left-over sum of money, it will be held on the balance sheet with no utility function.

The notional position to consider here is 'delete'. Effectively, the central bank will create money with a short-term and long-term view, and it will look to distribute the 'new' funds over a period of time. With a plan in place, if its variables coincide with the current market conditions, it will utilise the new form of money. This money will be roaming into the economy for a productive purpose, which corresponds to its fiscal or monetary policy. But, at the same time, the same means by which money is created, the 'unused' value should be deleted.

In times of a financial crisis, many spectators will judge an economy on its finances and will closely scrutinise the behaviours and practices of the central bank. This will be represented on its balance sheet and

Table 12.3 ***Participant's CBDC Account with CBDC***

Participant X's CBDC account (household, merchant, corporation)	
Amount	£200,000,000
CBDC or fiat currency	*CBDC (All)*

past financial transactions. If there are 'unused' sums of money with no means of function, it could reduce the level of confidence in the market and how this is perceived by the rest of the market. With this being said, the 'delete' function is 'more than what it says on the tin', but a viable resource to instil confidence in a market, where inflation or stagflation is a real concern in the economy.

Purchasing CBDCs in the Economy (Households and Corporations) and Deleting this Money

This is more complicated, but it is feasible in the given circumstances. In the above example, we explained that £200 million worth of CBDCs is in the economy. If the central bank requests this CBDC amount from all participants holding this amount, it can request the participant's amount, where it will denounce the CBDC from their accounts for fiat currency, namely GBP.

Example 1:

Depending on how CBDCs will be integrated is determined by the central banks and governments, whether it would be feasible to work with banking institutions or have a separate account with CBDCs, where these transactions remain digitised with no means of receiving cash from an ATM or a post office. We will assume this is done on a separate account called the 'CBDC Account', where participants can exchange, save, and spend their CBDC. The central bank can request the CBDC from the participant at any time if it wishes to do so, as long as it provides reasonable notice to the participant. It may purchase/buy-back the CBDC using its securities (asset), where the participant's CBDC account will be credited with fiat currency, and the central bank exchanges the security into GBP (fiat currency) to be debited into the participant's CBDC account (see Tables 12.3 and 12.5).

Table 12.4 ***Central Bank Uses Securities to Buy-Back CBDC from Public***

	Assets		Liabilities	
Bankers' Bank	Loans	£2 billion	Bank Accounts	£5 billion
Government's Bank	Securities	£10 billion – £200 million = £9.8 billion*	Currency (fiat currency)	£10 billion
	Foreign Exchange Reserves	£20 billion	**Central Bank Digital Currency (Pound Sterling)**	**£300 million**
			Government's Account	£2 billion
Total:		**£32 billion**		**£17.3 billion**

*The 'Securities' amount has now been reduced from £10 billion to £9.8 billion, which reflects the £200 million deducted from the purchase of the £200 million CBDCs in the economy.

From the participant's viewpoint, their ability to consume, invest, or save in the economy has not changed nor has it been affected because the CBDC is treated the same as a fiat currency. In this example, the central bank used its securities (asset) to purchase the liability (CBDC), where it would delete the £200 million worth of CBDC (see section 12.5). Simply put, the central bank used £200 million worth of securities to buy back its liabilities to delete, which becomes reflective on the balance sheet.

Example 2:

This example utilises the interchangeable nature of CBDCs to transfer value from CBDCs into fiat currency. If the central bank requests the participant to transfer their CBDC into fiat, they can see the request on

Table 12.5 ***Participant's CBDC Account with Fiat***

Participant X's CBDC account (household, merchant, corporation)	
Amount:	£200,000,000
CBDC or fiat currency	*Fiat (All)*

their account and accept this position accordingly. Once the request has been accepted, the account will substitute the central bank's fiat current liability with the Participant's CBDC account with fiat (see Tables 12.3 and 12.5). The central bank will receive the participant's CBDC in a seamless peer-to-peer manner.

In the first example, the central bank used its 'securities' to facilitate the buy-back of the participant's CBDC. In Example 2, the transaction involved the sale of its 'fiat currency' to finance the exchange of the participant's CBDC. In both scenarios, the participant has their funds intact and remains functional in the economy.

If the central bank converts and transfers its 'Fiat Currency' liabilities into CBDCs, and no longer needs it, it can 'delete' the CBDC value total to the initial transferred amount.

The Klair Effect should not simply delete a portion of the CBDC value on a central bank's balance sheet, but the central bank should be in a position to convert and transfer its 'fiat currency' to a 'CBDC' and set out the purpose and target for the same. Converting the 'fiat currency' liability to a 'CBDC' liability allows the debt to remain on its balance sheet.[13] There should be no problem in doing this because the debt is visible in one shape or form. Both currencies are government-issued by transferring the liability from one class to another form that can be actively used, where it can be held as a reserve or has an use-function instead of keeping the liability on the balance sheet without a real means.

It is not simple enough to transfer all fiat currency liabilities and convert them into CBDCs; however, it will need to assign a specific amount into CBDCs to integrate CBDCs in the economy, where consumers can spend CBDCs like fiat currencies. Once the economy is

[13] This can be held as an on – or off-balance sheet for the central bank's balance sheet.

Table 12.6 *Central Bank Balance Sheet with CBDCs*

	Assets	Liabilities
Bankers' bank	Loans	Bank accounts
Government's bank	Securities	Currency (fiat currency)
	Foreign exchange reserves	Central bank digital currency (Pound Sterling)
		Government's account

in a position of stability and growth, the central bank can consider minimising its liabilities and deleting the CBDC later.

This feature allows the liabilities to be functional in a society rather than 'do nothing' on its balance sheet. From the point of confidence in stagnate-to-poor economic conditions, the ability to digitise transactions creates a position of consumption in another means, and while it may not be enough to propel the economy from poor economic conditions to a substantial position, it creates new possibilities in the way we consume and interact with participants.

12.8 Klair Effect: How Will It Work?

In this section, the reader must understand that CBDCs and fiat currencies are interchangeable in the real world, and CBDCs have no relevance in a decentralised manner.[14] CBDCs have the same use functions and properties as fiat currencies, but their digital functionalities allow for ease of control and management of the currency. For the purposes of this chapter, there is £500 million worth of CBDCs, and each CBDC (in British Pound Sterling) is worth £1 (1:1).[15] It is also assumed that this CBDC is not traded or held as a reserve in other countries and is only available in the United Kingdom.

14 It is easier to understand CBDCs in this manner because CBDCs and fiat currencies will be valued at £1 and is government-issued.

15 In addition, CBDCs are deemed as a separate liability on the central bank's balance sheet.

The ability to appropriate the CBDC is much more accessible than a country's fiat currency because the entire process is digitised, and every participant uses the CBDC, including central banks, merchants, households, corporations, etc. Furthermore, it is easily controllable and manageable, extending to adding or 'deleting' the CBDC at any point in time.

The interchangeability of fiat currencies and CBDCs allows a central bank to hold the same balance sheet items for completeness, and allows the central bank to operate and function as it would without the CBDCs. Moreover, the agile nature of digital currencies allows all participants to engage in normal transactions without the fear of losing any value between their 'Fiat Currency Wallet' and their 'CBDC Wallet'.

The UK has been steady in controlling its inflation targets over the years, but like many countries, where there is financial turmoil, the use of quantitative easing to support corporations and households causes the inflation rate to rise, and this is typically followed by more quantitative easing over the years to sustain a smoother economy. In August 2008 and September 2011, we saw the inflation rate rise above 4%, and in the pandemic, we saw the inflation rate steadily rise above 2%.[16]

In view of the above inflation levels, a fiat currency will find it difficult to control or hedge its inflation rate because the country's economic circumstances may be gloomy or unforeseeable in the future. In September 2008, the inflation rate spiked to 4.8%, it took 9 months (June 2009) for the inflation rate to hit under 2% (1.9%). Later, the rate of inflation spiked to 4.5% in this level had dropped to 2% (1.9%) in October 2013.[17] Despite the fiscal and monetary policies that were applied to minimise the risk of inflation for the above years, it took several months to de-escalate the inflation rate. These time delays become problematic because it can take up to a year to see any possible change, and the majority of this is dependent on confidence. If confidence is high, businesses and consumers will continue to spend, despite raising the interest rates to deter lending.

[16] Office for National Statistic, 'CPIH Annual Rate 00: All Items 2015=100'. Available at: www.ons.gov.uk/economy/inflationandpriceindices/timeseries/l55o/mm23

[17] ibid.

12.9 CBDC Deletion: Foreign Exchange Reserves – CBDC Float

In the case of CBDCs, the funds can be deleted from its balance sheet to de-load its risks. In Table 12.7, you can see £300 million is held as a liability called 'Central Bank Digital Currency' and is not conflicting with the 'Currency (Fiat Currency)'. However, I propose that this amount is not just deleted and forgotten, but we use 'Foreign Exchange Reserves – CBDC Float' as a float/reserve for any complications along the way. This is placed as a separate matter on the balance sheet of the central bank.

There is an essential need for a float/reserve because there may be unidentified risks and repercussions that may happen as a result of 'deleting' large quantities of money in a short-term amount of time, including the 'deletion' of money for people that need it for a legitimate purpose. For example, if people are not rightfully included in the stimulus group, it will weaken overall market confidence. This float/reserve allows for swift coordination if anything goes wrong.

In Table 12.8, I have explained that 'Foreign Exchange Reserves – CBDC Float' should be used as the float/reserve, where money is transferred from 'Foreign Exchange Reserves – CBDC Float' to the

Table 12.7 *Central Bank Balance Sheet with Central Bank Digital Currency Held as a Liability*

	Assets		Liabilities	
Bankers' bank	Loans	£2 billion	Bank accounts	£5 billion
Government's bank	Securities	£10 billion	Currency (fiat currency)	£10 billion
	Foreign exchange reserves	£20 billion	**Central bank digital currency (Pound Sterling)**	**£300 million**
			Government's account	£2 billion
Total:		**£32 billion**		**£17.3 billion**

Table 12.8 ***Central Bank Balance Sheet with Central Bank Digital Currency Now "Deleted"***

	Assets		Liabilities	
Bankers' bank	Loans	£2 billion	Bank accounts	£5 billion
Government's bank	Securities	£10 billion	Currency (fiat currency)	£10 billion
	Foreign exchange reserves	***£19.9 billion***	**Central bank digital currency (Pound Sterling)**	£0*
	Foreign exchange reserves – CBDC Float	***£100 million***	Government's account	£2 billion
Total:		**£32 billion**		**£17 billion**

*The 'Central Bank Digital Currency' amount is now £0. To prevent any complications, the 'Foreign Exchange Reserves – CBDC Float' amount will be used as a reserve/float to compensate for any issues or leakages in the future.

corporation's and household's CBDC accounts. Once the central bank or primary issuer has provided the money to the individuals requesting their funds, the '*Foreign Exchange Reserves – CBDC Float*' will be reduced accordingly, and this will be added to the total 'Currency (Fiat Currency)'. If there is any unused 'Foreign Exchange Reserves – CBDC Float', it will be converted back to 'Foreign Exchange Reserves' for its intended purpose.

It can be argued that money has not been created to supplement the 'mass deletion' of CBDCs, but we use the central banks' assets (Foreign Exchange Reserves – CBDC Float) to transmit value to the individuals and businesses that need the funds. This keeps the inflation rate steady for an extended period and ensures predictability in the future for policymakers because CBDCs have not been created again to facilitate unexpected transactions.

While there is an amount of £500 million in CBDC value, £300 million worth of CBDC is on the balance sheet, the remaining £200 million will be roaming in the economy. Once the CBDC is in the economy, there is no way to recall this money unless it is exchangeable with fiat currency. It can be monitored to see how much has been converted from CBDC-GBP to fiat currency and vice versa, but other than that, it cannot be collected.

The £300 million worth of CBDC on the balance sheet will be held for several reasons, it may be used to hedge against future risks or used to inject into the economy at a later date. But if the central bank no longer needs the CBDC on its balance sheet, it can 'delete' this amount for whatever reason. This is seen in Table 12.8, which shows the 'Total' amount of liabilities decreasing due to deleting the 'CBDC'.

12.10 CBDC Deletion: CBDC Re-created in Times of Need

I have explained the use of assets to facilitate transactions to individuals and corporations in times of need. But I have not addressed re-creating the money and why this method may be beneficial in catastrophic scenarios.

In times of financial distress, the central bank will be looking at its assets to liability ratio, and its assets may be used in other forms to support the economy. By holding the '*Foreign Exchange Reserves – CBDC Float*', it means the money is not being utilised at all because the central bank anticipates that (X) amount will be used for the float, if 1/3 of (X) is used, the other 2/3 could have been utilised in the economy, but instead it is held and not functional for any beneficial means.

If the country is under stress, the central banks' securities would be used for other means rather than afloat. It is best to re-create the CBDC and provide the CBDC on an interval basis rather than provide a lump sum. This is important to ensure it does not hinder other monetary policies in place by the central bank. By 'deleting' and re-creating the money instantaneously, it allows the CBDC to hold a 'quantitative easing' function to support the economy, which is the case here. It should be noted that this method will accelerate inflation because the central bank's securities are not being utilised.

It is just as seamless to create new money (CBDCs), as it is to delete the money, so there should be no immediate administrative issues associated with the birth of new CBDCs. In times of a crisis, the government can create as much as it needs to support the economy. Our proposal suggests that the additional feature of 'deleting' money can further help the country.

12.11 Conclusion

The core concept of blockchain technology and digital currencies creates a new way to think about money. So long as the currency has a store of value, means of exchange, and a unit of account, individuals and corporations will utilise this new form of money (CBDCs). CBDCs are still in the early stages of their development, but their designs and functions are similar to crypto-assets.

The premise of this chapter was to enhance our thinking and usability of digital currencies. Initially, this idea stemmed from the application and dynamics of Satoshi's Bitcoin model. The deflationary model promotes its own incentives and interests for each participant on the Bitcoin blockchain, and those who partake will follow the Bitcoin protocol. This deflationary model was the basis of the 'delete button' for CBDCs and how central banks can control and monitor their liabilities more closely.

The start of the chapter explained the benefits of CBDCs, such as upholding confidence in central banks, especially where households and corporations believe that they will no longer have access to risk-free money, and the CBDC presence maintains this inherent value. In addition, the versatile nature of CBDCs allows for value to be transmitted simply and easily from one participant to another. Another advantage includes cross-border payment systems, where it has been suggested the use of CBDCs can maximise effectiveness and efficiencies in sending payments from and to, between domestic users and international residents.

It was explained that the central bank could control the money supply in three ways: (1) open-market operations; (2) foreign exchange intervention; and (3) discount loans. While these three options are used to control the money supply, there is no way to control or manage it, the central bank can use its toolkit to devise a strategy to hedge against inflation, but it cannot completely control the money supply in an economy.

The ability to control, manage, and organise an economy's monetary supply should place a country and its people in good standing. In light of the above, this is where the 'Klair Effect' comes into force. I have labelled it a form of 'quantitative tightening' because it decreases the monetary supply similarly to Quantitative Tightening. I explained the 'Klair Effect' is a form of quantitative tightening, but it does not use the apparatus of interest rates to control the inflation rate, but a 'delete' feature to control the money supply, mainly unused 'CBDCs/fiat currency' that can be removed on the central banks' balance sheet.

The deletion process can occur in a number of ways:

1. After the creation of the CBDC, if the CBDC is no longer needed, it can be deleted;
2. Purchasing CBDCs in the economy (households and corporations) and deleting this money; and,
3. If the central bank converts and transfers its 'Fiat Currency' liabilities into CBDCs, and then it is found that they are no longer needed because the purpose of this transfer is no longer valid, it can 'delete' the CBDC value total to the transfer amount.

While each scenario is different, the outcome remains the same – delete unused money. If there is no need for the money to be on the central banks' balance sheet, it should be removed. In addition, the ability for central banks to use the 'Klair Effect' to purchase CBDCs from their citizens and, later, delete the money allows further stability in inflation rates. The third process will be rare in some instances, but it can supplement a particular purpose for the central bank.

This chapter has focused highly on the control of inflation rates because governments, policymakers, and central banks focus on using quantitative easing to support households and corporations in this recessive period. The central bank's primary goal in the pre-COVID world was accelerating economic growth by lowering interest rates to promote spending and investment. Now, the central bank happens to be in a conundrum, where it continues to bolster quantitative easing at the cost of increased inflation. Over the years, the central bank must propel itself in a manner where it can control the prices of goods and services, and at the same time, ensure it has enough ammunition to control its 2% inflation rate target.

12.12 Annex 1: How Does Quantitative Easing Work

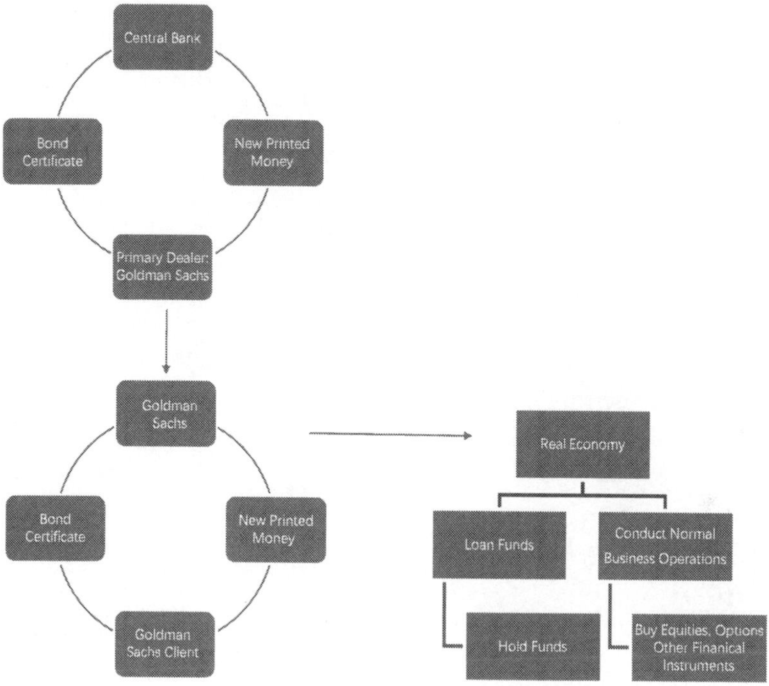

Abbreviations

5MLD	Fifth Money Laundering Directive
AAVE	Aave
AML	Anti-money laundering
AMM	Automated Market Maker
ATM	automated teller machines
BAC	Bank of America
BIS	International Settlements
BLK	BlackRock
BoE	The Bank of England
BRK.B	Berkshire Hathaway
C	Citigroup
CBDC	Central Bank Digital Currency
CBOE	Chicago Board Options Exchange
CCP	central counterparty
CDD	customer due diligence
CEA	Commodity Exchange Act
CeFi	Centralised Finance
CFTC	Commodity Futures Trading Commission
CME	Chicago Mercantile Exchange
COMP	Compound
CPI	Consumer price indices
CPMI	the Committee on Payments and Market Infrastructures
CPMM	Constant Product Market Maker
CQGR	Compound Quarter Growth Rate
CRSP	Center for Research in Security Prices
CRV	Curve
CSA	credit support annex
DAO	decentralised autonomous organisation
DApp	Decentralised Application
DBT	Distributed Book Technology

DCF	discounted cash flow
DeFi	decentralised finance
DEX	decentralised exchange
DJT	Distributed Journal Technology
DLT	distributed ledger technology
DMSPE	the discounted mean squared prediction error
DPA	Data Protection Act
EBA	European Banking Authority
ECB	The European Central Bank
EDD	enhanced customer due diligence
EIOPA	European Insurance and Occupational Pensions Authority
ETF	exchange traded fund
FATF	Financial Action Task Force
FCA	Financial Conduct Authority
FinCEN	Financial Crimes Enforcement Network
FIU	financial intelligence unit
FRED	Federal Reserve Economic Data
FSB	Financial Stability Board
GBTC	Grayscale Bitcoin Trust
GDP	Gross Domestic Product
GGM	Gordon Growth Model
GLR	General Ledger for Reporting
GLT	General Ledger for Transactions
GSC	global stablecoin
HyFi	Hybrid Finance
ICE	Intercontinental Exchange
ICO	Initial Coin Offerings
IDEA	Immutable Double-entry Accounting
IDLE	Idle Finance
IMF	International Monetary Fund
IOSCO	International Organization of Securities Commissions
IRA	Individual Retirement Account
IRS	Internal Revenue Service
JMLSG	Joint Money Laundering Steering Group
KYC	Know Your Customer
LLC	Limited Liability Company
LOIH	Large Open Interest Holders
LP	liquidity provider

LT	liquidity taker
MEV	miner extractable value
MiCA	Markets in Crypto-Assets
MLR	Money Laundering, Terrorist Financing and Transfer of Funds (Information on the Payer) Regulation
MS	Morgan Stanley
MSBs	money service businesses
NCA	National Crime Agency
NDAQ	Nasdaq
NSA	National Security Agency
OOS	out-of-sample
P2P	peer-to-peer
PLF	protocol for loanable funds
POCA	Proceeds of Crime Act
PoS	Proof-of-Stake
PoW	Proof-of-Work
PTA	Plain Text Accounting
RBA	risk-based approach
REIT	public real estate
SA	Securities Act
SAR	suspicious activity report
SEA	Securities Exchange Act
SEC	Securities and Exchange Commission
SMSF	self-managed superannuation fund
SPoF	Single Point of Failure
SR	Sharpe ratio
STRs	Shared Transaction Repositories
TACT	Terrorism Act
TEA	triple-entry accounting
TEB	triple-entry bookkeeping
TIP	Teachers' Innovation Platform
TradFi	Traditional Finance
TVL	Total Value Locked
UNI	Uniswap
VA	virtual asset
VASP	virtual asset service provider
VC	venture capital
WACC	Weighted Average Cost of Capital
WFC	Wells Fargo & Co.
YFI	Yearn Finance

Index

Printed in Dunstable, United Kingdom

71337389R00176